THE FRONTIER IN AMERICAN LITERATURE

AMERICAN CLASSICS

THE FRONTIER IN AMERICAN LITERATURE

Lucy Lockwood Hazard

FREDERICK UNGAR PUBLISHING CO., INC.
NEW YORK

Republished 1961
in the American Classics series

First published 1927

Second Printing, 1967

Printed in the United States of America

Library of Congress Catalog Card No. 60-13981

To

MY MOTHER

PREFACE

CHESTERTON has written of the joy that attends the discovery of an infinite debt; and what he writes of a great joy is true also of such lesser joy as goes to the making of a book. For no one can have attempted a task of creative scholarship without discovering first, his own unworthiness of his loved subject, his inadequacy in putting into words the significance of that which he has perceived; and second, his constant indebtedness and dependence upon those known and unknown friends without whom even his modicum of success would have been impossible. The joy of writing a preface is the opportunity which it affords for the acknowledgment of that unpayable debt.

For help of a personal nature, the value of which only they and I can understand, a word of appreciation to Mrs. Wilkinson, to Dr. Fletcher Taylor, and to Ellison Hazard. For help of a more devious sort, the value of which every reader of this book will realize, thanks are due to the publishers and individuals whose generous permissions have made possible the use of excerpts from copyrighted material: to Charles Scribner's Sons for the quotations from *The Autobiography of David Crockett* which has been edited for The Modern Students' Library by Hamlin Garland; to Harcourt, Brace & Co. for quotations from Sinclair Lewis' *Arrowsmith;* to B. W. Huebsch (Viking Press) for quotations from the writings of Sherwood Anderson; to Little, Brown & Co., publishers for the Atlantic Monthly

Press, for quotations from Lucy Furman's *The Quare Woman;* to the Johns Hopkins Press for quotations from Bentley's *Condition of the Western Farmer;* to the Arthur H. Clark Co. for quotations from Dale's *Ashley-Smith Explorations;* to Mr. Hamlin Garland for the use of quotations from his play *Under the Wheel;* to Miss Mary V. George for quotations from Henry George's *Progress and Poverty;* to Mrs. Carnegie for quotations from the writings of Andrew Carnegie; to Professor Frederick J. Teggert, editor of *The Diary of Nelson Kingsley,* and Professor John Spencer Bassett, editor of *The Writings of William Byrd;* to Boni & Liveright for quotations from the writings of Theodore Dreiser; to Harper & Bros. for quotations from Mark Twain; to Houghton Mifflin Co. for material quoted from Royce's *California,* Willa Cather's *O Pioneers* and *My Antonia,* and from the writings of Bret Harte, Emerson and Thoreau; to The Macmillan Co. for quotations from Robert Herrick's *Memoirs of an American Citizen,* Hamlin Garland's *A Son of the Middle Border,* John G. Neihardt's *Song of Three Friends, Song of the Indian Wars,* and *The Splendid Wayfaring.*

Less tangible, but no less real, is the debt to those pupils and teachers of mine whose interest in American history and American literature has been contagious. Special acknowledgment is gratefully made to those classes at Mills College whose eager discussion of American backgrounds suggested this study; to Professor V. L. Parrington of the University of Washington, who first taught me the economic interpretation of American literature; to Professor H. E. Bolton whose seminar at the University of California has been an inspiration to so many pioneers in Western history; to my colleague, Professor C. L. Goodwin, head of the Department of History at Mills College, who read the book in manuscript and offered valuable suggestions for its revision; above all, to Professor B. H. Lehman of the Department of English at the University of California, who has accompanied every stage of this work with that unfailing helpfulness, that eager interest, that keen criticism, that stimulating scholarship which he spends so generously on all his students, and to which we in return can offer only our grateful recognition of the far-reaching influence of his creative intention.

In anticipation I hope to owe a debt of gratitude to my readers; to their intelligence in recognizing that this book is by its title defined as the study of only one phase of influence upon American literature, and not as a general and all inclusive survey; to their tolerance, if beloved figures or philosophies have been unfavorably adjudged; to their awakened interest in carrying further lines of investigation which it has been possible only to indicate within the limits of his book.

LUCY LOCKWOOD HAZARD.

MILLS COLLEGE,
Oakland, California.
December 9, 1926.

CONTENTS

CHAPTER I

THE PURITAN FRONTIER

CHAPTER II

THE SOUTHERN FRONTIER: A STUDY IN ROMANTICISM

CHAPTER VI

THE GILDED AGE OF INDUSTRIAL PIONEERING

CHAPTER VII

THE FRONTIER AND THE NESTER

CHAPTER VIII

INTRODUCTION

THE SIGNIFICANCE OF THE FRONTIER IN AMERICAN LITERATURE

PROFESSOR LEON KELLNER in his study of *American Literature* remarks the contrast between "the greatness of American history and the mediocrity of American literature." Impressed with the epic grandeur of the westward march of the pioneer on an ever receding frontier, he marvels that this unique factor in American life has not found an echo in American literature.

If instead of turning to a German critic to see ourselves as others see us, we turn to the Brahmins of American criticism, to the Woodberrys and Wendells, we find the same verdict, but with a different interpretation. It is true, admit these cultured gentlemen, that the best that has been thought and said in American literature bears little relation to the crude hurly-burly of contemporary American life. And they thank God for it. For literature to them is something far too bright and good to be associated with Jacksonian democracy, furtrading posts, and Homestead Laws. Her soul is like a star that dwells apart—not like the star that marks the westward course of empire.

Within the last quarter of a century we have had a re-definition of the significance of American history. Professor Turner has told how as a graduate student he was stirred to indignant denial by his professor's urbane announcement that the seminar had exhausted the subject of American history. Finished the study of American history?—flashed back Turner—we have only begun.

And out of that conviction was born the address on "The Significance of the Frontier" which revolutionized the treatment of United States History.

The time is ripe for a similar re-definition and interpretation of American literature. Old gods are toppling on their pedestals; new gods are claiming homage. Mr. Pattee in his *History of American Literature Since 1870* recognizes that the westward movement changed the balance of power in American literature. The dilettanti who imitated European forms and sentiments, the Aldriches and Stedmans and Gilders are relegated to the cheerful yesterdays. The critical judgment of today has different standards. The judgment of the purchasing public sends *Main Street* and *Miss Lulu Bett* and *The Education of Henry Adams* to the top of the list of best sellers. The judgment of the professional critics is likewise swayed by the demand for the indigenous product; even Professor Stuart Sherman deserts the Olympians and makes a bid for popularity with a brochure on "The Significance of Sinclair Lewis."

The history of American literature from Henry Wadsworth Longfellow to Nicholas Vachel Lindsay, from Thomas Bailey Aldrich to Sherwood Anderson, is a fulfillment of the vision of Walt Whitman as he looked down Democratic Vistas for the inspired literatus who should sing the song of these states. It is quite aside from the point to enter here into the old debate as to whether the highest type of literature is not that concerned with universal aspects of human experience rather than with local and temporary issues. We are not measuring either Lindsay or Longfellow against Shakespeare. But in measuring them against each other, we are conscious that it was as natural for the one to retell the Golden Legend as for the other to write the Golden Whales of California and the Golden Book of Springfield. In one case, we have something decorative, imitative, conventional—that is what we used to call literature in America; on the other, we have something brilliant, bizarre, original—that is what we now call literature in America.

In other words, we used to lay the emphasis on "literature"—the polish, the form; now we lay it on "American" and estimate the value of a piece of writing very largely by its fidelity to the American scene, its significance as an interpretation of these states. It is in this more recent sense that the phrase "American literature" is used in this study. No attempt is made to assert that every writer conventionally included in the histories of American literature was consciously or subconsciously influenced by the presence of a frontier. An attempt has been made to study the use of the frontier by those writers who, like Cooper and Bret Harte, have deliberately chosen it as a setting; an attempt has also been made toward the analysis of a much more difficult and much more important problem: the indirect but powerful influence of the frontier in shaping the conditions of American life and the resultant American philosophies.

Obviously, this study necessitates the use of the word "frontier" with varying connotations; but this apparent looseness of terminology is inherent in the very shifting nature of the frontier, which meant at one time one thing, at another time, another, and yet which was indispensable alike to the farmer and to the furtrader, to the Puritan and to the profiteer, to the Argonaut of the gold rush and to the Titan of railway finance. In every case where the word may appear to have been wrested from its simple meaning, the connotation of the word has been vouched for on the authority of such distinguished specialists on the frontier as Professor Turner and Professor Paxson.

Mr. Turner has pointed out in his brilliant essay on "The Significance of the Frontier in American History," that life in America has been conditioned by the perennial rebirth of the frontier. The successive frontiers present a moving picture of American life—moving geographically and chronologically from the Atlantic settlements of the 17th century to the California mining camps of the 19th century; moving economically from the pathfinder, the trapper, to the exploiter, the land-speculator. These successive frontiers present differences in location and occupation; but they display a common factor which we may call the pioneering spirit; a spirit of determination, of endurance, of independence, of ingenuity, of flexibility, of individualism, of optimism; we conceive of the American type as the product and embodiment of this frontier spirit.

But according to the statement of the Superintendent of the Census of 1890 which serves as text for Mr. Turner's thesis: "The free lands have gone; the frontier has vanished." The democracy of the frontier has been succeeded by the oligarchy of Big Business; the fluidity of the frontier has been succeeded by the standardization of Main Street. What is the effect upon the American type? And to what extent is it reflected in American literature?

It is the purpose of this study to trace in American literature reflections of the pioneering spirit; first, on the frontier of regional pioneering, which is primarily concerned with man's attempt to control nature; second, on the frontier of industrial pioneering, which is primarily concerned with man's attempt to control the labor of his fellowmen; finally, on the frontier of spiritual pioneering, which is primarily concerned with man's attempt to control himself.

The most obvious influence of the frontier on American literature is found in the exploitation of the picturesque and melodramatic aspects of life on regional frontiers. Cooper and Bret Harte are the best examples of this direct functioning of the frontier. Much more significant, however, are the portrayals of pioneering life given by writers who not only exploit but explain the frontier, recognizing it as a focal point in American character. In suggestive contrast stand two such first-hand representations of pioneer life: Crèvecoeur's *Letters from an American Farmer* is a record of success explicitly attributed to abundance of free land; Garland's *A Son of the Middle Border* is a record of failure explicitly attributed to the disappearance of free land. The indirect influence of the frontier may be seen by tracing the characteristic moods of American literature from Crèvecoeur to Garland.

The era of regional pioneering, of which Crèvecoeur is one of the earliest and most enthusiastic representatives, was a Golden Age aglow with the expectation of success. Franklin, Emerson, Thoreau, and Whitman exemplify the characteristics engendered by the presence of abundant natural resources affording equal opportunity to all. Optimism, self-confidence, belief in man's control over his environment, are the keynotes in the glad forward song of the pioneers. By almost imperceptible degrees the Golden Age merges into the Gilded Age; the average man is perhaps less confident in his expectation of success; so much the greater the glorification of the success of the superman of industry, the Harrington, the Cowperwood, heroes of industrial pioneering. But for one superman who succeeds there are a hundred average men who fail; hard upon the heels of a philosophy which glorifies success must follow a philosophy which rationalizes failure. With the disappearance of free land disappeared the rosy illusion upon which characteristic American optimism was based. Naturalism, product of the disillusioned Old World, for the first time flourished in the soil of the New. Naturalistic writers such as Frank Norris, Sinclair Lewis, and

Edgar Lee Masters, presented their characters no longer as triumphing over their environment, but as victimized by it. The Gilded Age began with optimism and complacency, the spirit of the Booster, and ended with pessimism and protest, the spirit of the Muckraker. But the great despisers are close akin to the great adorers; out of the bitter despair of America's *Domesday Book* shines the "vision of a new Republic." Again the frontier is reborn, and American writers voice a new challenge to the pioneer spirit. The Coming Age in American literature is an age of spiritual pioneering, of contempt for material success, of sublimation of failure, of a new idealism, based on the acceptance, not on the denial of limitations. The energies of the American people, long extraverted to the conquest of the continent, are now introverted to the perfecting of human relationships. In the impatient analysis of the American scene by the younger intellectuals, in Vachel Lindsay's rhapsodical Gospel of Beauty, in Sherwood Anderson's mystical Gospel of Love, in Arrowsmith's passionate pursuit of passionless Science, in Jurgen's eternally frustrated search for the Eternal Womanly, speak the representatives of "America's Coming of Age," repudiating the mess of pottage, and claiming their birthright.

THE FRONTIER IN AMERICAN LITERATURE

CHAPTER I

THE PURITAN FRONTIER

I. THE CHRONICLES OF OLD NEW ENGLAND

However far American history and American literature may diverge from each other in their treatment of later men and events, they conventionally take a common starting point from Plymouth Rock. Until very recently, historians have treated the landing of the Pilgrims, not as part of the colonizing activities of the English Puritans, but as a dramatic turning point in world affairs, an inspired beginning of American history. Historical writers and literary historians have agreed that some mysterious metamorphosis was accomplished by contact with the Rock; that fairy-tale fashion, those who had been Englishmen became Americans upon taking the fatal step.

An interesting by-product of the recent interpretation of American history in terms of the frontier has been the fluent coupling of the terms "Puritan" and "pioneer" by those younger critics of American literature who see in the Puritan only the sour fanatic, in the pioneer, only the unimaginative drudge. According to such interpreters as Waldo Frank and Van Wyck Brooks, Puritan and pioneer were by nature diabolical affinities. Either type would have been a heavy handicap to a young nation; the alliance of the two damned it from the start. Proceeding from the premises of this perverted Calvinism, these gloomy apostles of the *joie de vivre* ascribe whatever is wrong in our moral and industrial America to the fatal gifts which these evil geniuses brought to its christening.

The only logical way to evaluate these criticisms is to go back of them to the sources. It is easy to construct a Puritan or a pioneer from a little desultory reading pieced out with imagination; it is not quite so easy, but on the whole more profitable, to find in the chronicles of Massachusetts and Plymouth, the Puritan pioneers' own account of their motives, their struggles, their successes, their ways of looking at life. One peculiar advantage we have in studying the Puritan frontier: in forming our estimate of subsequent frontiers, we have to differentiate sharply between the contemporary accounts and their utilization by literary artists; the latter only are dignified by the name of literature; but the chronicles of the Puritan frontier are claimed not only by the historian, but by the literary critic. Histories of American literature do not begin with Hawthorne, the artist of the Puritan world, but with John Smith, with William Bradford, with Cotton Mather. Rightly: for what other literature was there in the America of the seventeenth century than these records of the spirit of the first frontier? Here we may find the portrait of the Puritan pioneer drawn from life by writers who were not only men of affairs but men of letters.

II. THE MOTIVES OF THE PURITAN MIGRATION

The sophisticated adventurer, John Smith, writing a *Description of New England* in 1616 emphasized economic opportunities: "I am not so simple to think that ever any other motive than wealth will ever erect there a commonweal or draw company from their ease and humors at home to stay in New England to effect my purposes." Within fourteen years there were in New England some fourteen hundred people who professed to have torn up stakes in their old home and braved the hardships of the new with no other motive than the love of religion pure and undefiled. We find the early divines gloating with masochistic satisfaction over their renunciations. Cotton Mather calls the emigration to Massachusetts Bay, "a banishment rather than a removal . . . sufficiently afflictive to men of estate, breeding, and conversation." Samuel Whiting says, "I am going into the wilderness to a sacrifice unto the Lord." Captain Edward Johnson compares the New England colonists with "any other people, who have left their countryes, as the Gothes, Vandals, etc., to possesse a fatter, as Italy, or warmer, as Spaine. But these forsooke a fruitful Land, stately Buildings, goodly Orchards, yea, deare Friends and neere relations to goe to a desart Wildernesse, thousands of leagues by Sea, both turbulent and dangerous—here the onely encouragements were the laborious breaking up of bushy ground, with the continued toyl of erecting houses for themselves and cattell, in this howling desart; all which they underwent with much cheerfulnesse, that they might enjoy Christ and his Ordinances in their primitive purity."

It was long the custom to accept the Puritan emigrants at their own valuation. Such effusive eulogies as Rufus Choate's "The Age of the Puritans the Heroic Period of our History" are sufficient illustrations of this hero-worshiping tendency. Of late years it has become the fashion to deride the Puritan, to make him a convenient scapegoat for all American sins of omission and commission. H. L. Mencken immediately comes to mind as the most brilliant *advocatus diaboli.* Well, Mencken is gloriously free to indulge in "Prejudices," but the student of history is not. In attempting to find the safe middle ground between indiscriminate eulogy and indiscriminate abuse, our hardest task is that of estimating the motives of the Puritan migration. It is probably safe to conclude that they were mixed motives. Modern historians of the founding of New England emphasize the economic urge of the Great Migration, and agree that "Land hunger was the master passion which brought the men of the seventeenth century across the sea and lured them on to the frontier." Even Bliss Perry, while leaning to the traditional idealistic interpretation, admits that the Puritan pioneer was "both a mystic and a bargain hunter." A delightfully naive combination of these attitudes characterizes the various "arguments for removing to New England," such as Robert Cushman's *Reasons and Considerations touching the lawfulnesse of removing out of England into the parts of America,* John White's *The Planter's Plea,* John Winthrop's *General Considerations for Planting New England,* John Cotton's *God's Promise to His Plantations.* While differing in details, this emigration propaganda presents a curious sameness that enables us to reduce it to a formula. The orthodox thing is to begin with parallels from Hebrew history, the Puritans being confident that by grace of a non-apostolic succession, they were now Jehovah's Chosen People. Fortified by Biblical precedents, they proceeded with a perfunctory remark or two about the duty of converting the Indians, sometimes for the benefit of the over-scrupulous, setting forth elaborate distinctions between "natural rights" and "civil rights," and proving to their own satisfaction that the Indians had no real claim to the lands they occupied. Besides, probably they were the devil's children anyway, and was it not downright impious to acquiesce in the fiend's possession of that fair land? After these casuistical rationalizations, the Puritan got to the point: the economic opportunities in an undeveloped country, the manifest destiny of the dominant race to profit by them. Calvinism, says Leon Kellner, "is the natural theology of the disinherited." There is an odd mixture of religious zeal and economic dissatisfaction in Winthrop's *Considerations*: "Sixthly: The whole earth is the Lord's garden and hee hath given it to the sons of Adam to be tilled and improved by them, why then should we stand starving here for places of habitation—and in the meane tyme suffer whole countryes as profitable for the use of man, to lye waste without any improvement?" "Seventhly: What can bee a better worke and more noble and worthy a Christian, than to helpe to raise and support a particular church while it is in its infancy?" There is a curiously Rotarian mingling of the aim of service and the appeal to self interest in Cushman's *Reasons* for exchanging "the present consumption which groweth on us here" for "the easinesse and plentifulnesse of living in those remote places" since "a man must not respect only to live and doe good to himselfe, but he should see where he can live to doe most good to others."

III. THE CHARACTER OF THE PURITAN EMIGRANTS

Closely connected with the presentation of motives are the specifications for would-be emigrants. Even the enthusiastic John Smith, prototype of sanguine realtors, admits that it is not every one who can make a success of pioneering in New England: "it requires all the best parts of art, judgment, courage, honesty, constancy, diligence and industry to do but near well." But the Puritan Fathers were comfortably confident that they had a monopoly of these as of all other virtues. "God sifted a whole nation," boasted William Stoughton in the Election Sermon of 1668, "that He might send choice grain into this wilderness." In the fathers of New England we find highly developed that inspired illusion which persisted, sometimes under grotesque transformations, throughout American pioneering: the illusion that the pioneer's private adventure is part of a Divine Mission, that the pioneer is "an instrument ordained of God to conquer the wilderness." This belief harmonized with and was fortified by Calvinistic theology; the combination of the two rendered the Puritans well nigh invulnerable. "It is not with us as with other men whom small things can discourage or small discontentments cause to wish ourselves at home again." In this often quoted assertion of Brewster's we hear both the Puritan's justifiable pride in his own fortitude, and his less justifiable contempt of individuals who were less thick-skinned. A ludicrous instance of this contempt is found among Bradford's answers to anticipated objections. He imagines a pusillanimous person hesitating to come to New England because, "The people are much anoyed with muskeetos," to which Bradford replies with scathing scorn: "They are too delicate and unfitte to begine new plantations and collonies that can not enduer the biting of a muskeeto; we would wish such to keepe at home till at least they be muskeeto proof."

Industry came next to fortitude in the hierarchy of Puritan virtues. Thoroughly imbued with the belief that his Satanic Majesty was especially active in times of unemployment, the promoters of emigration urged the need of constant vigilance as the price of material and spiritual safety. The general Letter of Instructions from the Governor and Deputy of the New England Company admonishes "that all be kept to labor, as the only means to reduce them to a civil, yea, a godly life, and to keep youth from falling into many enormities, which of nature we are all too much inclined unto." The second

General Letter of Instructions repeats the caution and makes it clear that no "idle drone" will be tolerated in the community. Incompetents have often sought relief from the pressure of a complex society in the less exacting environment of the frontier; but they sought it in vain on a frontier dominated by Puritans. To be "diligent in business, not slothful in spirit" was a large part of the Puritan's conception of serving the Lord. When the people of Mr. Weston's less godly plantation at Wessagusett were reduced to starvation "by their folly and profuseness," the Puritan historian comments on their plight with the grim satisfaction of the ant rebuking the grasshopper. In his own select community the Puritan wanted not "men nourished up in idleness, unconstant, and affecting novelties, unwilling, stubborn, inclined to faction, covetous, luxurious, prodigal" but men who were "willing, constant, industrious, obedient, frugal, lovers of the common good,"

We have heard the not unduly modest characterizations of the Puritan pioneer as he saw himself. It may be well to close with a characterization of the Puritan pioneer as his neighbors saw him. Thomas Morton (the Morton of Merry Mount fame, naturally not prepossessed in favor of the Puritans) writes in his *New English Canaan* of his experiences in New England: "where I found two sortes of people, the one Christians, the other Infidels, these (the Indians) I found most full of humanity and more friendly than the other."

IV. THE PURITAN *EN VOYAGE*

Matthew Arnold, after paying a carefully qualified tribute to the virtues of the Puritans, points out that had Shakespeare or Virgil been stowed away among the ancestral furniture on the Mayflower, they would have found the Pilgrim Fathers "intolerable company." The terror of storms, the miseries of seasickness, the tragedies of sea-burials, the countless discomforts of the long voyage in crowded quarters—a sporting spirit and a grim determination would carry one through these. But Virgil or Shakespeare would have balked "even as you and I" at what for the Puritans constituted the one great compensation for all these trials: "preaching and expounding of the word of God every day for ten weeks together by our ministers." On John Cotton's voyage to America there were "sermons or expositions" not only every day but three times a day: "Mr. Cotton in the morning, Mr. Hooker in the afternoon, Mr. Stone after supper in the evening." Small wonder that one well-meaning passenger who had committed the almost unpardonable sin of "diverting himself with an hook and line on the Lord's Day," when called to account, "protested *that he did not know when the Lord's Day was; he thought every day was a sabbath day; for, he said, they did nothing but pray and preach all the week long.*"

The one secular delight which is recorded in the journals of Puritan voyages speaks even more eloquently than the interminable "exercisings" of the temper of the Puritan pioneers. A porpoise "for bigness not much less than a hog" is harpooned and hauled on deck. Richard Mather dwells with great gusto upon the details of the disembowelling, "in view of us all . . . marvellous merry sport, and delightful to our women and children."

V. THE FINDING OF THE FRONTIER

And so to land. It is not our purpose here to tell the old, old story of Plymouth Rock, of Squanto and Massasoit, of the rigors of the first winter of 1620–21 when half the colonists died, and of the survivors at one time only seven were able to be about and tend the sick, of the "loyal hearts and true" who refused to go back in the Mayflower; nor to recount the annals of the more aristocratic and prosperous settlement on Massachusetts Bay. Our interest lies rather in seeing what the Puritan thought of the frontier, what he did to it, and perhaps, what it did to him.

The chronicles of these New England frontiersmen present an interestingly incongruous emphasis on two phases of the New England frontier; its privations and its plenty. Roger Clap gives one of the most painfully realistic accounts of the scarcity of provisions. "Frost-fish, muscles and clams were a relief to many . . . When I could have meal and water and salt boiled together, it was so good, who could wish better?" But what the Puritans lacked in diet they made up in piety. Johnson pictures the women resorting to the clambanks "where they daily gathered their Families' food with much heavenly discourse of the provisions Christ had formerly made for many thousands of his followers in the wildernesse." Cotton Mather celebrates the godly content of a pioneer who having invited a friend to share his supper of clams "gave thanks to Heaven who had given them to suck the abundance of the seas and of the treasures hid in the sands." Perhaps it was in a similar mood of pious exaggeration that Winthrop wrote: "My dear wife, we are here in a paradise."

It is not enough to say that the frontiersmen endured with fortitude, though evidences of such fortitude abound. The Puritan pioneer combined the endurance of the zealot with the enthusiasm of the realtor. The Puritans' glowing accounts of the resources of their new country would put to shame the most roseate "literature" sent out by our Chambers of Commerce. No Californiac could outdo the Rev. Higginson's tributes to the climate. When a Puritan saw the frontier environment as it was, "withered grass on the surface of the cold earth," it was only as a fitting background for his spiritual drama, an effective contrast to the godly civilization which he intended to build. Johnson gives a picture of Endicott's men which in its sturdy vigor smacks of Elizabethan England: "They made shift to rub out the Winters cold by the Fireside, having fuell enough growing at their very doores, turning down many a drop of the Bottell and burning Tobacco with all the ease they could, discoursing betweene one while and another, of the great progresse they would make after the Summers-Sun had changed the Earths white furr'd Gowne into a greene Mantell." This picture is hardly representative of the Puritan; Johnson half apologizes for its humanly delightful aspects, explaining that Endicott's men were "a mixt multitude" and that the glorious work in New England really began the ensuing year with the arrival of "three godly ministers." But if it inadequately represents the mood of the seventeenth century Puritan, it admirably renders the mood of the eternal pioneer—turning from the frontier as it is to the frontier as he is going to make it, forgetting cold, hunger, danger, in plans "of the great progresse they would make."

VI. THE PURITAN COMMUNITY: ATTITUDE TOWARD THE INDIANS

So rapidly was this "progresse" effected that in reading William Wood's account of the New England towns in 1634, his description of "faire corne-fields" and "pleasant kitchen-gardens" and handsome country towns whose residents were "all very rich," one wonders if such staid and comfortable communities ought to be included under the heading of the frontier. But the pioneer settlements quickly displayed a characteristic Puritan civilization, and it is in the organization, attitudes, and ways of life of these communities that the spirit of the Puritan frontier must be studied.

One hardly expects to find that leisure class complaint, the servant problem, listed among the hardships of frontier life. But Wood particularizes that "men of good estates may doe well; always provided that they goe wel accommodated with servants." Margaret Winthrop and her stepdaughter exchange commiserations over the shortcomings of their maids. A generation later Sewall plaintively enters in his diary: "Just now wanted a Maid very much, courted Goodwife Fellows' daughter; she could not come till spring: hard to find a good one." Under such trying circumstances, it must have seemed logical to the Puritans to conscript the labor of the Indians. Traditional accounts of the Puritan frontier have featured the Indian as enemy or as ally; now it can be told that he also figured as a slave.

According to the Charter of the Colony of Massachusetts Bay: "To win and invite the natives of this country to the knowledge and obedience of the only true God and Saviour of mankind and the Christian faith, in our royal intention, and the adventurer's free profession is the principal end of this Plantation." Since an avowed purpose of the Puritan migration was the conversion of the Indians, it seems not unreasonable to consider the attitude of the Puritan community toward their savage neighbors. We all know that the New England colonists did little or nothing in the way of carrying out their much vaunted missionary designs—that jibe has become hackneyed. We all know that the English lacked the French facility in mingling with the natives—that comparison has become hackneyed. Hackneyed too has become the lament of that gentle soul John Robinson: "Oh, how happy a thing had it been if you had converted some before you had killed any." As for the allegation that the pioneers outraged the Indians' sense of justice by delivering for punishment, not the real culprit, but "a poor, decrepit, old man that was unserviceable to the company"—that ingenuous substitution was attributed by Morton to the Puritans, and by the Puritans indignantly ascribed to Mr. Weston's godless colony—and Butler has perhaps made sufficient anti-Puritan capital out of that in *Hudibras*—so let it pass. Nor will we belittle the motives or achievements of the "apostle to the Indians," John Eliot. But John Eliot is no fair representative of the typical New England attitude toward the Indians, which was at the best aloof; at the worst, vindictive. With monotonous unanimity the Puritan chronicles agree that the disease which had reduced the Massachusetts from 30,000 to 300 was a special interposition of Providence on their behalf. As Johnson voiced it, "God cast out the heathen to make room for his people." From the rifling of the grave of an Indian child by the Plymouth colonists, to the systematic extermination of the Pequot War, the journals of Puritan New England breathe the proverbial conviction that "the only good Indian is a dead Indian."

VII. THE THEOCRACY

If the Puritans were unsuccessful in inflicting their peculiar form of religion upon the Indians, they more than compensated for it by the vigor with which they applied their religion to themselves. Blackstone's familiar epigram that he had not "left the rule of the Lord Bishops to come under that of the Lord Brethren" suggests the audacious assumption of authority which made life worth living for the Puritan Divines.

On the occasion of the departure of Winthrop's expedition was delivered a farewell address supposed to have been prepared by the Rev. White of Dorchester. This address makes an explicit repudiation of separatist intentions and with expressions of tender devotion acknowledges the Church of England as spiritual mother.

Whether because of Puritan hypocrisy or frontier freedom, the Puritans, once safely arrived in Massachusetts, took a very different tone. Two misguided members of Endicott's company who read together the Book of Common Prayer were shipped home in disgrace. The installation of Mr. Higginson and Mr. Skelton into their New England charge was accompanied by an improvised system of ordination; the details of the ceremony need not concern us here; the significant point is that such a service was tantamount to a repudiation of Episcopal orders, and that the Massachusetts colonists had become as openly non-conformist as their more lowly brethren at Plymouth. The decisive step having been taken, the Puritans proceeded to demand assent to eighty-nine articles of faith where only thirty-nine had been essential for salvation via the Church of England; to establish a coalition of church and state as tyrannical as the wildest dreams of Charles I or Archbishop Laud; to hound heretics as ruthlessly as was ever done by the most unholy work of the Holy Inquisition. No one could be a freeman: *i.e.,* entitled to civic rights, unless he were a member of the Puritan church. No one could be a member of the Puritan church unless by detailed and public account of his conversion and profession of his faith he had proved his claim to be numbered among the elect. Unless one passed this ordeal successfully, he and his children were excluded from the sacraments of the church and the rights of citizenship. But even in this despised and outcast state one was not exempt from attendance on Puritan meetings or permitted to seek comfort in private devotions. Small wonder that Lechford described the Puritan machine as among the things which he "misliked."

One must read such a record as Winthrop's Journal to appreciate in detail the working of the Puritan machine: the sweeping power of the magistrates, the swift suppression of all unfavorable criticism, the persistent petty interference in the details of private life. Perhaps because of the allure of alliteration, we usually couple "freedom" and "frontier" as if they were inevitable companions. But on the Puritan frontier, even the dictatorship of Winthrop was regarded as too lenient by his colleagues who finally convinced him: "that strict discipline, both in criminal offences and in martial affairs was more needful in plantations than in a settled state, as tending to the honor and safety of the gospel."

VIII. INTOLERANCE

"If Religion be Worth anything," wrote Cotton Mather, "it is worth everything." The New England Puritans, by virtue of the independence of their isolated position on the frontier, had a chance not only to enjoy their own religious opinions, but to enforce them upon others. As we read their accounts of what we should call religious persecutions, we must, of course, bear in mind that toleration is a modern virtue—often synonymous with indifference; that about the things which we think really matter—business prosperity, for instance—we are as rabid as the Puritans were about sanctification; that we love an I. W. W. as little as they did a Quaker. Yet any arguments which excuse John Wilson and Thomas Dudley, also excuse Charles I and Archbishop Laud; if we expunge from the Puritan the stain of persecution, we also rob him of the halo of martyrdom.

The Puritans made no pretense of regarding toleration as a virtue. Pious Thomas Dudley breathed a dying curse "on all who do a toleration hatch." John Cotton argued with shameless casuistry that the heretic was "not punished for his conscience but for sinning against his conscience"; if people followed their consciences, of course, they would all be good Puritans! And so we find the chronicles of the Puritan frontier filled, not with the building of homes, the planting of fields, the conquest of the wilderness—but with hairsplitting theological discussions, vituperative railings against the Quakers, the Anabaptists, the Antominians, the Familists, We find the community convulsed, not over terrors of famine, or cold, or disease, or Indian warfare, but over Hugh Blewett who held publicly that he was free from original sin; over Roger Williams who became so holy that even his wife was not sufficiently regenerate for him to eat with; over Deborah Wilson walking naked in the streets of Salem to show the inhabitants the nakedness of their sins; over Anne Hutchinson preaching the "two dangerous errors: 1. That the person of the Holy Ghost dwells in a justified person. 2. That no sanctification can help to evidence to us our justification." One goes to the chronicles of the New England pioneers seeking to learn how they won their daily bread; and one learns only how they threw the persecuting stone.

IX. SUPERSTITION

But if the things which were seen on the New England frontier did not seem to the Puritans worth recording, the things which were unseen were of eternal interest. Superstition has been defined as "a faith which we don't share." It is doubtful if the most religious of us today shares that unquestioning assurance of a persistent interference of the Deity in our private affairs in which Cotton Mather wrote of "Demonstrations of the Divine Providence in remarkable Mercies and Judgments." Therefore we call this belief in special providences, this complicated supernatural explanation of natural phenomena and fortuitious circumstances—superstition. Call it what we will, it loomed high on the horizon of the Puritan frontier. The Puritan God was a general utility character. Nothing was too petty or too vindictive to be ascribed to his machinations; with Him all things were possible.

The Puritan had a comfortable "heads I win, tails you lose" formula for all the changes and chances of this mortal life. If any misfortune befell him or his, it only proved that "the Lord chasteneth whom he loveth." If any misfortune befell his adversaries, it was an equally positive proof of the vengeance of Jehovah upon the wicked. The Indian attack on Mrs. Hutchinson is evidence of God's displeasure with her heresies; the Indian attack on Mrs. Rowlandson is evidence of "the soveraignty and goodness of God together with the faithfulness of his promises." The Puritan was as skillful as Job's friends in tracing misfortune to the innate depravity of the sufferer. A ship "lying before Charltown" was "blown in peeces with her owne powder" and some fifteen lives lost; "wherein the judgment of God appeared, for the master and company were many of them profane scoffers at us." Two fishermen lose their boat and are drowned; "it was an evident judgment of God upon them for they were wicked persons." Any disrespect to the clergy was a sure way of inviting the displeasure of Jehovah. Cotton Mather details exultantly the repeated judgments of the Lord upon those who were rude to the Rev. Francis Higginson. Nor is parsimony in dealing with God's elect to escape unpunished. "A town in this countrey, enrich'd with two very *eminent ministers* did one year pass a town vote that they could not allow their ministers above *thirty pounds* apiece that year for their salaries; and behold, the God who *will not be mocked* immediately caused the town to lose *three hundred pounds* in that specie of their cattle by one disaster."

The annalists of New England scrutinize the trivial occurrences of every-day life in search of Providential interpositions. Sewall notes that he neglected private prayer in the morning and was duly punished with a sore throat before night. Winthrop acknowledged "a special providence of God that my wife taking upp a messe of porridge before the children or anybodye had eaten of it, she espied therein a greate spider." In this case, it appears fortunate for Mrs. Winthrop that her husband was more disposed to praise God than to criticize her housekeeping. But the interferences of the Almighty are not always of so kindly a nature. A man of Boston anxious to finish a piece of work, fails to stop at the canonical hour of sunset on Saturday night. The next day one of his children falls into a well and is drowned, and the bereaved father "freely in the open congregation did acknowledge it the righteous hand of God for his profaning his holy day." Even the fauna of New England have developed correct theological sensibilities. Out of Winthrop's library of more than a thousand books, the mice select for destruction the Book of Common Prayer!

X. INTROSPECTION

Closely allied with the superstitious habit of referring every event to the interposition of a special providence, is the introspective tendency of weighing every act and thought "as ever in a great taskmaster's eye." If the Puritan took a malicious joy in plucking out the beam from his brother's eye, he suffered morbid agonies over the mote in his own. Winthrop regards such self-torture as essential to the religious life: "Where there is not a reverend trembling at the committinge of smale sinnes . . . there is not feare of God and where there is no feare there is no faithe." Thomas Parker, hearing his more frivolous relatives "laughing very freely" squelches their innocent mirth with this cheerful remark: "Cousins, I wonder you can be so merry unless you are sure of your salvation." The effect of this gloomy self-examination upon impressionable natures is painfully evidenced throughout the New England journals. John Winthrop Junior at the age of fourteen "was for months held under such affliction of mind that he could not be brought to apprehend any comfort in God, being much humbled and broken for his sins." Little Betty Sewall worries for fear "she should goe to Hell" and accuses herself of being a "Reprobate" and not "loving God's people as she should." These exhibitions of religious hysteria may be discounted as ascribable partly to the excitability of adolescence, partly to the Puritan convention whereby conviction of sin was a necessary precursor to assurance of salvation and ultimate church membership. But we cannot dismiss so lightly the all too frequent manifestations of religious melancholia or religious mania which found no happy ending. There is the man of Weymouth who cried out one stormy night, "Art thou come, Lord Jesus?" leapt in his night attire out of the window into the snow and was found dead seven miles away the next morning. There is the woman of Boston who, unable to attain assurance of salvation, puts an end to the torturing suspense by throwing her baby into a well, "and then came into the house and said now she was sure she should be damned for she had drowned her child." Dorothy Talbye also murders her little daughter under the delusion that she is obeying a divine revelation "to free it from future misery." With the same benevolent motive a cooper's wife of Hingham attempts to drown her daughter, after having worked herself into a state of frenzy by brooding over her fancied sins against the Holy Ghost. These pitiful cases might be multiplied indefinitely, but the point is clear and we may omit the harrowing details. Conventional eulogies of the pioneer pay tribute to his habitual stoicism without tracing its periodical relief in religious frenzies. But first-hand accounts of pioneer life from Winthrop's *Journal* to Garland's autobiography, from the Book of Mormon to *The Tales of the Argonauts,* bear witness that a gloomy fanaticism has been the characteristic religion of the frontier.

XI. REPRESSIONS

There is an equally painful side of frontier life in New England which is difficult to discuss frankly in a generation more reticent than that of the Puritans. For with all the much boasted and much berated modern frankness of speech concerning sexual matters, the flapper or the Freudian would blush to read aloud certain passages in the chronicles of the godly fathers of New England. Suffice it to say that the only light that shines over the Puritan wilderness is the lurid gleam of the Scarlet Letter. The wonder is not that Hawthorne gave us one Dimmesdale, one Hester Prynne, but that he did not give us a dozen. It is hard to estimate whether the deviations from normality which are grouped under the general head of "immorality" were more frequent proportionally on the Puritan frontier than in other communities—our own for instance. We should resent being judged by future historians on the evidence of headlines and Hollywood; and we must remember that the Puritan Inquisition gave a relentless publicity to irregularities which are discreetly ignored in a more sophisticated society. But it is beside the question to debate whether the percentage of immorality in the Puritan community was relatively high or low; the significant point is that the very men of God whose religious and secular duty it was to ferret out and punish vice, betray an indecent interest in all its disgusting details.

The Puritan home has been the last stronghold from which to repel the assaults upon Puritanism. When

Mencken sneers his nastiest, Stuart Sherman reminds us that Winthrop wrote affectionate letters to his wife; he fails to mention that the Mrs. Winthrop in question was the governor's third wife, the first two, like the wives of many Puritan leaders, having died from neglect in childbirth. Such a bereavement might be bewailed as a practical loss, but it received a speedy condolence. Neither woman's rights nor birth control flourished in the Puritan community. The ideal wife was one who, like Margaret Winthrop, "made it her whole care to please, first God and then her husband." If young wives were inclined to have ambitions outside these pious duties, let them take awful warning from the sad fate of Mrs. Hopkins who lost her mind through "giving herself wholly to reading and writing. . . . If she had attended her household affairs and such things as belong to women, and not gone out of her way and calling to meddle in such things as are proper for men whose minds are stronger, she had kept her wits and might have improved them usefully and honorably in the place God had set her."

Of course, human nature is human nature in Puritans as in other men; even the staid Samuel Sewall after living in praiseworthy but monotonous domesticity for forty-three years, becomes quite animated when left a widower and goes a-courting gallantly—until rejected by the lady on whom he has lavished "a pair of Shoebuckles cost 5s 3d" and "a Psalm-Book neatly bound in Turkey Leather." Whereupon, with characteristic Puritan unctuousness, Samuel remarks, "I think God directs me in His Providence to desist."

But this Indian-summer courtship of Samuel Sewall's is unique in Puritan annals. Marriage on the frontier was a severely practical proposition; large families were expected and their labor utilized. For the New England frontier fostered no sentimentality on the subject of child labor. Higginson points out as one attraction of *New England's Plantation* that "Little Children here by setting of Corne may earne much more than their owne maintenance." Johnson praises the industry of the citizens of Rowley who "built a fulling mill, and caused their little ones to be very diligent in spinning cotton wool." Religion was robbed of the beauty of holiness; marriage was robbed of the beauty of romance; childhood was robbed of the beauty of tenderness; the only emotions which the Puritan felt free to express were those of hate and cruelty. It is no mere accident of history that the first head of the first Puritan college was found guilty of saddistic abuse of the boys entrusted to his care.

XII. DISSENSIONS

Another outlet of emotional energy was found in the perpetual wranglings which accompany the "Dissidence of Dissent." Even leaving out of account the innumerable heresy hunts and the mutual recriminations between those who were under the covenant of grace and those who were under the covenant of works, the chronicles of New England bristle with antagonisms. The feud between Dudley and Winthrop is an outstanding example. Sometimes the source of friction lies in a pet antipathy, like Sewall's aversion to periwigs. Sometimes trivial occurrences lead to momentous consequences, as in the famous sow case when a dispute about a stray pig ended in a debate over the principle of a bicameral legislature. Often the argument bears fruit in an exchange of controversial and uncomplimentary pamphlets. Child tells of "New England's Jonas cast up at London," and Winslow replies with "New England's Salamander." Cotton Mather writes "A Memorial of the Present Deplorable State of New England"—a vicious attack on the Dudley administration—and "A Disinterested Hand" —presumably Dudley himself—replies with "A Modest Inquiry into the Grounds and Occasions of a Late Pamphlet entitled 'A Memorial of the Present Deplorable State of New England' "; in spite of which Mather issues another pamphlet alleging that the state of New England is still deplorable, "by reason of a Covetous and Treacherous Governor and Pusillanimous Counsellors." Roger Williams accuses the Puritans of holding "The Bloody Tenent of Persecution"; John Cotton denies the charge in a pamphlet bearing the picturesque title of "The Bloody Tenent washed and made white in the Blood of the Lamb," to which Roger Williams rejoins with "The Bloody Tenent made still more bloody through Mr. Cotton's attempt to wash it white." On this literature of controversion the New Englanders of the seventeenth century lavished all the intellectual ingenuity which their contemporaries in Old England were expending in getting pretty ladies in and out of embarrassing situations in the comedies of intrigue; the results in each case were about equally edifying. One wonders if in their exhaustive researches upon the nature of the Holy Ghost, the Puritans had ever come across the simple text which tells us that "the fruit of the Spirit is peace." "I have only Two Comforts to Live upon," said Nathaniel Ward to Increase Mather, "the one is in the Perfections of Christ; the other is in the Imperfections of all Christians." And I fear of the two, he found in "the imperfections of all Christians" the more enduring satisfaction.

XIII. INDIVIDUALISM

Individualism is traditionally accounted a trait of both the Puritan and the pioneer; it is only reasonable to expect the Puritan pioneer to be an arch-individualist.

Bradford tells of the failure of the communistic experiment at Plymouth: "The strong or man of parts, had no more in division of victuals and cloaths than he that was weake and not able to doe a quarter ye other could; this was thought injustice." The Rev. Cushman preaches in vain against "The Sin and Danger of Self-Love." Robinson urged upon the departing band of Pilgrims the necessity of suppressing the individual for the benefit of the community: "Let every man represse in himselfe and the whole bodie in each person as so many rebels against the common good, all private respects of mens selves, not sorting with the generall convenience." But at Plymouth as at Massachusetts, "it was a very sad thing to see how little of a public spirit appeared in the community, but of self-love too much."

But in at least two respects, the community succeeded in stamping out individual variations. The first, extermination of heresy, has already been mentioned. This insistence upon standardization in religion is peculiar to the Puritan and to the Mormon frontiers. But there is another manifestation of the tyranny of the majority which has been more persistent and more significant in American life: the suppression of unfavorable criticism of the community. We find the seventeenth-century frontiersman extremely touchy about real or fancied slurs on his new home. One of the most amusing instances of this is the calling of John Pratt into court to explain "a letter which he wrote into England . . . wherein he raised an ill report of this country." The shameful slander with which he was charged was the report "that here was nothing but rocks and sands, and salt marshes, etc." John Pratt's *Apology* is a masterpiece of conciliatory but carefully qualified retractions: "and as for the barrenness of the sandy grounds, I spoke of them as then I conceived, but now I find that such ground as before I accounted barren, yet being manured and husbanded, doth bring forth more fruit than I did expect."

A less amusing aspect of this spirit is seen in the arbitrary denial of the right of petition and the summary punishment of petitioners. After reading the interchange of courtesies in *New England's Jonas* and *New England's Salamander,* one is moved to wonder, not that John Cotton advocated throwing overboard the petition, but that he refrained from recommending the same treatment for the petitioners. It is a very delicate, almost impossible task to dissociate human motives: to know how much of this suppression of criticism ought to be ascribed to political and military conditions which had no immediate connection with the influence of the frontier. But making all due allowance for these factors, we recognize in this attitude two leading characters in the American drama: the pioneer and the "knocker." That impatience with the knocker which is a characteristic American attitude, is part of our inheritance from the pioneer: the pioneer, who has worked desperately to achieve something which to him is so precious that criticism is profanation.

XIV. THE DISTINGUISHING FEATURES OF THE NEW ENGLAND FRONTIER

Samuel Sewall enters in his diary two consecutive items with no apparent thought of their incongruity: "Three men are carried away from Lancaster from Mr. Sawyer's sawmill [by Indians]. "This day I made this Distich:

> Roma inhonesta jacet. Sanctae gaudate puellae
> Vindicis et vivi vivitis Urbe Dei."

This is one of the unconscious bits of self revelation that illuminate the Puritan frontier: a frontier where scholars wrote Latin distichs and elaborated theological subtleties while their neighbors were carried into the wilderness by savages; a frontier where transplanted Old World prejudices were intensified and embittered by the very isolation which gave them free play.

"The wilderness masters the colonist. It finds him a European in dress, industries, tools, modes of travel and thought," says Professor Turner, and then details the changes by which the colonist becomes an American. I cannot find that this metamorphosis had taken place in the seventeenth century Puritan. What did the frontier mean to him? Not the scene of romantic adventure; Chesterton calls the love of adventure for its own sake "a peculiarly Christian trait," but it was missing from the Puritan form of Christianity. The seventeenth century Puritan was entirely free from sentimentality about the "noble savage" or "the pleasure in the pathless woods." The noble savage might be useful as an ally or profitable as a slave; most frequently, he was obnoxious as an enemy. The pathless woods furnished abundant cheap fuel; and if one's neighbors didn't agree with one about the technic of justification, it was always possible for a community to pick itself up bodily and make a path through the woods until they found a site which was safe for 100 per cent orthodoxy.

Nor did the frontier mean to the Puritan the challenge of a great exploit for King and country. John Smith had repeatedly appealed to this motive of expansionist patriotism; but even the haziest knowledge of English and American history in the seventeenth century will remind us that it was not a motive paramount in the Puritan mind.

Nor, in spite of their perfunctory protestations, did the frontier mean to the Puritans the field of missionary endeavor. The most casual comparison of Father Kino's sacrificial devotion to his "children" with the Puritans' contemptuous toleration of "praying Indians" will show the negligible part that missionary motives played on the Puritan frontier.

But the frontier did mean to the Puritan the opportunity to exercise to the full his will to power: economic power, in a New World abounding in what seemed to him inexhaustible natural resources; political power in a theocracy that for half a century held absolute sway; religious power as self-constituted priests in a public confessional where confessions were neither respected in confidence nor comforted with absolution.

The Puritan frontiersman was not a chronic pioneer. The chronic pioneers are recruited from the incompetent, who dodge the pressure of organized society; from the restless, who are always like Samuel Chapdelaine in Hemon's novel, "homesick for the place farther on that they have never seen"; from the solitary, who like Daniel Boone long for "more elbow room." On the Puritan frontier, as we have seen, the incompetent were not wanted and were ruthlessly weeded out; the restless ones turned their energies to new theories concerning heaven and the best way to get there, instead of to earthy explorations; when more elbow room was needed, it was a church, not a solitary individual who made the move.

The Puritan frontiersman was not a primitive pathfinder, but a land-hungry "nester." As such he displays the characteristic traits of those who love the frontier, not for what it is but for what they are going to make of it: the optimism, the endurance, the intolerance of the creative pioneer. The optimism of the pioneer is born of a faith that is really "the substance of things hoped for"—the vision of the possibilities of things. It is because of this vision that the pioneer has the endurance to "stay with it" until he sees it through.

> The heroes that I've read about,
> Were only fools that stuck it out
> To end of mortal breath

sings the cowboy of a later frontier. Because he is willing to endure anything in the furtherance of his project, the pioneer is intolerant of anything or anybody who obstructs the accomplishment of his purpose. He is so aglow with enthusiasm in his dream, that he can only regard those who having eyes see not, as deliberately blind, disobedient to the Heavenly Vision. He hates them with a holy hatred; for have they not blasphemed that which he holds sacred? And so we say, the pioneer is intolerant. Faith, endurance, intolerance: these, aggravated by Calvinistic theology, characterize the Puritan frontier; these, mitigated and metamorphosed by varying circumstances, characterize the succeeding frontiers in American history and in American literature.

XV. HAWTHORNE: THE RELUCTANT PURITAN: THE TIMID PIONEER

It is a commonplace of literary criticism that the frontiersmen have neither the time nor the inclination to sing the epic of the pioneer; that is the work of emotion recollected in tranquillity and must be performed by a generation who, in the leisure made possible by the efforts of the pioneer, work over his raw material, bring it to life in an artistic recreation. The story of the Puritan frontier was told indeed by contemporaries, but told not as mere literature but as a day to day chronicle of community life, or as a pious propaganda designed to rebuke the laxness of the always unsatisfactory younger generation by inspiring them with admiration for their fathers and their fathers' God. The story was retold by Hawthorne with the selection, simplification and interpretation of conscious literary art; with the ironic consequence that most of us see New England in terms of Hawthorne and Hawthorne in terms of early New England. Only an antiquarian interest leads the historical or literary student to the once told tales of Winthrop, of Johnson, of Sewall. The squirming urchin in grammar school is conscientiously put through the *Twice Told Tales* of Hawthorne, simultaneously with heroic legends about Miles Standish and Plymouth Rock. The usual result is that by the almost ineradicable influence of early training, we ascribe the vices of the Puritan Fathers to Hawthorne, while we think of their virtues as peculiarly their own. To the popular mind, Hawthorne becomes an admittedly great, but certainly gloomy writer of very unexciting fiction which is "seven-eighths conscience and the rest remorse."

A critical study of American literature confirms the student in the impression that the mantle of the Puritans fell upon Hawthorne, well nigh smothering his creative genius. A well coined phrase speaks of Hawthorne as "the ghost of old New England." Erskine tells us that Hawthorne "was unable to see life except as a Puritan world from a Puritan standpoint." Brownell calls Hawthorne "a very genuine son of the Puritans." Barrett Wendell says, "Beyond anyone else he expresses the deepest temper of that New England race which brought him forth." Woodberry goes even farther in aligning Hawthorne with the Puritan *Weltanschauung*: "The genius of Hawthorne involved a reversion to the Puritan past, and not only that, but to what was grim, harsh, and terrible in its spirit. His genius worked in a reactionary way upon the theme of his brooding, and he throws open the doors of the past rather than the gates of the future." Hawthorne is thus traditionally stamped as a Puritan; he is never thought of as a pioneer. And it must be admitted that Hawthorne's writing lends itself readily to this interpretation. The reader of *Roger Malvin's Burial* for instance, can scarcely fail to notice the slight emphasis given to the frontier environment, although it is that environment which conditions the tragedy. Roger and Reuben have been members of an expedition for the defence of the frontier. Roger's dying request springs from the almost superstitious regard with which the frontier inhabitants, revolted by the Indian practice of mutilating the dead, insisted upon the rites of sepulture. The tragic expiation is made possible through the perennial rebirth of the frontier which enables the unsuccessful Reuben to pull up stakes and start over again in the virgin bosom of the wilderness. Hawthorne, however, is not telling the story of a frontiersman, but of a moral coward; he seems all impatience to get through the brief introductory paragraph with its mention of Lovell's flight, and to begin the story of a tortured soul. Yet this emphasis is by no means peculiar to Hawthorne; it is exactly the emphasis that would have been given in a contemporary chronicle by a Puritan pioneer.

As part of the modern reaction against Puritanism an attempt has been made to snatch Hawthorne from the side of the angels and parade him stamped not as Puritan but as artist. This attempt, of course, proceeds on the assumption which to its promulgator seems self evident, that artist and Puritan are incompatible terms. Exonerated from the charge of Puritanism, an emasculated Hawthorne is acclaimed by the younger critics of American literature as "a verbal melodist without any ethical intention whatsoever."

Is it then only an ironical misinterpretation that has persistently associated Hawthorne with the Puritan scene and the Puritan ideal? Which is right—the critic who identifies him with Puritanism or the critic who detaches him from Puritanism? Neither—and both. In the words of Professor Percy Boynton, Hawthorne was at once "a product of his ancestry and a living protest against it."

If Hawthorne, the product of a Puritan ancestry, the

inheritor of a Puritan environment, instinctively transcribed Puritan materials and Puritan attitudes, he made the very transcription a commentary on the inadequacy of the Puritan world. Whether in implicit inference or explicit comment, he gives us not only a representation but a criticism of the ideal which brought the Puritans to the New England frontier.

This criticism is by no means always destructive. Hawthorne honors the idealism of the Puritan. But even at the moment that Hawthorne recognizes Puritan idealism, he condemns Puritan cruelty. It is a mistaken idealism that makes, a false ideal that demands, human sacrifices. "Had Aylmer reached a profounder wisdom he need not thus have flung away the happiness which would have woven his mortal life of the self-same texture with the celestial." Thus Hawthorne anticipates the modern exposure of the Puritan fallacy.

In many cases Hawthorne's condemnation of Puritan cruelty is more evident than his respect for the motivating ideal. As he records the persecuting spirit of his own ancestors, he fears that their hard severity will outweigh their many good deeds, and as their representative he takes shame upon himself for their sakes. He admires the Endicott who defied pope and tyrant, but hopes that even that implacable Endicott was touched at the inevitable blight of early hopes when his vengeance lighted on the newly married lovers of Merry Mount. For the relentless malevolence of the Puritan community to the Gentle Boy and his charitable protectors, he has no word of extenuation. We feel that he shares the conviction of the ringing words in which Hester denounces the subtle malice of Roger Chillingsworth: "That old man's revenge was blacker than our sin." The sins of love carry their own atonement; the sins of hate make their own hell. If in this conclusion Hawthorne has departed far from the spirit of the persecuting Puritan, he goes even farther in his assault upon the very stronghold of the Puritan position;—the Puritan sense of obligation as his brother's keeper which Hawthorne stigmatizes as "the terrible egotism which he mistook for an angel of God." When Zenobia speaks to Coverdale, I hear Hawthorne speaking to Winthrop, to Dudley, to John Cotton and John Wilson—to all the self-righteous despots who ruled the Puritan frontier:

> O this stale excuse of duty! I have often heard it before from those who sought to interfere with me, and I know precisely what it signifies. Bigotry, self-conceit; an insolent curiosity; a meddlesome temper; a cold-blooded criticism, founded on a shallow interpretation of half-perceptions; a monstrous skepticism in regard to any conscience or wisdom except one's own; a most irreverent propensity to thrust Providence aside, and substitute one's self in its awful place—out of these and other motives as miserable as these, comes your idea of duty!

Just as Hawthorne repudiates the Puritan ideal of duty, does he repudiate the Puritan ideal of aloofness. The Puritan was forever setting himself up as judge; and a judge must stand apart, must be untouched by a feeling for human infirmities, unswerved by sympathy with human delights. But to Hawthorne there is "no fate in the world so horrible as to have no share in either its joy or sorrows." Hawthorne's feeling on this point was intensified by the unnatural loneliness of his early life. That he regretted its dehumanizing influence is evident from his letter to his college classmate, Longfellow: "I have made a captive of myself and put me into a dungeon and now I cannot find the key to let myself out." Repeatedly in his novels and short stories he gives us characters in whom solitude has bred not strength but weakness — Clifford, for instance, crippled so that his spirit cannot walk, a plaintive ghost, longing for and yet shrinking from contact with the bustling world of his more normal fellows. More than one of Hawthorne's protagonists share the conviction of the Puritans that isolation from humanity means superiority to humanity; in every case their pride goes before their destruction. The Man of Adamant, both a Puritan and a frontiersman, seeks solitude in the wilderness that he may "hold no communion with those abominable myriads which Heaven hath cast off to perish"; he petrifies in his desolate cave. Ethan Brand finds the Unpardonable Sin in his own stony heart. Lady Eleanore wraps herself in pride as in a mantle and dies from its pestilential influence. Septimius Felton is somewhat like Dostoevski's Raskolnikoff in his desire to prove though by a crime, that he is beyond good and evil; the outcome of his experiment is equally ironic. He purchases immortal life at the price of the surrender of all human emotions—and finds it in truth, a Devil's bargain.

Like the Puritans, Hawthorne betrays interest in the unpardonable sin; unlike them, he identifies it with the Puritan distrust of human nature. The most clinching evidence of Hawthorne's repudiation of Puritanism is found in the story of Young Goodman Brown. The witches' Sabbath attended by the Puritan youth bears as little resemblance to the traditional Walpurgisnacht as the essentially ascetic Devil's bargain subscribed to by Septimius Felton does to the traditional barter of an immortal soul for sensual delights. The devil lures Septimius Felton not to gratification but to suppression of emotions. The devil's gift to Young Goodman Brown is not the kingdoms of the earth and the glory thereof, not the vision of that matchless beauty which burnt the topless towers of Ilium;—but the power to discern the hidden evil in the hearts of his fellow men. "I hate cynicism," wrote the genial R. L. S. "a good deal worse than I do the devil; unless indeed, they are the same thing." They are identical in the story of Young Goodman Brown. The devil who lures him to the unhallowed altar is "der Geist der stets verneint"; he bears "no slight similitude, both in garb and manner, to some great divine of the New England churches."

Most audacious of all Hawthorne's departures from Puritanism is his suggestion of the possibility of purification by sin. "Some rise by sin and some by virtue fall" was a paradox incomprehensible to the Puritan mind, but not to the writer of *The Scarlet Letter*. Hester works out "a purity more saintlike than that which she had lost, because the result of martyrdom." She becomes such a power for good in the community that the people who had branded her interpret the mark of her shame to signify ABLE. The faun-like Donatello achieves a soul through the very crime which tortures it. "Sin has educated Donatello," comments Kenyon. The strait-laced Hilda is shocked at the irreverent suggestion, and we may assume that Hawthorne himself does not care to be too positive upon this point, but leaves his own attitude undefined, half way between that of Kenyon and that of Hilda. It indicates a radical protest against Puritanism that he even raises the question: "Is sin then—which we deem such a dreadful blackness in the universe—is it like sorrow, merely an element of human education, through which we struggle to a higher and purer state than we could otherwise have attained? Did Adam fall that we might ultimately rise to a far higher Paradise than his?"

These tentative questionings, which mark Hawthorne as an unwilling Puritan, mark him also as a hesitant pioneer—the first artist in American literature to dissent from the established and expand the spiritual frontier. The Puritan frontier, as we have seen, was primarily an adventure in spiritual pioneering. Life in the forest primeval was not to the Puritans an end in itself, as it may be to the chronic pioneers, but a means to an end; a freedom to work out an experiment in community living. The Puritans, hard as it may be for us to appreciate it, were the radicals of their day. They worked to realize their dream of a Congregational Commonwealth with the same rabid zeal with which modern radicals work for the realization of a Soviet Republic. They began in America two types of pioneering which have conditioned and colored the national life and consequently the national literature. The adventure in regional pioneering which began with their settlements on the Atlantic frontier, swept across the continent. It was in part an "expansion of New England" achieved by the lineal and spiritual descendants of the Puritan pioneers. But the sea to sea advance of the frontier was achieved in larger part by men of a very different type: trappers, pathfinders, cowboys, Mormons, gold-diggers, land speculators. The adventure in regional pioneering which the Pilgrim Fathers had inaugurated, became, as Professor Turner has told us, the distinguishing factor in American history. Whether in the primary stage of exploration, or in the secondary stage of exploitation, the conquest of the continent absorbed the energies of American life.

And what of the adventure in spiritual pioneering which Bradford's little band of dauntless souls had initiated at Plymouth? We have seen that by the end of the seventeenth century it had ceased to be a heroic adventure and had become an established church. The heresy of old England had become the orthodoxy of New England. Now it takes a Chesterton to find orthodoxy exciting; for the average mortal it becomes "verra praiseworthy but verra monotonous." We need a perennial rebirth of the spiritual as of the geographical frontier. The intellectual and emotional stimulus which vitalized New England life while Puritanism was persecuted or persecuting, subsided into the tameness of toleration. Puritanism as a negative, an inhibiting force survived; Puritanism as a positive, an energizing force died; or rather, suffered a sea change into something rich and strange that was transcendentalism.

"Ours is the first generation consciously engaged in spiritual pioneering," asserts Waldo Frank with a touch of the fatuousness of Goethe's Baccalaureus, confident that "Die Welt sie war nicht eh ich sie erschuf." One wonders how Mr. Frank explains the certainly self-conscious spiritual pioneering of the transcendentalists. We shall consider later the golden age of transcendentalism which coincided with the golden age of regional pioneering. But Hawthorne was no more a transcendentalist than he was a Puritan. His spiritual life was lived "between two worlds, one dead, the other struggling to be born." He was no more the devotee of the new than he was the idolater of the old. He was a pioneer—but he was not a partner in any great general migration, but a solitary pathfinder. True, it was but a tiny trail that he broke through the wilderness; true he easily became discouraged and finding the way threatening or obscure, turned his face toward Main Street. He was a timid pioneer; but nevertheless he did leave Main Street sometimes and roam in the thickets dreaming of a better city beyond.

To abandon the figure: just as critics have differed as to whether Hawthorne were a Puritan or a Transcendentalist, so they have differed as to whether he were a reformer. The consensus of literary criticism seems to be that he is a moralist, but one well content to apply the old Puritan pattern to mankind in the making. Hawthorne has generally been acquitted of "any attempt to change, rectify or spiritualize society." Bliss Perry speaks of Hawthorne as "moving wholly within the framework of established institutions with no desire to shatter the existing social order."

Now the most casual reading of Hawthorne shows his distaste for professed reformers. But with all his contempt for the cocksureness of professional philanthropists, Hawthorne has a deep reverence for the Will to Utopia. He speaks of Holgrave as having "that sense of inward prophecy—which a young man had better die at once than not to have, and a mature man had better never have been born than utterly to relinquish—that we are not doomed to creep on forever in the old, bad way, but that this very now there are harbingers abroad of a golden era to be accomplished in his own lifetime." Writing in *The Blithedale Romance* of his venture at Brook Farm, he says: "Whatever else I may repent of, let it be reckoned neither among my sins nor follies that I once had faith and force enough to form generous hopes of the world's destiny—yes! and to do what in me lay for their accomplishment." Hawthorne was no mere dilettante languidly retouching the faded daguerreotype of the Puritan world; he was no mere mystic, rapturously soaring to the heights of transcendentalism; he was, however ineffectually, a Utopian; that is to say, a spiritual pioneer.

The latent radicalism of Hawthorne may best be illustrated in one strain that runs throughout his fiction—his feminism. This differentiates him sharply from the Puritan who thought of "good" women as child-bearers and housewives, and of other women as snares of the devil. On occasion, it is true, Hawthorne assumes the Puritan attitude toward women as well as utilizing the Puritan materials. In writing a biographical sketch of Mrs. Hutchinson he speaks of the intellectual activities of that strong-minded woman in language that might have been taken from Winthrop's *Journal*. Hawthorne justifies the banishment of Mrs. Hutchinson as a case "in which religious freedom was wholly inconsistent with public safety." He traces the downfall of Mrs. Hutchinson to her presumptuous intellectual ambitions, and asks: "Is it good for woman's self that the path of feverish hope, of tremulous success, of bitter and ignominous disappointment should be left wide open to her? . . . Fame does not increase the peculiar respect which men pay to female excellence and there is a delicacy that perceives or fancies a sort of impropriety in the display of woman's natal mind to the gaze of the world with indications by which its inmost secrets may be searched out." For the equally strongminded and disturbing woman of his own day, Margaret Fuller, he had equally scant sympathies. And if we turn for evidence to the ladies of his imagination, we find abundant proof of Hawthorne's admiration of the traditional womanly woman. Woman's constancy and unselfishness in love are celebrated in "The Shaker Bridal," in "Edward Fane's Rosebud," in "The Prophetic Pictures"—"The White Old Maid," "The Minister's Black Veil," "The Maypole of Merry Mount," "Egotism"—the list becomes tedious, and we might continue indefinitely cataloguing the conventional use of *das ewig weibliche.* But just as Hawthorne's embodiment of Puritanism is in curiously ironic contrast to his protest against Puritanism, so his eulogy of the time-honored feminine virtues is coupled with recurrent wonder whether these virtues form an all-sufficient expression of a woman's nature. Sometimes in the same story the simple conventional girl is contrasted with the complex restless woman: Priscilla with Zenobia, Hilda with Miriam. In Zenobia and Miriam, Hawthorne has given us the rebel, raging against the conventional routine for women. In Sibyl, Hawthorne has given us the skeptic, doubting the conventional mission for women. In Hester, he has given us the free woman who has translated her feeling and thinking into action. In his treatment of Hester, the dual personality of Hawthorne is evident; now he seems to judge her as her Puritan contemporaries judged her; now to admire her with the untrammeled respect which she inspires in a modern reader. It is impossible to draw any conclusions from one point of view which cannot be effectively refuted by quotation from another. It is impossible to draw a consistent brief for one point of view without arbitrarily ignoring the other. It is impossible to reconcile the two without putting a strained interpretation on clear statements. Rather than attempt such a reconciliation, let us admit frankly that Hawthorne's advocacy of Hester as a free woman progresses like the Sabine army of Andreyeff's play, "two steps forward and one step back." Hawthorne is a timid pioneer on these perilous paths into forbidden territory; but he does take some forward steps. The very creation of such a personality as Hester as the wearer of the Scarlet Letter is a forward step.

Hester is a faint precursor of the feminist type. In her relation to her lover she displays the traditional self-abnegating devotion of a Gretchen or a Heloise. In her relation to her child she displays the fierce intensity of a Magda. But neither her child nor her lover fills the whole of her life; she is not entirely a creature of emotion; her salvation lies in her indomitable will. Life is a bigger thing to her than her affair with Dimmesdale, profoundly as that had entered into her soul. When love was denied her, she made for herself a world of daring thoughts, thoughts even more reprehensible from the point of view of Puritan orthodoxy, than her passionate sin. "The Scarlet Letter was her passport into regions where other women dared not tread."

The merciless illumination of the Scarlet Letter exposes the rottenness of the foundations on which society is built. Under its baleful radiance, Hester challenges the validity of accepted conventions. Let the Puritan community cast her out marked with the brand of shame;

she knows that her union with Dimmesdale had "a consecration of its own." Let the Puritan magistrates attempt to take away her child, and she defies Religion and Respectability with the assertion of her God-given right to the Pearl for which she had paid so great a price. Even while abandoning hope that she may be the prophetess of a better era, she cherishes "a firm belief that at some brighter period when the world should have grown ripe for it, in Heaven's own time, a new truth would be revealed in order to establish the whole relation between man and woman on a surer ground of mutual happiness."

Thus the very romance which takes its title and inspiration from the Puritan code, rejects that code and prophesies another. The very artist who recreates the Puritan world dreams of reshaping it nearer to the heart's desire. The spiritual frontier like the geographical one, must move forward. With Hawthorne it is true, it does not move very far; but in him is seen the twofold influence of the frontier on American literature; the direct influence which lends to American fiction characters, situations, and settings peculiar to frontier life; and the indirect but even more potent heritage from the first frontier, the tradition of spiritual pioneering, with its refusal to abide by accepted dogmas and practices, its effort to remake human nature and human society in accordance with a new ideal.

BIBLIOGRAPHY

I. Primary Sources.

BRADFORD, WILLIAM
A Descriptive and Historical Account of New England in verse
in Mass. Hist. Coll. series 1, vol. 3

BRADFORD, WILLIAM
Letter Book (1624–30)
in Mass. Hist. Coll. series 1, vol. 3

BRADFORD, WILLIAM
History of Plymouth Plantation (1620–1647)
Boston; 1856

BRADFORD, WILLIAM and WINSLOW, EDWARD
Mourt's Relation (Nov. 1620–Jan. 1622) New York, 1848
(also in Mass. Hist. Coll. series 1, vol. 7–8)

BULKLEY, JOHN
Inquiry Respecting Indian Rights to Lands in America
Mass. Hist. Coll. series 1, vol. 4

CHILD, JOHN
New England's Jonas cast up at London (1647)
in Mass. Hist. Coll. 2nd series, vol. 4

CLAP, ROGER
Memoirs (1676)
in Young's *Chronicles of Mass. Bay Colony*

COTTON, JOHN
God's Promise to His Plantations (1630)
Boston, 1894

CUSHMAN, ROBERT
On the Sin and Danger of Self Love (1622)
in Masefield's *Chronicles of the Pilgrim Fathers*

CUSHMAN, ROBERT
Reasons and Considerations touching the lawfulness of removing out of England into the parts of America (1622)
published with Mourt's relation in Mass. Hist. Coll. series 1, vol. 7–8

DUDLEY, THOMAS
Letter to the Countess of Lincoln, (1631)
Washington, 1838

HIGGINSON, FRANCIS
A True Relation of the last voyage to New England (1629)
in Young's *Chronicles of Mass. Bay Colony*

HIGGINSON, FRANCIS
New England's Plantation (1630)
in Young's *Chronicles of Mass. Bay Colony*

JOHNSON, EDWARD
The Wonder-Working Providence of Sion's Saviour (1628–1652)
New York, 1910
Also in Mass. Hist. Coll. 2nd series vol. 2–8

JOSSELYN, JOHN
An Account of Two Voyages to New England, (1675)
in Mass. Hist. Coll. 3rd series, vol. 3–4

LECHFORD, THOMAS
Plain Dealing: or News from New England (1642)
in Mass. Hist. Coll. 3rd series, vol. 3–4

MATHER, COTTON (writing under pseudonym of Philopolites)
A Memorial of the Present Deplorable State of New England, (1707)
also the reply
"By a Disinterested Hand" (probably DUDLEY)
A Modest Enquiry into the Grounds and Occasions of a Late Pamphlet entitled A Memorial of the Present Deplorable State of New England. (1707)
and Mather's reply

MATHER, COTTON (Philopolities)
The Deplorable State of New England by reason of a Covetous and Treacherous Governor and Pusillanimous Counsellors. (1708)
The three pamphlets are published with Sewall's *Diary*, Mass. Hist. Coll. 5th series

MATHER, COTTON
Magnalia Christi Americana (1620–1698) 2 vol.
Hartford, 1820

MATHER, INCREASE
Remarkable Providences illustrative of the earlier days of American colonization (1684)
London, 1890

MATHER, RICHARD
Journal (1635)
in Young's *Chronicles of Mass. Bay Colony*

MORTON, THOMAS
New English Canaan (1632)
in Force's Hist. Coll. vol. 2

PRATT, JOHN
Apology (1635)
in Mass. Hist. Coll. 2nd series, vol. 7

SEWALL, SAMUEL
Diary (1674–1729) 3 vol.
in Mass. Hist. Coll. 5th series
SHEPARD, THOMAS
Memoir (1634)
in Young's *Chronicles of Mass. Bay Colony*
SMITH, JOHN
A Description of New England (1616)
in Force's Hist. Coll. 5th series
SMITH, JOHN
Advertisements for the unexperienced Planters of New England or anywhere, or, The Pathway to erect a Plantation. (1631)
in Mass. Hist. Coll. 3rd series, vol. 3–4
SMITH, JOHN
New England's Trials (1622)
in Force's Hist. Coll. vol. 2
THACHER, ANTHONY
Narrative of his Shipwreck (1635)
in Young's *Chronicles of Mass. Bay Colony*
WHITE, JOHN (supposed author)
The Planters' Plea (1630)
in Force's Hist. Coll. vol. 2
WINTHROP, JOHN (supposed author)
General Considerations for planting New England (1629)
in Young's *Chronicles of Mass. Bay Colony*
WINTHROP, JOHN
Journal: History of New England (1630–1649) 2 vol.
New York, 1908
WINSLOW, EDWARD
Good News from New England (1625)
in Mass. Hist. Coll. 1st series, vol. 7–8
WINSLOW, EDWARD
Hypocrisie Unmasked (1646)
Providence, 1916
WINSLOW, EDWARD
New England's Salamander (1647)
in Mass. Hist. Coll. 3rd series, vol. 1–2
WOOD, WILLIAM
New England's Prospect (1634)
Boston, 1898

II. Collections of Primary Sources

FORCE, PETER (editor)
Tracts relating to the Origin, Settlement, and Progress of the Colonies in North America
Washington, 1836

LINCOLN, CHARLES (editor)
Narratives of the Indian Wars
New York, 1913

MASEFIELD, JOHN (editor)
Chronicles of the Pilgrim Fathers
New York, 1910

YOUNG, ALEXANDER (editor)
Chronicles of the first planters of the Colony of Massachusetts Bay
Boston, 1846

III. Secondary Sources

ADAMS, CHARLES F.
Three Episodes of Massachusetts History
Boston, 1903

ADAMS, JAMES T.
The Founding of New England
Boston, 1921

ANDREWS, CHARLES M.
The Fathers of New England
New Haven, 1921

BEST, MARY AGNES
Rebel Saints
New York; Harcourt Brace & Co., 1925

DOYLE, J. A.
The English in America: The Puritan Colonies. 2 vol.
London, 1887

EARLE, ALICE M.
Margaret Winthrop
New York, 1895

EGGLESTON, MELVILLE
The Land System of the New England Colonies
Baltimore, 1886

FISKE, JOHN
The Beginnings of New England
Boston, no date given

HUBBARD, WILLIAM
A General History of New England to 1680
Cambridge, 1815

HUTCHINSON, THOMAS
The History of Massachusetts from the first settlement thereof in 1628 until the year 1750
Salem, 1795, 2 vol.
MATTHEWS, LOIS K.
The Expansion of New England
Boston, 1909
MURDOCK, KENNETH B.
Increase Mather: The Foremost American Puritan
Cambridge; Harvard University Press, 1925
OSGOOD, HERBERT L.
The American Colonies in the Seventeenth Century
New York, 1904, 3 vol.
PALFREY, JOHN G.
A Compendious History of New England
Boston, 1873, 4 vol.
SEARS, LOUIS M.
"The Puritan and his Indian Ward"
in Amer. J. Soc. vol. 22, July, 1916
WEEDEN, WILLIAM B.
Economic and Social History of New England
Boston, 1891, 2 vol.
WENDELL, BARRETT
Cotton Mather, the Puritan Priest
New York, 1891
WINTHROP, ROBERT C.
Life and Letters of John Winthrop
Boston, 1869, 2 vol.

IV. On Hawthorne

NATHANIEL HAWTHORNE: Works. The Date given is of the first edition.
Twice Told Tales—1837
Grandfather's Chair—1841
Mosses from an Old Manse—1846
The Scarlet Letter—1850
The House of the Seven Gables—1851
The Blithedale Romance—1852
The Marble Faun—1860
American Notebooks—1868
English Notebooks—1870
Septimius Felton—1871
Between 1871 and 1904 there have been eighteen editions

of Hawthorne's Collected Works in from six to eighteen volumes.

Critical articles on Hawthorne appear in the following:

Boynton, Percy
A History of American Literature
Boston, 1919

Brooks, Van Wyck
America's Coming of Age
New York, 1915

Brownell, W. C.
American Prose Masters
New York, 1909

Erskine, John: article on Hawthorne in Cambridge History of American Literature Volume II, Book II, ch. XI
New York, 1918
also in
Leading American Novelists
New York, 1910

Macy, John
The Spirit of American Literature
New York, 1912

More, Paul Elmer
"The Solitude of Nathaniel Hawthorne" in *Shelburne Essays,* 1st series
New York, 1909

Wendell, Barrett
A Literary History of America
New York, 1907

Woodberry, George E.
America in Literature
New York, 1903

For more extended biographical and critical data:

Woodberry, George E.
Nathaniel Hawthorne
Boston, 1902

Woodberry, George E.
Nathaniel Hawthorne and How to Know Him
Indianapolis, 1918

CHAPTER II

THE SOUTHERN FRONTIER: A STUDY IN ROMANTICISM

I. PLANTATION AND FRONTIER

THE South is generally conceded to be less solid for the purposes of literature than for the purposes of electioneering. William P. Trent writing in *The Atlantic Monthly* for January, 1897, on "Dominant Forces in Southern Life" points out the distinctive differences which cause "the typical Charlestonian to differ as much from the average inhabitant of Nashville as the typical New Yorker does from his rival of Chicago, the tidewater South to differ from the Southwest as much as New England does from the Middle West." If these differentia are perceptible even in this era of uniformity and standardization, how much more obvious must they have been in the days of the frontier? How shall we characterize the hetrogeneous elements that the frontier of the Old South contributed to the Southern Confederacy? How shall we reduce to a least common denominator such various factors as the landed aristocrats of Virginia, the poor whites of North Carolina, the mountaineers of Kentucky, the Creoles and Acadians of Louisiana?

The complexity of the problem tempts one to evade it in one of the two traditional methods for disposing of Southern literature. The first and the most frequent, tacitly defining literature as synonymous with belles lettres, limits its discussion to the decadent effusions of

Southern dilettanti,—the pseudo-classical, pseudo-European poetizings of Timrod, Hayne, and Lanier, whose writing, thin and imitative, belongs entirely to the academic side of literature and has no connection with the author's geographical or social habitat. The second method follows the more recent but equally fallacious assumption that state lines are of abiding validity in literature, and that however trivial the literary product that may be associated with a particular state, there is some mysterious merit in collecting, let us say, all the stories of Mississippi, even to such a piece of conventional romanticism as Miss Murfree's *The Fair Mississippian,* while conversely, a star of larger magnitude like Poe is dimmed or enhanced in glory according to whether his scintillations can be proved characteristically Virginian. By this method an interesting tabulation of Southern writers may be made, but the abundant undergrowth on which our attention is focused obscures the forest; while cataloging writings about the South, we have lost sight of the fundamental problem: what is the distinctive element in the spirit of the South and what influence has it had on American literature?

We find our answer as we go back to origins. The northeastern frontier was a Mecca of zealous fanatics obsessed with their project of a Congregational Commonwealth; the far western frontier was an Eldorado for emigrés who desired to find new fortunes and lose their old selves; the Middle Border was the frontier of embattled farmers steadily pushed farther west by the forces of landlordism; the southwestern frontier was the Utopia of gallant adventurers. Whether we look to the carnival gaiety of the Louisianian Creole, or the stolid somnolence of a Tennessee mountaineer, or the serene magnificence of a South Carolinian planter, everywhere we find the spirit of the South the spirit of romance,—a reverent cherishing of the past, an easy-going enjoyment of the present, a lighthearted challenging of the future. The extent to which this romantic, loyal, masterful, chivalric, adventurous spirit of the South is rooted in the economic condition of the pioneer settlements is recognized by Ulrich Phillips in his introduction to the "Plantation and Frontier" volumes of *The Documentary History of Industrial Society in the United States.* The ante-bellum South, says Professor Phillips, was "preëminently the region of plantation and frontier. The most perfect types of plantation and frontier occurred in the Southern colonies. . . . In the north the Indians and the popular government was (sic) administered directly under the Federal authority. In the southwest the settlers in general did their own fighting, their own land office work, their own legislating, when any was done, and their own administering of the laws. . . . The temper and philosophy of the people were formed chiefly by the combined and interacting influence of the frontier and plantation systems."

It is then to plantation and frontier that we should look for the genesis of all that is peculiar in Southern literature. Instead of paying perfunctory respects to the conventional headliners of Southern literature, instead of swamping ourselves among the throng of minor writers who specialize in the local color of Southern sections, we shall consider three types of Southern pioneers and trace from each a vital impulse in Southern romanticism. First, as first not only in Southern literature but in American literature, that Sir John Mandeville of the New World, the father of Virginia, arch romancer and adventurer, Captain John Smith; the journals of Colonel William Byrd, second of the name, furnish the second example of the Cavalier as frontiersman; and in Davy Crockett, Congressman and bear-hunter, we have the first contribution of the Southern mountains to the folk epic of American history.

II. CAPTAIN JOHN SMITH: ELIZABETHAN IMPERIALIST

The reputation of Captain John Smith as a veracious chronicler of history has in recent years suffered an eclipse. But the more fictitious Smith's narrative can be proved from the standpoint of history, the more significant it becomes from the standpoint of literature. We lose only one of many journalistic recorders of colonizing activities; we gain the one unique among many frontiersmen for whom the frontier was a theater of romance, who consciously posed center stage, the hero of his own drama. Out of Captain John Smith, discredited historian, emerges the first American writer to create romance from contemporary realism.

John Smith was representative of a generation elated over the defeat of the Spanish Armada, eager to emulate the feats of the Spanish adventurers. They could not forget how nearly the prize of American settlement had been within England's grasp, how in one of those moments that determine destinies the offer of Columbus had been let slip and the memorable expedition had been made under the auspices of Spain. The gallant adventurers of England felt that it was not too late to retrieve the error, to wrest the prize of empire from Spain on the new continent as they had done on the high seas. The motive of nationalistic glory pulses through Smith's propaganda for emigration as strongly as does the motive of sectarian bigotry through the propagandist appeals of the Puritan Fathers. 'Leave the City of Destruction and build Zion in the Chosen Land to which Jehovah will guide his people,' urge in effect the persuasions of the Dissenting Divines. 'For the love and glory of Old England spread her empire into the New World where fame and fortune await you,' is the challenge flung by Smith to his torpid countrymen. In the difference between these two appeals lies the distinctive difference between the frontier of the Puritan and the frontier of the cavalier. Smith preached the campaign against Spain as fervently as Winthrop conducted the campaign against the Devil. But Smith at least gave his devil his due and admitted that England must deign to learn the lesson of effective expansion from her detested rival:

> Who seeth not what is the greatest good of the Spanyard but these new conclusions, in searching those unknowne parts of the unknowne world? By which meanes hee dives even into the verie secrets of all his Neighbours, and the most part of the world: and when the Portugale and the Spanyard had found the East and West Indies; how many did condemn themselves that did not accept of that honest offer of Noble Columbus?

Smith anticipates H. G. Wells in the impatience with which he sees his fellow Englishmen muddling through. They might well emulate the very people they despise:

> It would bee an historie of a large volume to recite the adventures of the Spanyards and Portugals, their affronts and defeats, their dangers and miseries; which with such incomparable honour and constant resolution so farre beyonde beleefe they have attempted and indured in their discoveries and plantations as may well condemne us of too much embecillitie, sloth and negligence. . . . I could wish every English man to carry alwais this Motto in his heart; why should the brave Spanish souldiers brag: The Sunne never sets in the Spanish dominions, but ever shineth on one part or other we have conquered for our King: who within these few hundred of yeares was one of the least of most of his neighbours, but to animate us to doe the like for ours who is in no way his inferior?

The story of these earliest, gallantly desperate attempts at colonization by the English is familiar. Twice had devoted bands of colonists been sent out under the inspiration of Raleigh—only to perish on the desolate shores of North Carolina leaving no clue to their fate.

Smith joined the third band of undaunted adventurers which set sail from the Downs on New Year's Day, 1607. The mismanagement and no-management of this ill-assorted company of gentlemen enthusiasts is a historical fact which does not depend altogether on Smith's narratives of the jealousies, the follies, the complainings and the factiousness which well nigh wrecked the settlement. "There is no misery worse than to be conducted by a foole or commanded by a coward," wrote Smith in his "Advertisements to the Inexperienced; or the Pathway to erect Plantations." With how much poignant emotion wrung from his own tussles with folly and cowardice Smith penned that maxim all who have read his record can realize.

When his companions wasted time and supplies in the fatuous task of forcing a crown upon the uncomprehending Powhatan, Smith looked on in helpless disgust, but without abandoning his more practical diplomatic negotiations with their fickle ally. When Wingfield with sentimental pacifism and self-laudatory freedom from race prejudice opposed any fortification and insisted on treating the redmen as brothers, Smith realized the precarious position of one hundred and five unorganized, incompetent fortune hunters on the outskirts of an alien barbarism—and took measures of defense accordingly. When the improvidently generous commissioners bartered their supplies at a ruinously low rate of exchange, giving their all to the Indians in return for a pitifully inadequate supply of grain, Smith came to the rescue by creating a demand for some blue beads with which he procured the needed food for his people.

It was Smith who steadily opposed the fatal indiscretion of placing firearms in the hands of the savages. It was Smith alone who kept his head when his fellow colonists lost theirs over the "phantasical gold dust" which they madly dug from the Virginia streams when their labor was imperatively needed in hoeing their grain. It was Smith who, when starvation threatened went fearlessly into the heart of the enemy country, negotiating for supplies. And what were the rewards a grateful country offered for his leadership? Upon his almost miraculous escape from captivity after the memorable expedition which saved the colony, he returned to his own—to face indictment by the pedantical Archer under a curiously perverted construction of the Levitical law whereby the colony presumed to hold Smith as captain responsible for the deaths of two of his party who had lost their lives by deliberately disobeying his express orders for their safety.

From the prolonged misery of the voyage out during which Smith was accused of mutiny and imprisoned under martial law, to the torturing accident which sent him back to Old England a shattered sufferer, Smith's life on the Virginia frontier was a heroic drama of maligned leadership, resolute, shrewd, and cheerful, not only through terrifying crises, not only through the long discomforts of inadequate food and shelter, but under the daily bickering, shortsightedness, incompetence, and pettiness of the men with whom and for whom he was working. And the gallant adventurer looks upon it all and sees that it is good. In words whose indomitable spirit recalls the death boast of Beowulf and links the first folk hero of Teutonic England with this, the first folk hero of English America, he praises his God for the welfare of the colonies which with no mere sentimental affectation he calls his children:

> For they have bin my wife, my hawks, my hounds, my cards, my dice, and in totall my best content.—and notwithstanding all those miracles of disaster that have crossed both them and me, yet were there not one English man remaining (as God bee thanked there is some thousands) I would yet begine againe with as small meanes as I did at the first.

American literature begins with John Smith's summons to a new frontier of romantic adventure. That is to say, American literature begins with romanticism at its best: not dodging but transfiguring the stern actualities of existence, not mooning in the past, but pressing forward to the future, glorying in disappointments and hardships, unshaken by defeat, unembittered by failure. What honor Smith holds out to the magnanimous spirits that dare the enterprise for empire:

> Truly there is no pleasure comparable to that of a generous spirit; as good imploiment in noble actions, especially among Turks, Heathens, and Infidels; to see daily new Countries, people, fashions, governments, strategems; to releeve the oppressed, comfort his friends, passe miseries, subdue enemies, adventure upon any feazable danger for God and his Country. It is true it is a happy thing to be borne to strength, wealth, and honour; but that which is got by prowesse and magnanimitie is the truest lustre: and those can the best distinguish content that have escaped most honourable dangers.—If he have but the taste of virtue and magnanimite what to such an inde can bee more pleasant than planting and building a foundation for his posterie gotte from the rude earth by God's blessing and his own industrie without prejudice to any? —What so truly suits with honour and honestie as the discovering things unknowne? erecting Townes, peopling Countries, informing the ignorant, reforming things unjust, teaching virtue, and gaine to our Native mother-countrie a kingdom to attend her.

The honor which Smith bestows upon the valiant is equalled only by the contempt in which he holds the ignoble spirits satisfied with a stay-at-home existence: "Then who would live at home idly (or thinke it in himselfe any worth to live?) onely to eate, drinke and sleepe and so die?"

Romantic in his vision of the ultimate goal of his efforts, Smith is romantic also in his spontaneous delight in the nature and natives encountered by the way. Strikingly in contrast to the introspective and dogmatic entries in the Puritan journals are his observant comments on flora and fauna and folkways. To be keenly aware of life, of the flower by the trail, the bird in the tree, the details of Indian dress and dance; to share in that renaissance of wonder which has been called the essence of the romantic spirit—all this was as instinctive to the adventurer of the Old South as it was foreign to the zealot of New England. It is only a part of this romantic response to life that Smith was as enjoyably conscious of his own role in the drama as he was of the details of staging.

Thus American literature begins in the South with a proud inheritance from Elizabethan England. But curiously enough it is the most Anglophile commentators on American literature who lay most stress on the genesis of American literature from Plymouth Rock to the subordination or complete omission of the cavalier colonists. Two of the textbooks on American literature which are most prominent in the high school and junior college field make no mention of Captain John Smith while devoting detailed chapters to Winthrop, Bradford *et al.* It has been left for an English critic, Gilbert K. Chesterton, to remind us that "before there was any New England in the north there was something very like Old England in the South," to ask why we have forgotten "the great state of Virginia, the first in foundation and long the first in leadership; why a few crabbed nonconformists should have the right to erase a record that begins with Raleigh and ends with Lee and incidentally includes Washington." It is in the colonial records of Virginia and not of Massachusetts that we recognize the Elizabethan heritage. This spiritual kinship has been skillfully suggested in a little known romance, *My Lady Pokahontas* by the Southern novelist, John Esten Cooke. The story, purporting to be told by one Anas Todkill, a member of the Virginia expedition, is given in language borrowed from Smith's narratives, the writer's imaginative contribution consisting only of a reading between the lines of a romantic attachment between Smith and his Lady Pocahontas, and of the not improbable supposition that Smith and Shakespeare were acquaintances. Undisturbed by the findings of the Variorum Shakespeare, Todkill, or rather Cooke, ascribes the theme of *The Tempest* to a conversation between Smith and Shakespeare. We remember Matthew Arnold's saying that it is impossible to conceive of Shakespeare as associating intimately with the Pilgrim Fathers. No such sense of incongruity prevents us from imagining the man who wrote dramas as the confrere of the man who lived dramas. American literature, says Norman Foerster, should be studied in the light of its European origins and its American environment. Nowhere do we find this interaction of forces better illustrated than in the chronicles of the Southern frontier.

III. COLONEL WILLIAM BYRD OF WESTOVER IN VIRGINIA, ESQUIRE

As the Southern frontier of the seventeenth century is best revealed in the narratives of Captain John Smith, the Southern frontier of the eighteenth century is best revealed in the journals of William Byrd, gentleman, planter, scholar. The Byrd family is representative of the colonial society of tidewater Virginia at its best. The restoration of the Stuarts in Old England was reflected in a Cavalier aristocracy across the sea. Land grants multiplied in size until it is said that the average well-to-do Virginian at the opening of the eighteenth century owned as much as three thousand acres. Slavery spread in direct ratio to the extension of land grants; the type of society was determined by the feudal character of the large slaveholding estates. With the flower of the population controlling the land, the government, and the society of Virginia, it was inevitable that those less generously endowed by nature or circumstance should move on to a new frontier and seek their fortunes in a more democratic, more fluid society. Hence the new generation of frontiersmen, the typical immigrants with their way to make in the New World, passed on to North Carolina. The resultant social cleavage between two types of Southern colonies and colonists is depicted for us in the journals of William Byrd's surveying expedition to North Carolina.

The period of the supremacy of Virginia tidewater society almost exactly corresponds with the period covered by three generations of William Byrds. The first of the name came to America in 1670, the last of the name died in 1777. William Byrd the second furnishes the most brilliant example of the Virginian cavalier. Born in Virginia in 1674 he succeeded in 1704 to his father's vast estate. His epitaph is a happy epitome of the many-sided interests of his long life:

> being born to one of the amplest fortunes in this country
> he was early sent to England for his education
> where under the care and direction of Sir Robert Southwell
> and ever favoured with his particular instructions
> he made a happy proficiency in polite and varied learning.
> By the means of the same noble friend
> he was introduced to the acquaintance of many of the first persons of the age
> for knowledge, wit, virtue, birth, or high station
> and particularly contracted a most intimate and bosom friendship
> with the learned and illustrious Charles Boyle, Earl of Orrery.
> He was called to the Bar in the Middle Temple
> studied for some time in the Low Countries,
> visited the court of France
> and was chosen fellow of the Royal Society.
> Thus eminently fitted for the service and ornament of his country
> he was made receiver general of his majesty's revenues here
> was thrice appointed public agent to the court and ministry of England
> and being thirty-seven years a member

at last became President of the Council of this colony.
To all this were added a great elegance of taste and life
the wellbred gentleman and polite companion
the splendid economist and prudent father of a family
was the constant enemy of all exorbitant power
and hearty friend to the liberties of his country.

William Byrd's contribution to the literature of the American frontier dates from the Indian summer of his variedly interesting life, when, after his return from his third residence in London as agent for the colony, he settled in his mansion at Westover "devoting himself to the dignified and courteous pursuits of a cultivated English country gentleman." The most important of his annals of this period are *The History of the Dividing Line, The Journey to the Land of Eden,* and *The Progress to the Mines,* all narratives of his business travels through the frontier country, all giving invaluable pictures of the places and people he observed, and more illuminating glimpses of the personality of a typical gentleman of eighteenth century Virginia.

The History of the Dividing Line grew out of Byrd's appointment as one of the commissioners for Virginia in the longstanding dispute over the Virginia-North Carolina boundary. Its basis was the journal Byrd kept during that surveying expedition of 1728; in spite of the insistence of his English friends, Byrd did not find time to put his rough notes into finished form until the winter of 1737–38. "It will seem like a joke when I tell you that I have not time to finish the work," he wrote in reply to Mark Catesby's compliments; "but 'tis very certain I have not, for I am always engaged on some project for the improvement of our Infant Colony." The journal in its literary form takes on added interest from being the work of an author who regarded literature as a by-product in his absorbing projects for government. This subordination of mere literature to the designs of constructive statesmanship is noteworthy as characteristic of Southern literature in the full flush of its energies, tossed off incidentally by men whose vigor was more concerned with deeds than with words.

The Dividing Line justifies its name metaphorically as well as literally, for in this journal crops up repeatedly the scorn of the prosperous and efficient Virginia land-owner for the poor white trash of North Carolina. Byrd is repelled by the churlishness with which a certain type of frontier incompetent has always shielded his inferiority complex. "In North Carolina," Byrd writes, "everyone does what seems best in his own eyes." Insolence and inertia seem to him to characterize the North Carolinians. "To speak the truth 'tis a thoro aversion to Labor that makes people file off to North Carolina where Plenty and a warm Sun confirm them in their Disposition to Laziness for their whole lives." Perhaps Byrd's pictures of the Carolinians should be discounted because of their obvious state prejudice. But the part of Byrd's record that carries indubitable conviction is the unconscious picturing of himself and his companions. This band of Virginians may be seen most clearly if placed in direct contrast to the Puritans as we have seen them in their annals of the same period.

One marked difference concerns the attitudes of the Virginians and of the Puritans toward "inferior" races. We have seen the contemptuous cruelty visited by the Puritans upon the savages for whose conversion they had expressed such unctuous hopes. The Virginians with chivalrous naïveté accept the Indian civilization as one entitled to respect on an equal footing. It was the graceful tribute of John Smith to Pocahontas that first made her the rage in London society, investing her royalty with such mythical divinity that the pompous pedant James Stuart rebuked the English gentleman Rolfe for presuming to mate with the blood of kings. With similar exaggerated courtesy Byrd respects the contemporary state of the Indians, while cherishing perfectabilian hopes of their further educability. He records with approval the provision of Robert Boyle for the education of Indian youths at the college of William and Mary. He regrets that this and other well-meaning attempts at the education of the Indians have not been conspicuously successful, and repeatedly gives it as his opinion that the English would do well to follow the example of the French and intermarry with the natives as "the one way of Converting these poor Infidels and reclaiming them from Barbarity." In eighteenth century America it was the Southerner and not the Northerner who was free from race prejudice. The spirit of eighteenth century egalitarianism speaks through Byrd, not through Mather. "All nations of men have the same natural dignity," asserts the compatriot of Thomas Jefferson; "very Bright Talents may be lodged under a very dark skin. The principal Difference between one People and another proceeds only from the differing Opportunities for Improvement." The Southern gentleman and not the Yankee merchant was the friend and advocate of abolition. Byrd wrote to Oglethorpe congratulating him on his exclusion of negroes and rum from Georgia, but predicting that both measures would be frustrated by the profiteering proclivities of "the Saints of New England." "Nothing else could slip through a penal statute like the New Englanders. They import so many Negroes hither that I fear the colony will some time or other be Confirmed by the name of New Guinea."

In their attitudes toward religion also we expect a marked contrast between Puritan and Cavalier. Our expectations are not mistaken. Byrd runs as true to Catholic form as Bradford does to Protestant. He accepts his God in the sacraments as simply, as naturally as he accepts God's gifts of sunlight and air. With Byrd we find none of that agony of spiritual wrestling, none of that arrogance of spiritual triumph which makes the inner drama of the Puritan. And so, as the Puritan would put it, Byrd's religion is largely a matter of form. Religious ceremonies are scrupulously observed. A chaplain accompanies the surveying expedition. Halts and detours are made, to the sacrifice of the avowed business of the party, in order to bring the privilege of baptism to the children of backwoods settlers. But Byrd adds disapprovingly that the good women who brought their children to be baptized "brought no capons along with them to make the solemnity cheerful." The cavalier acted in good faith upon the admonition to be joyful in the Lord and saw no irreverence in making "a solemnity cheerful." Contrast Samuel Sewall opening the family vault on Christmas Day, determined, we may say, to reverse the process and make a day of cheer as solemn as possible! Byrd says little about Bible or dogma; his religious comments are concerned with the Church and her ritual. He passes animadversions upon the absence of churches or the presence of cheap, unsightly churches along the route. He is shocked to discover pioneer couples whose union has been sanctioned only by a contract before a local magistrate—the form of marriage preferred in the anti-sacramental Puritan community. Byrd makes a practice of honoring Sundays by a service and a rest; but though the service is faithfully observed, however adverse the conditions, the abstinence from work is interpreted leniently, and Byrd chronicles without compunction making of maps and making of marches on Sunday when the work had been pronounced necessary by the chaplain—infringements of the Sabbath which the Puritan would have looked to see punished by sudden and violent death.

Relieved of the Puritan preoccupation with the things of the next world, Byrd and his company are free to observe what is curious or lovely in the world about them. Like the narratives of Captain John Smith the narratives of Colonel William Byrd are full of remarks on the natural history of the country through which he is traveling and the amusing or annoying idiosyncrasies of the folk he encounters. Poetical people, a modern critic has told us, are people who realize life as they go along, people to whom life is an end in itself, not a means to the end of piling up profits on earth or treasures in heaven. William Byrd was one of those poetical people. The object of his expedition was a preëminently practical one with a definite political motive. But this motive does not obsess Byrd's consciousness. He revels in the gypsy life by the way as keenly as though it were the *raison d'être* of his journey. At one place he writes: "Our Landlord had a tolerable good House and Clean Furniture and yet we could not be tempted to lodge in it. We chose rather to lie in the open Field for fear of growing too tender. A clear sky spangled with stars was all our Canopy which being the last thing we saw before we fell asleep gave us Magnificent Dreams." Again he writes of their pitching tent in an orchard "where the Blossom of the Apple Tree contributed not a little to the sweetness of our Lodging." Like a breath from the forest of Arden comes this idyllic entry: "We had no other Drink but what Adam drank in Paradise, though to our comfort we found the Water excellent, by the Help of which we perceived our appetites to mend, our Slumbers to sweeten, the Stream of Life to run cool and peaceably in our Veins, and if ever we dreamt of Women they were kind."

But Byrd's zest for life is not the fair weather kind that shrivels under annoyance. He recounts some nights' lodgings less refreshing than these nights *à la belle étoile*, when, forced "to put up at a wretched Hovel where we were almost devoured by Vermin of various kinds. However, we were above complaining, being all philosophers enough to improve such slender Distresses into Mirth and Good Humour." Housebound with the rains on his progress to the mines, he diverts himself by reading *The Beggar's Opera* aloud to amuse his companions. This last entry betokens one of the resources of the man of the world which is most suggestive of the difference between his view of life and that of his other-worldly Puritan contemporaries. We have as evidence of the personality of William Byrd II not only this trio of travel narratives, but a catalogue of the books in his library at Westover. The library is classified under the headings of History, Voyages and Travels, Law, Tryalls, etc., Physick, etc., Entertainments, Poetry, Translations, Divinity, French Books chiefly of entertainment, Classicks and other Latin and Greek Authors. A perusal of the voluminous and varied entries under each classification is the most illuminating evidence of the world in which the mind of the Virginian gentleman was at home while his body pushed through the dismal swamps of the North Carolina frontier—a larger and more gracious world than that in which the Bradfords and the Winthrops, the Sewalls and the Mathers toiled up the rocky road to their austere and exclusive heaven, looking neither to the right nor to the left at the enticing glory and loveliness of this world, nor back at the treasures of the mighty though unregenerate dead.

IV. CONGRESSMAN DAVY CROCKETT: THE BACKWOODS POLITICIAN

The Elizabethan adventurer and the Virginian planter were not the only typical frontiersmen of the South. Reluctantly, perhaps, we must pass from the giants of the heroic period of colonization, from the gentlemen of the gallant period of development to meaner days and smaller folk. We must take into account another typical pioneer, the individual immigrant who for purely personal motives, without vision except for his immediate necessities, lived under primitive conditions, a primitive himself in mental reaction as well as in physical prowess. It is peculiarly in the South that we find this type of settler. The expansion of New England was, as we have seen, an expansion through town units. The frontiers of the West found a common focus in the cattle camp or logging camp or around a mining lode. No such common center of attraction bound together the pioneers of the Southern Piedmont or the Southern Appalachians. From the long list of solitary pathfinders shine the names of Adair, of Boone, of Sevier, of Robertson. Less heroic but more representative than these trailblazers of the early days is a rustic home-hewer of the nineteenth century frontier—the braggart bearhunter and petty politician, Davy Crockett.

If John Smith suggests the England of Shakespeare, and William Byrd the England of Steele, Crockett foreshadows the America of D. W. Griffith. His heroisms are all of the cinema variety; his strutting center stage is as different from the grandiose self-glorifications of Smith as it is from the large-minded native dignity of William Byrd. If *The Narrative of the Life of David Crockett of the State of Tennessee* were less obtuse in its self-esteem it would be intolerable; but the imperturbable aplomb of Crockett's swagger is so superbly sustained that it outbrazens criticism. In fact, Crockett himself disposes of possible critics of his "plain, honest, homespun account" in his preface: "They are a sort of vermin that I shan't so much as stop to brush off. If they want to work on my book, just let them go ahead; and after they are done, they had better blot all their criticisms than to know what opinion I would express of them and by what sort of a curious name I would call them, if I were standing near them and looking over their shoulder."

We read of Crockett in the book which he boasted was "the exact image of its author" that he was born in 1786 of an Irish father who had drifted from Pennsylvania to North Carolina, and from there on to Tennessee and who continued to drift farther along the frontier throughout all Davy's childhood. Crockett senior had married a Maryland woman of whose family their son appears to know nothing; he fought in the Revolutionary War, taking part in the battle of King's Mountain; but evidently fighting Tories had been tame compared to fighting redskins, for the tales which David remembers are those of Indian encounters: his grandfather and grandmother Crockett had been murdered in their cabin by the Creeks, and a brother of his father's had been carried away and kept captive among the savages for over seventeen years when he was discovered and ransomed by his brothers. The pioneers who like Crockett carried their fearless homesteading into the very heart of the red country were less likely to cherish sentimental illusions concerning the equality of races than were the comfortably housed theorists of the tidewater. If Crockett's account of his campaigns in the Creek War seems utterly inhuman in its ferocity, we must plead in extenuation his intimate knowledge of the barbarities of Indian warfare.

With true pioneer self-assertion, Crockett begins his career as a runaway. Having played truant from school and fearing the discipline of his father who was hot in pursuit with a "two year old hickory," Crockett hides in the bush until his father has given up the hunt and then joins an acquaintance who is driving his cattle out for sale. Instead of returning with his neighbor, Crockett joins himself to another and then another casual employer, roaming through Maryland, Virginia, and Pennsylvania, until, rather by chance than forethought, he finds himself back at home after two years' absence and creates the desired sensation by walking in and begging a night's lodging from his family, who at first fail to recognize their prodigal son in the stalwart youth who had "attained so advanced an age, the age of fifteen," and, in spite of the paternal hickory, "without knowing the first letter of the book."

That Crockett's wanderings were inspired rather by the pioneer wanderlust and impatience of restraint than by filial callousness is attested by his hiring himself out to two successive creditors of his father's and delighting that embarrassed pioneer by presenting him with the redeemed notes on which he had been unable to make payment. Having helped the old man out of his difficulties, Crockett sets about improving himself, entering a new term of service to earn some clothes. An impetus is given to his ambition by his falling in love with his employer's niece. Grotesque is the language in which Crockett records the violence of his emotions: "If all the hills about there were pure chink and all belonged to me I would give them if I could just talk to her as I wanted to; but I was afraid to begin, for when I would think of saying anything to her, my heart would begin to flutter like a duck in a puddle; and if I tried to outdo it and speak, would get right smack up in my throat and choak me like a cold potatoe." After all this uncouth anguish, it transpired that the lady's affections were promised elsewhere. The disappointed Crockett by some illogical mental process, conceived the idea that all his troubles were due to his lack of "learning." Accordingly Crockett started going to school four days a week and working the other two to earn his board and lodging. At the end of six months, says Crockett, "I learned to read a little in my primer, to write my own name, and to cypher some in the first three rules in figures. And this was all the schooling I ever had in my life up to this day." Feeling that he had followed knowledge like a sinking star quite far enough for all practical purposes, Crockett, now aged eighteen, decided that it was high time to take a wife, and after various infatuations and various rebuffs which he recounts with thick-skinned insensitiveness, he married a "little girl," "sweeter than sugar" whom he "loved almost well enough to eat." The bride brought as dowry two cows and calves and a good wheel, "and knowed exactly how to use it." Crockett's employer gave a munificent wedding present of a fifteen-dollar order upon the general store for such house furnishings as the bride might pick out. Thus started in life Crockett "rented a small farm and cabin and went to work," until he got disgusted with paying rent and determined to strike out for free land. So with a capital of one horse, two colts, and two sons, Crockett and his wife are away across the mountains till they find land to their liking on the Mulberry Fork of Elk River. "It was here," writes Crockett with the gratification of a successful man looking back to humble beginnings, "that I began to distinguish myself as a hunter and to lay the foundation for all my future greatness."

Crockett's "greatness" both as a hunter and as a politician is elaborated through the rest of his autobiography. He describes with gusto the hunting exploits by which he provided his constantly increasing family with venison and bear meat. It was nothing for Crockett and his son striking alone into the woods around their little clearing "to kill three bears in less than no time," ten bears during a few days' hunt, and pile up a total of fifty-eight bears during the fall and winter months with forty-seven more in a month of the spring hunt. With even more ingenuous self-satisfaction, Crockett recounts his accumulation of votes. Unlike Smith and Byrd in all else, Crockett shares with them that love of fame which may be an infirmity in noble minds; which in the ignoble degenerates into a mere itch for publicity.

Allied with Boone as the Leatherstocking of the Southwest, Crockett is allied with Lincoln as a pioneer legislator. His public career began with his appointment as a local magistrate—an appointment typical of the pragmatic justice of the frontier. "We remained here [on Shoal Creek] some two or three years without any law at all: and so many bad characters began to flock in upon us that we found it necessary to set up a sort of temporary government of our own. . . . We lived in the backwoods and didn't profess to know much and no doubt used many wrong words. But we met and appointed magistrates and constables to keep order. We didn't fix any laws for them though; for we supposed they would know law enough whoever they might be; and so we left it to themselves to fix the laws." In Crockett's case this assumption was optimistic, to say the least, for not only had he "never read a page in a law book," but he could barely write his own name, let alone keep the required record of his proceedings. But a mere trifle like that did not distress the resourceful Crockett; he told his constable that a warrant was superfluous between friends; "when he should happen to be out anywhere and see that a warrant was necessary and would have a good effect, he needn't take the trouble to come all the way in to get one, but he could just fill out one." Crockett's régime as magistrate and later in the more elevated position of squire, met the great American criterion: it worked. "My judgments were never appealed from and if they had been, they would have stuck like wax as I gave my decisions on the principles of common justice and honesty between man and man and relied on natural born sense and not on law learning to guide me."

Inflated with success, Crockett proceeded on the theory that he who has been faithful in a few things should aspire to be ruler over many cities. Crockett entered with zest into a campaign as representative of his county in the Tennessee legislature. He is a trifle embarrassed at first in his electioneering because of the fancied necessity of telling the people "something about the government and an eternal sight of other things that I knowed nothing more about that I did about Latin and law and such things as that." But though Crockett is handicapped by never having read even a newspaper which might inform him in contemporary political science, he has the supreme advantage of having been "born for luck," and he is quick to perceive that votes are born of laughter and liquor rather than of law or logic. A good joke and a good drink place Crockett first in the hearts of his countrymen. After two sessions in the Tennessee legislature, Crockett runs for Congress and thrice represented his native state in Washington—the representation, if we are to judge from his own narratives, consisting chiefly in tours through the north and east where large crowds hailed him as an eccentric, a sort of Buffalo Bill of the cane brake, and where Crockett made interminable speeches bitterly railing against his former leader, Andrew Jackson, whose autocratic removal of the "deposites" had incurred Crockett's animosity. "It was a hard road to hoe," as Crockett put it, to oppose Old Hickory in those days, but a road along which Crockett moved with stubborn tenacity and with sturdy pride that no man could see on his hands any "party handcuffs" or on his neck any collar with the engraving, "My Dog, Andrew Jackson." Crockett's ambition growing by the adulation he fed on, grasped with touching seriousness at the jocular suggestion that he run for the Presidency. "Cut to the hollow" by his disappointment, not only in this hope but in his reëlection to Congress, Crockett, like Coriolanus, turned his back on his ungrateful country and marched away "to lend the Texans a helping hand on their way to freedom." And while *Colonel Crockett's*

Exploits and Adventures in Texas is now generally admitted to be spurious, no disillusioning research has as yet thrown doubt on that heroic death in defense of the Alamo through which Crockett was vested with a tragic dignity that life had denied.

V. THE SOUTHERN FRONTIER IN AMERICAN LITERATURE

We might go on indefinitely adding to the file of frontiersmen whose own accounts of pioneer life as they lived it in the South and Southwest are of intrinsic interest. But these frontier journals, fascinating and illuminating as they are, are not all of Southern literature. The more polished and sophisticated writings of the later nineteenth and of the twentieth century are conditioned by curious echoes from the plantation and frontier of colonial and revolutionary days. If we have limited our consideration of Southern frontiersmen to Smith, to Byrd, to Crockett, it is because from each may be traced a line of descent that brings the modern literature of the South in touch with the vanished frontier.

The dream of empire led John Smith to Virginia, inspired his pen to take up the task where his sword had been forced to drop it, cried from the wilderness to prepare the way for England's dominion beyond the sea. Long after the dream of a dissenting theocracy which built New England had cooled into a tepid Protestantism, the glory of the dream that had built Old England in the South still beat strong in the hearts of Southern statesmen. Turn to any standard history of Southern literature and you cannot but mark the preponderance of statesmen among Southern men of letters. Boynton in his college text on American literature apologizes for "the non-mention of any Southern writers for nearly two centuries" on the ground that "the richest culture of the South devoted itself to statesmanship and expressed itself in oratory." In fact "mere literature" plays a negligible part in the output of Southern writers until after the Civil War—that is to say, until after the first impulse of Southern romanticism had met a violent death. How far its death struggle was a struggle between the Southern ideal of a tropical empire and the northern ideal of a creditor nation has been powerfully delineated by Eskenrode in his recent biography of Jefferson Davis.

The resultant phenomenon is familiar enough to students of psychology. Defeated on the plane of the actual, man has always comforted himself with easy victories in a dream world. Romance is the twin of adventure: it woos real women, the more refractory the better; it challenges real perils; it cherishes faith in a Real Presence of its God under the guise of the commonest necessities of daily life. Romanticism dreams of ethereal maidens who vanish if touched, whom all poets may adore but no man may wed; it triumphs over impotent adversaries; it makes graceful gestures of reverence before empty symbols. Romance transfigures the actual with the glory of an all-embracing vision; romanticism escapes from the actual into wish-fulfillments which it is unable to achieve within the limitations of a realistic universe. When a great romantic urge has spent itself in vain we have the decadence of romance into compensatory romanticism.

Such a decadence of romance is the history of Southern literature. The urge of empire descends from Captain John Smith through intervening generations of Southern statesmen to—William Gilmore Simms. The grandiose ambition which failed of realization is feebly reflected in a type of historical fiction of which the South has furnished the best—or the worst—examples.

It is beside the point here to reopen the controversy

as to the merits of historical fiction *per se.* It is very much to the point to suggest a question seldom if ever raised in connection with this type of writing which has been accused of being mongrel history and mongrel fiction. Why has it been left to Americans, a people proverbially forwardlooking, proverbially proud of their emancipation from ancestor-worship, to be most prolific in the production of ephemeral romances anent their own past? When Scott initiated the vogue for historical romances it is obvious that he did so in accord with the romantic revival of his age, stirred by an antiquarian curiosity, by a theatrical feeling for effective settings, but certainly never moved by nostalgia for the past. We remember Mark Twain's savage accusation that Scott kept alive in the South an obsolete tradition of romantic chivalry long after the rest of the practical world had discarded the feudal ideal. May not one explanation be that while the "progressive" north was eagerly concentrating its energies on the romance of business, the South, balked in its designs of empire, broken in industrial resources, found solace in the evocation of a heroic past?

Preëminent among the writers whose stock in trade was the exploitation of the past is William Gilmore Simms. For intrinsic interest of thrilling plot, for felicitous descriptions of the unconquered wilderness, for grandiloquent speeches of the unconquered redmen, Simms' *Yemassee* compares very favorably with Cooper's more famous romances of the frontier. The marked point of contrast which determines the inferiority of Simms' novels is the absence of the hero, or rather, the attempt to palm off upon the reader as hero a mere lay figure. Cooper's novels have been assailed in respect to his Indians, his "females," his woodcraft, and his rhetoric —but the shafts of criticism fall harmless from the unscathed figure of the Leatherstocking. He lives though all other elements of the novels fall; he lives because he lived in not one but many frontiersmen, because he was the archetype of the American pioneer—the distinctive American. Consider in contrast the young Governor of South Carolina who, incognito, posing as a mere Captain among the soldiers who guard the frontier, lightheartedly wooes his pretty Bess under the frowns of her Puritan father, saves the settlers from massacre in the Yemassee War, and in the end, theatrically disclosing his real station as Palatine, returns in triumph to Charlestown "with his peerless forest flower."

If we analyze the attributes which Simms bestowed upon Governor Craven we shall have a fair idea of the frontier hero of Southern fiction. In the first place, he is well born, well educated, a man of the world, and a gentleman. The indigenous frontiersmen are all very well for minor characters; they may prove their huskiness by defending the blockhouse, or their denseness by opposing (ineffectually of course) the program laid down for them by the hero; but their creator never falls into the democratic fallacy of believing that they are of essentially the same caliber as their commander. Then his heroisms are of the gallant variety that is tempered with sprightliness. The old Puritan preacher is pained by what he considers the Captain's undue levity "unbecoming in one having an immortal soul." The Captain answers his prospective father-in-law: "My levity does not unfit me for business—never interferes with my duties. I shall undertake to reform it when you shall satisfy me that to laugh and sing and seek and afford amusement are inconsistent with my duties either to the Creator or the creature." If this dashing young Lochinvar of the Carolinas is a less appealing figure than the simple minded, serious-minded Leatherstocking, it may be because he moves through the narrative with a rather too evident superiority complex. Even his wooing of his "forest flower" is rather playfully patronizing than passionate; he is quite as much interested in discomfiting the father as in winning the daughter. The frontier is not his native setting; it is merely an obstacle over which he must triumph, a region which must be subdued and civilized to smooth the path of empire. The Southern hero was a military gentleman who, with drawn sword and prancing steed confronted the wilderness undaunted. When the wilderness that he had conquered and civilized was reconquered and laid waste by Sherman, reduced again to barbarism by the carpetbaggers and the freedmen, historical fiction offered a refuge from the pressure of contemporary fact.

VI. THE CULT OF THE COLONEL

Another group of Southern writers features the typical military figure, not of the glorious victories that attended colonial and revolutionary campaigns, but of the glorious failures that attended the Confederate cause. While Simms and Kennedy revived the audacious young warriors of the empirebuilding period, Thomas Nelson Page, James Lane Allen, Owen Wister, Irvin Cobb, O. Henry, George Washington Cable, F. Hopkinson Smith, and a host of lesser luminaries dwelt lovingly on the gentle and pathetic figure of the Civil War Colonel—the fragrance and loveliness of the Old Dominion, "befo' the wah," the gallant losing, the mournful acquiescence in a new régime.

The cult of the Civil War colonel with his faded dignity, his quixotic honor, his pathetic impracticability, made the most popular literature of the South. The author of "Mississippi, Heart of Dixie" in *The Nation* symposium on *These United States,* recognized as the appropriate atmosphere of Southern fiction: "wisteria, live oaks, and soft voices, and faithful old mammies, and courteous squires, and benign old colonels, and mint juleps, and charming belles and white columned plantation houses." In his recent *Notebook* Sherwood Anderson, perhaps with the trite tale of the professional Southerner in mind, reflects that "the literature of the South is far removed from the soil. The stench is gone out of it. New Orleans, for example, is a city of smells. It reeks with smells from the earth, the sea, the rivers, the houses, the markets, the swamps. In the moist heavy air the smells hang all day and all night, but in Southern stories nothing is mentioned but the magnolia."

Like the bloom beloved by Southern romancers is the heavy-scented, sickly sweet, pallid waxen substance of the literature of the Southern gentleman. It runs true to its eighteenth century traditions in being a literature of decorous gestures, of gracefully skimming over the surfaces of life, of grandiloquent phrases and theatrical posturings, of superficial cultivation cloaking meannesses and lusts.

So far removed is this typical Southern literature of the present from the heroic impetus of the frontier that it would be straying too far from our thesis to dwell in detail on the diminished specimens of Southern gentility who continue the tradition of the cavalier colonel, William Byrd. Romance has become a fragile decoration, a languishing sentimentality. Let us regard some of its more familiar manifestations. Page's Old Virginia is an album of reverently preserved if somewhat stiffly posed daguerreotypes. The capricious Southern beauty, the ardent young wooer, the faithful family retainer, the bellicose martinet of a parent who inevitably if inexplicably succumbs in the end with a bless-you-my-children gesture—the longstanding family feud, originating in some trivial umbrage and dissolved even more inconsequentially by the smile of an innocent child—the prim but lovable maiden aunt, secretly cherishing an unrequited affection; smiling, insubstantial wraiths these float before us, beguiling perhaps an idle hour, but awakening no tragic pity or terror, provoking no responsive recognition, demanding no effort of analysis.

James Lane Allen, somewhat more vigorous in his delineation, is equally fanciful and tenuous in his substance. In *The Choir Invisible* he purports to tell a story of Kentucky in the pioneer days. In reality, his story is only by accident a tale of Kentucky; in essence it is the story of a Tennysonian lady and gentleman whose finespun scruples are nicely contrived to frustrate their love, but who are evidently so much more in love with their irrational conception of honor than they are with each other that the reader is unlikely to waste any tears over their blighted lives. In the conventionally moral dénouement of his fictions Allen may suggest Hawthorne; but while the taboo may be the same, the motive of the inhibition is different. Hawthorne's Dimmesdale prefers open ignominy to free love with Hester because of what he fancies due to his God. John Gray prefers to carry through a loveless engagement rather than marry the now unencumbered Mrs. Falconer; his decision is determined by what he considers due to himself as a gentleman. Both motives are emasculated until the impatient reader is likely to consider them mere rationalizations of moral cowardice; nevertheless, in genesis one is the motive of the Puritan and the other of the Cavalier.

A Kentucky Cardinal and its sequel *Aftermath* are a fair basis on which to judge Mr. Allen's contribution to the literature of the Southern gentleman. The chaste delicacy of the diction, the punctilious polish of the manners, the overfine attempt to extract from the material more emotional values than the material warrants, are characteristically dilettante. The sensitive feeling for nature, the bookish culture, the tolerant acceptance of human weaknesses, particularly where a pretty girl is concerned—these are of the caliber of William Byrd. But the healthy-minded energy, the constructive enterprise of the oldtime Southern gentleman have given way to the dawdlings of a philanderer who potters at odd jobs around his garden and with much the same languid affectation, pursues his courtship with the fair neighbor next door. It is not essential to his life to have either strawberries or Georgiana; the cultivation of either is a leisure time avocation. The lovers' quarrel, which is introduced for no apparent purpose except prolonging the slender thread of narrative, is occasioned by the trapping of the Kentucky Cardinal. Allen's hero is so exquisitely sensitive in emotional susceptibilities that he suffers the requisite amount of excruciating mental anguish in making this supreme sacrifice to the whim of his ladylove. But Georgiana is also endowed with the exquisite sensibilities by which the Southern aristocrat like the roseleaf princess proves his finer fiber. It transpires that she didn't want to have the redbird put in a cage. He ought to have known that when she said she did, she really meant the opposite. And with this much-ado-about-nothing the lovers continue to quarrel and the pages of the book to increase, until, for no apparent reason, the lovers make up and the story ends. In the *Aftermath* Georgiana gives additional proof of her proper feminine delicacy by dying from the chill of a strawberry blossom which her sentimentally dutiful husband has brought her in commemoration of their anniversary. A hero who storms and rants over the sufferings of a caged bird, a heroine who dies from the chilling touch of a frosted blossom—to such hypersensitive neurasthenics has rotted down the vigor of Southern romance.

George Washington Cable deserves mention apart

from the other popularizers of the Southern gentry, for he more than the other writers of this school has associated himself with a definite region and in his treatment of that region has preserved some flavor of its pioneer past. The pioneer past of Louisiana, Cable's chosen territory, is a Latin past, Cable renders that past rather less justice than does the less well-known raconteur of French America, Grace King, who appreciates to the full the Parisian quality of New Orleans. Cable, although a soldier in the Confederate army (or perhaps *because* he fought on the losing side in the Civil War) throws in his lot with the angels and never misses a chance to correct the fascinating charm, the rollicking gaiety of his Louisiana by the intrusion of impeccable Puritan and abolitionist sentiments. Lafcadio Hearn, himself a dabbler in the legends of New Orleans, hailed *The Grandissimes* as "the most remarkable work of fiction ever created in the South." But in this as in *Old Creole Days* and *Strange True Stories of Louisiana,* the sympathies of the writer are with the quadroons and free men of color for whom he pleads a full social recognition, with the Grandissime of the New South who shamelessly goes into business partnership with his quadroon bastard brother, rather than with the Grandissime of the Old South who holds tenaciously to his belief that "the yankee government is a failure, a driveling failure," and who dies with the cry upon his lips, "Louisiana forever!" But while Cable extols the "propressive" régime which obliterates lines of class and color, he employs for decorative purposes the characters and settings of old Creole society. It is something that the Old World fragrance of that decaying society has been preserved even in the pages of an unsympathetic critic; but always it is a musty fragrance, a decorative, not a vital, element in modern life. With the passing of the feudal plantation has passed the prestige of the feudal aristocrat whom it established as a distinctive type of the Southern frontier.

VII. THE FAD OF THE PRIMITIVE

In this day when to dissent from Darwin is to write oneself down a Fundamentalist, it is perhaps periling one's reputation for intelligence to suggest that the survival of the fittest means literally and logically only the preservation of that which is fittest to survive. Not every lost cause, says Chesterton writing of the Old South, should have been lost; conversely, not every survival is a cause for rejoicing. Whatever the student of economics and history may think about the downfall of the Southern Republic, the student of literature must regret that the frontier impulse of the South which has proved its sturdiness by surviving owes its inspiration not to the adventurous empire building of Captain Smith nor to the gallant chivalry of Colonel Byrd, but to the superb self-satisfaction of Congressman Crockett. The analyses of Southern States by the various contributors to *The Nation* symposium offers one line of evidence. South Carolina is plaintively mourned by Ludwig Lewisohn as "a lingering fragrance." Mencken laments that Maryland once the home of fierce wars and faithful loves, has now shrunk to "the apex of normalcy." "Where," cries Basil Thompson, "are the Louisianians of the past?" And so the tributes to the great states of the Confederacy unite in a minor key. For a picture of a happy commonwealth, "the only happy, the only successful people in America" we look to Arkansas, an isolated rural community of "landscratching people moving through forests of free land," a state where unhurried by the mechanisms of civilization, undisturbed by the subtleties of culture, frontier conditions and frontier psychology still prevail.

The evidence of Southern literature bears out this conclusion. The literature of triumphant imperialism has died to a feeble echo in the historical novel. The literature of culture has sunk to the feeble sentimentalities of hackneyed romance mongering. But the literature of the people, the untutored, unlettered speech of the mountaineer, the crude expression of primitive passions, is the only Southern literature with sufficient vitality to save it from putrefaction.

The cult of the primitive has had a twofold expression in recent American literature. One aspect is concerned with the unearthing of native ballads and folklore. The recent interest in such investigations is another sign of awakening national consciousness in the realm of literature. The independent compilation of Paul Bunyan yarns by Esther Shepherd and by James Stevens betokens an effort to recapture and conserve for our children the literary heritage of the frontier. Fritz Rickaby's *Ballads of the Shanty Boys* is another publication to preserve the native poetry of the lumber camps. But while Paul Bunyan is of the stature of the nation, striding from Niagara Falls to Puget Sound, most of the American folklore is centered not in occupation but in section. By far the largest proportion of this indigenous literature belongs to the isolated districts of the South. Here have been gathered a goodly number of the *American Ballads and Songs* edited by Louise Pound. From the far Southwest come the *Cowboy Songs and Ballads, Songs of the Cattle-Trail and Cow Camp* gathered by Professor Lomax. Frank Dobie and his collaborators have brought together a delightful volume of Texas folklore. Students of the University of North Carolina under the direction of Professor Koch have utilized native stories as a basis for one act plays. Kentucky legends have furnished material for Percy Mackaye's *Tall Tales from the Kentucky Mountains,* Josephine

McGill's *Folksongs of the Kentucky Mountains,* and Loraine Wyman and Howard Brockway's collection of *Lonesome Tunes.* So the list might be continued, and no list could be finally exhaustive since from month to month new volumes appear indicating that American scholars no longer think it beneath their dignity to consider the literature which springs from the frontier past of their own country. How large a proportion of this primitive poetry belongs to the South may be judged from the fact that the most extensive repository of such ballads is Campbell and Sharp's *Folk Songs from the Southern Appalachians.*

So fascinating is this literature of the primitive that one is tempted to linger over it with that profuseness of quotation, that fullness of appreciation which can be afforded only in a book devoted exclusively to the subject. But while the more intrinsically meritorious it is less popular than the literature about the primitive. Associated with the mountaineers as Bret Harte is with the fortyniners are John Fox and Mary Noilles Murfree (writing under the pseudonym of Charles Egbert Craddock). The meretricious mountaineering of John Fox may be dismissed with a few words. His romances have already received the damning encomium of cheap melody and cheap movie. *The Trail of the Lonesome Pine* sang itself with such easy sentimentality into one's ear full ten years ago that the title now suggests a once popular tune rather than a once popular novel. The *Little Shepherd of Kingdom Come* is typical of the author's favorite *modus operandi.* The hero starts out in the picturesquely forlorn condition dear to fairy tales —sans family, sans money, sans education, sans name— sans everything. But this is only by way of accentuating the heights of glory to which he rises figuratively as he goes down literally—into the Blue Grass region where he finds not only the education he was ostensibly seeking, but an uncle and a sweetheart of the F. F. V. type. Fox, for all his professed preoccupation with the mountaineers, evidently did not think well enough of them to trust his hero in that class throughout the book. Chad's story from the time that beneficent coincidence brings him to his unknown uncle, belongs to the cult of the colonel rather than to the cult of the primitive and degenerates into the wearisomely familiar story of friends and kinsmen tragically divided in the Civil War, but with remarkable facility wiping out old scores the moment the war was over, marrying and living happy for the remaining page or so of the book.

Miss Murfree's stories of the Great Smoky Mountains are worthy of more respectful consideration, for however vitiated her tales may be by the conscientiously appended moral tag, they are sincere studies of a people who approximate the rank and file of the pioneers more closely than do any other contemporary Americans. Her sketches are well entitled stories of the Tennessee Mountains, for the mountains rather than the mountaineers are the dominant factors in the situation. In every tale the somber grandeur of the ranges is set beside the cramped and barren lives of the natives. Shut in by the impassive mountains, the men and women of the settlements adopt a similar impassivity and stoically resign themselves to frustration. The externals of their lives Miss Murfree reproduces with care: the feuds, gambling, and revivals which afford the chief emotional outlets, the superstitions which afford the chief imaginative expression, the pathetic simplicity which strengthens their devoted attachment to those they love, and facilitates their fleecing by those shrewder than themselves, their proclivity for moonshining, their antipathy for sheriffs, their hospitality to strangers, their unspoilt natural dignity.

But in Miss Murfree's stories of the Tennessee Mountains, as in all local color stories, there is a tendency to substitute picturesqueness for penetration, to emphasize details of location, dialect, and customs, and ignore the human mind. We have a suspicion that Miss Murfree over simplifies and prettifies her people. Repeatedly she closes their stories with a flourish of self-sacrifice on which she comments approvingly. Miss Murfree does not succeed in convincing us that Budd Wray, with his revenge finally within his grasp, would have spared his rival, that Ike would meekly resume slaving for his harsh stepfather, that the Prophet of the Great Smoky Mountains would substitute himself in the best Sydney Carton manner for his doomed foe. These touches of melodramatic nobility are suspiciously suggestive of the conventional romantic idealization of human conduct.

But we should not lay this literary sin—if it be a sin—solely to Miss Murfree's charge. It is a curious characteristic of the local color story whether practiced by Mary Wilkins Freeman or by Bret Harte. Always a painstakingly realistic and scrupulously differentiated account of locality is counterbalanced by a stereotyped set of sentimental situations. So the one tendency toward realism which began in the South with Longstreet's *Georgia Scenes* with Baldwin's *Flush Times in Mississippi and Alabama* borrows a protective coloration from romance; while purporting to present primitive man in all the pristine simplicity of industry and culture, it delights to assume that primitive man was intuitively possessed of those refinements of emotion which have been superimposed upon human nature by the slow evolution of moral fastidiousness.

Entertaining as are Miss Murfree's stories, for an account of the mental processes of the mountaineers we may more safely depend upon such a *bona fide* narrative as Lucy Furman's *The Quare Woman* which, for all its patronizing attitude, approaches a faithful interpretation of the people. It is doubtful whether the Uncle Ephraim of her sketches could have explained himself in the words which she puts into his mouth. But though such an effort of self-analysis might be beyond him, it is nevertheless a sound analysis, and one which links the mountaineer of today with the pioneer of the days:

> when our forbears fust rid acrost the high ridges from old Virginny or North Caroliny and along these rocky creeks and tuck up land in the narrow valleys. A rude race they was, but a strong, with the blood of Old England and bonny Scotland in their veins and in their hearts the fear of naught; a rude race but a free, chasing the deer and the bar and the wild turkey and the Indian, tending their crops with a hoe in one hand and a gun in t'other; a rude race but a friendly, banding together agin all foes, helping one another in all undertakings. Some of 'em like my grandsir, the old cap'n, come in to live on land that was granted 'em because they had fit under Washington, t'others jest wandered in and tuck up what pleased 'em.
>
> Well after they had settled themselves in this rugged, penned-in land, then what happened to 'em? Well right thar was the trouble; nothing never happened. Here they was shut in for uppards of a hundred year, multiplying fast, spreading up from the main creeks to the branches and hollows but never bettering their condition, you might say worsening hit. For before long the game was all kilt off and life became the turrible struggle hit still is jest to keep food in our mouths, raising crops on land that's nigh straight up and down like we have to.

This is the plight of the David Crockett of today: the bears "kilt off," Texas annexed, Congress civilized, liquor prohibited—his last stand among the mountains invaded by lady philanthropists and lady philologists eager to collect his songs and correct his customs.

VIII. THE ESCAPE TO POICTESME

With these forlorn survivors of a great race the chronicles of the Southern frontier logically end. But one cannot close a consideration of any phase of Southern literature without a mention, however brief and inadequate, of two men of genius whom the South has given to American literature: Edgar Allan Poe and James Branch Cabell. No study of the romantic tradition which hails from the Southern frontier is complete without recognizing that the first and the latest great figure in American romanticism are Virginians. They have no connection with the regional frontier or with any region except those to which their magic has given a local habitation and a name. They have no connection with the industrial frontier on which the enterprising Yankees piled up fortunes from the new territories to which the ambition of Southern imperialists had blazoned the way. But there is a frontier of the spirit on which they are at home, where Americans of today view them askance, afraid to follow.

It is one of the satirical instances of that appeal to posterity of which Mr. Cabell writes that Edgar Allan Poe, that enigmatical waif in complacent America, so long belittled as a writer and sermonized upon as a man, has recently been claimed by the fellow citizens who left his very grave unmarked, who finally, to Mr. Mencken's grim delight, adorned it with "a thumping misquotation from his poetry." We now have it upon the authority of the official oratory of the University of Virginia that Poe was what he was because of the influence of his Alma Mater. Dr. Robinson and Mr. Krutch in their recent biographies have done much to rescue Poe from neglect and misconstruction. James Branch Cabell has not had so long to wait; the suppression of *Jurgen* achieved for him the success of scandal; with the reversal of the censorship he became mentionable even in the best academic circles, and now, according to his official biographer, Carl Van Doren, he is already a classic.

But however much the tide of pious disapprobation may have ebbed, neither Poe nor Cabell will ever be popular in the sense in which Page and Cable are popular. It is diverting to be lulled by the romance that depends on decorative costumes; it is disturbing to be stirred by the romance that is the demiurge of the cosmos. Romance as handled by Poe and Cabell is as "morbid" as conventionalized romance is "wholesome": it is something disquieting, exotic, perverse; embarrassingly indelicate in its recognition of the devastating impulses and sly camouflages of the sex instinct; gruesomely explicit in its delineation of decay and death; its heroes are curiously incapacitated for effective heroisms.

The wizardry, the haunting despair, the yearning for beauty, the unearthly melody of Poe are found again in the art of James Branch Cabell. But Cabell has a wider range than Poe; in him we find a recapitulation of the successive stages of romanticism. Beginning with *Domnei* and *Chivalry* in which the fine gesture is made with the splendid futility of the best knightly traditions, he traces *The Line of Love* to *Gallantry* whose secret, as he defines it, is "to accept the pleasures of life leisurely and its inconveniences with a shrug." His chronicles of Lichfield upon superficial reading seem to belong to the cult of the colonel. But John Charteris and Rudolph Musgrove, Robert Townsend and Felix Kennaston are much more than so many additions to the ranks of antiquated gentlefolk. Cabell's treatment is ironic where Page's and Allen's were sentimental. Consider *The Rivet in Grandfather's Neck* reviewed by Clement Wood as "a conventional Southern story." The usual maiden aunt, in the Musgrove menage is a dipsomaniac; the old family servant carries out a completely passive, completely fiendish revenge upon the Musgroves for the wrongs she and hers had received at their hands; the quixotic self-sacrifice by which Rudolph Musgrove shields the woman he loves is born of vanity; the disclosure of ties of blood fails to deter Charteris in his pursuit of his brother's wife.

And so, says Cabell through his mouthpiece Charteris, while "the legend of Lichfield" may seem to belong to the Old South, the real Lichfield is "a hamlet of Hamlets" and its tale would not be a romance but a tragedy. This real Lichfield, Cabell has demonstrated by a whimsically elaborated genealogy to be linked with Poictesme; the romantic attitudinizing of the Southern gentleman is but an accidental localization of the incorrigible romantic "who alone among animals plays the ape to his dreams." Whether in Lichfield or in Poictesme, Cabell has but one hero: the eternal dreamer in search of a life that will find employment for every faculty—and eternally baffled in his quest; one heroine: "the ageless lovable and loving woman of whom all poets have dreamed"; one villain: that God of things as they are who is Cabell's devil. This dissatisfaction with the actual which has so recently crept in as a disturbing note in the "glad" literature of adolescent America, has expressed itself both through romance and through realism. With Dreiser it produces *An American Tragedy;* with Cabell it produces a series of comedies: a comedy of justice, a comedy of shirking, a comedy of appearances, a comedy of redemption. The baffled desires of Clyde Griffith bring him to the electric chair; the baffled desires of Felix Kennaston bring him to Ettarre. Both naturalistic tragedy and romantic irony agree in the verdict: the American scene is inadequate to satisfy human aspirations.

Cabell heads the reaction against the provincially patriotic American literature which specialized in photographic representations of neatly subdivided localities. From the forward-looking romanticism of industrial and imperial ambition, from the backward-looking romanticism of reminiscent sentimentality, he leads the escape into Poictesme, into that "life beyond life" which creates and controls all through the "dynamic illusions" of romance.

BIBLIOGRAPHY

The Southern Frontier

I. General References

A. On History

HENDERSON, ARCHIBALD
The Conquest of the Old Southwest
New York; The Century Co., 1920

PHILLIPS, ULRICH B. (ed.)
Plantation and Frontier (1649–1863)
(vol. II Documentary History of American Industrial Society)
Cleveland: Arthur H. Clark, 1909

SKINNER, CONSTANCE L.
Pioneers of the Old Southwest
New Haven; Yale Univ. Press, 1919

TRENT, WILLIAM P.
"Dominant Forces in Southern Life," in *Atlantic Monthly*, vol. 79, pp. 42–54

B. On Literature

FULTON, MAURICE G.
Southern Life in Southern Literature
Boston; Ginn and Co., 1917

HALLIDAY, CARL
A History of Southern Literature
New York; Neale Publishing Co., 1906

MANLY, LOUISE
Southern Literature from 1579 to 1895
Richmond, 1900

MOSES, MONTROSE J.
The Literature of the South
New York; Thomas Y. Crowell & Co., 1910

II. Captain John Smith

Travels and Works of Captain John Smith (2 vol.)
(Arber edition revised by A. G. Bradley)
Edinburgh; John Grant, 1910

These originally appeared as follows:

The True Relation—1608
Generall Historie—1624
True Travels—1629–30
Advertisements for the Inexperienced—1631

Adams, Henry
"Captain John Smith" in *Historical Essays*
New York; Chas. Scribner's Sons, 1891

Cocke, John Esten
My Lady Pokahontas
Boston; Houghton Mifflin Co., 1885

Simms, William Gilmore
The Life of Captain John Smith, the Founder of Virginia
New York; Geo. R. Cooledge & Bros. 1846

III. Colonel William Byrd

Bassett, John Spencer (ed.)
The Writings of Colonel William Byrd of Westover in Virginia, Esquire
New York; Doubleday Page & Co., 1901

IV. David Crockett

Abbott, John S.
David Crockett: His Life and Adventures
New York; Dodd, Mead & Co., 1902

Anonymous
Sketches and Eccentricities of Colonel David Crockett
Louisville, Ky. Morton & Griswold, no date given

Crockett, David
Autobiography
New York; Chas. Scribner's Sons, 1923
(First edition 1834)

Sprague, William C.
Davy Crockett
New York; Macmillan Co., 1915

V. William Gilmore Simms

Beauchampe; or the Kentucky Tragedy
Chicago; Donohue, Henneberry & Co., 1890

Border Beagles; a tale of Mississippi
Chicago; Donohue, Henneberry & Co., 1890

Charlemont; or the Pride of the Village; a tale of Kentucky
Chicago; Donohue, Henneberry & Co., 1890
Eutaw, a sequel to the forayers
Chicago; Donohue, Henneberry & Co., 1890
The Forayers; or the Raid of the Dog-days
Chicago; Donohue, Henneberry & Co., 1890
Guy Rivers, a tale of Georgia
Chicago; Donohue, Henneberry & Co., 1890
The history of South Carolina from its first European discovery to its erection into a republic
Charlestown; Babcock, 1842
Katherine Walton
Chicago; Donohue, Henneberry & Co., 1890
The life of Francis Marion
New York; G. F. Cooledge, 1844
Mellechampe, a legend of the Santee
Chicago; Donohue, Henneberry & Co., 1890
Richard Hurdis; a tale of Alabama
Chicago; Donohue, Henneberry & Co., 1890
The Scout; or the Black Riders of Congaree
Chicago; Donohue, Henneberry & Co., 1890
The Wigwam and the Cabin
Chicago; Donohue, Henneberry & Co., 1890
Woodcraft; or Hawks about the dovecote
Chicago; Donohue, Henneberry & Co., 1890
Yemassee
Chicago; Donohue, Henneberry & Co., 1890

VI. James Lane Allen
A Kentucky Cardinal
New York; Harper & Bros., 1895
Aftermath
New York; Harper & Bros., 1896
The blue grass region of Kentucky
New York; Macmillan Co., 1907
The choir invisible
New York; Macmillan Co., 1898
Flute and violin
New York; Harper & Bros., 1904
The mettle of the pasture
New York; Macmillan Co., 1903

The reign of Law
New York; Macmillan Co., 1900
Summer in Arcady
New York; Macmillan Co., 1896

VII. George Washington Cable
The cavalier
New York; no publisher given, 1909
The Creoles of Louisiana
New York; Chas. Scribner's Sons, 1885
Dr. Servier
New York; no publisher given, 1910
The flower of the Chapdelaines
New York; Chas. Scribner's Sons, 1918
Lovers of Louisiana
New York; Chas. Scribner's Sons, 1918
Old Creole Days
New York; Chas. Scribner's Sons, 1897
Strange True Stories of Louisiana
New York; Chas. Scribner's Sons, 1889

VIII. Grace Elizabeth King
Balcony Stories
New York; Macmillan Co., 1925
Creole Families of New Orleans
New York; Macmillan Co., 1921
De Soto and his Men in the land of Florida
New York; Macmillan Co., 1898
Jean Baptiste Le Moyne, Sieur de Bienville
New York; Dodd, Mead & Co., 1893
Monsieur Motte
New York; A. C. Armstrong, 1888
New Orleans, the Place and the People
New York; Macmillan Co., 1907
The pleasant ways of St. Medard
New York; H. Holt and Co. 1916
Stories from Louisiana History
(with John N. Ficklen)
New Orleans; L. Graham and Co. 1905

IX. Thomas Nelson Page
Bred in the Bone
New York; Chas. Scribner's Sons, 1904

Elsket and other stories
New York; Chas. Scribner's Sons, 1893
Gordon Keith
New York; no publisher given, 1912
In ole Virginia
New York; Chas. Scribner's Sons, 1887
John Marvel, Assistant
New York; no publisher given, 1912
The old gentleman of the white stock
New York; Chas. Scribner's Sons, 1902
The old South; essays social and political
New York; Chas. Scribner's Sons, 1892
Pastime Stories
New York; Harper & Bros., 1894
Red Rock; a chronicle of reconstruction
New York; no publisher given, 1909
Social life in old Virginia before the war
New York; Chas. Scribner's Sons, 1897
Under the crust
New York; Chas. Scribner's Sons, 1911

X. John Fox
Christmas Eve on Lonesome and other stories
New York; Chas. Scribner's Sons, 1910
Erskine Dale, pioneer
New York; Chas. Scribner's Sons, 1920
The heart of the hills
New York; Chas. Scribner's Sons, 1913
The Kentuckians; A Knight of the Cumberland
New York; Chas. Scribner's Sons, 1910
The little shepherd of Kingdom Come
New York; Chas. Scribner's Sons, 1910
A mountain Europa; A Cumberland vendetta
New York; Chas. Scribner's Sons, 1910
The trail of the lonesome pine
New York; Chas. Scribner's Sons, 1923

XI. Lucy Furman
Mothering on Perilous
New York; Macmillan Co., 1914
The quare woman; a story of the Kentucky Mountains
Boston; Atlantic Monthly Press, 1923

XII. Mary Noilles Murfree (Charles Egbert Craddock)
Down the ravine
Boston; Houghton Mifflin Co., 1885
The fair Mississippian
Boston; Houghton Mifflin Co., 1908
In the clouds
Boston; Houghton Mifflin Co., 1886
In the Tennessee Mountains
Boston; Houghton Mifflin Co., 1886
The mystery of Witchface Mountain
Boston; Houghton Mifflin Co., 1895
The Prophet of the Great Smoky Mountains
London; no publisher given, 1891
The raid of the guerrilla
Phil. J. B. Lippincott Co., 1912
The story of Keedon Bluffs
Boston; Houghton Mifflin Co., 1888
Where the battle was fought
Boston; Houghton Mifflin Co., 1895
The young mountaineers
Boston; Houghton Mifflin Co., 1897

XIII. James Branch Cabell
Beyond Life
New York; R. M. McBride & Co., 1919
Chivalry
New York; R. M. McBride & Co., 1921
The Cords of Vanity
New York; R. M. McBride & Co., 1920
The Cream of the Jest
New York; R. M. McBride & Co., 1919
Domnei; a comedy of womanworship
New York; R. M. McBride & Co., 1923
Figures of Earth
New York; R. M. McBride & Co., 1922
From the Hidden Way
New York; R. M. McBride & Co., 1924
Gallantry; an eighteenth century dizain in ten comedies
New York; R. M. McBride & Co., 1907
The High Place
New York; R. M. McBride & Co., 1923

Jurgen
New York; R. M. McBride & Co., 1920
The Line of Love; Dizain des mariages
New York; R. M. McBride & Co., 1921
The Rivet in Grandfather's Neck
New York; R. M. McBride & Co., 1921
The Silver Stallion
New York; R. M. McBride & Co., 1926
Straws and Prayerbooks
New York; R. M. McBride & Co., 1924
VAN DOREN CARL
James Branch Cabell
New York; R. M. McBride & Co., 1925

CHAPTER III

HUNTER AND TRAPPER: HEROES OF THE FUR TRADE

I. NEW TYPES OF FRONTIERSMEN

WE have seen the adventurers of the South both in the stalwart substance of their own pioneer journals and in the shrunken shadows of subsequent Southern literature. We have seen the 17th century English Puritans who colonized the first Northern frontier: as they saw themselves, the chosen of the Lord, building a new Zion in the heart of the wilderness; as Hawthorne saw them, bigoted zealots whose adventure in spiritual pioneering was directed by a warped view of human nature and a limited view of human destiny. But the story of the frontier is not so much a story of the Old South or of the Old North as of the ever New West.

The part of the South in the building of the nation and the nation's literature has been unfairly minimized. The New England influence on American history and American literature is in no danger of like disparagement. For better or for worse, the American heritage from the Pilgrim Fathers has been so exaggerated that it is generally accepted as the core of the American tradition. But the New England influence, however potent, was but one of many forces in the development of the straggling Atlantic settlements into thirteen colonies and of the thirteen colonies into forty-eight states. New England Puritanism is not the only spirit that animated American literature from Bradford's *Plymouth* to

Masters' *Spoon River,* from Mather's *Magnalia* to Lewisohn's *Upstream.* Other types and other motives must be reckoned with. New characters come upon the scene, born of non-Puritan ancestry, brought up under frontier conditions. The "expansion of New England" is but one of many types of the westward movement in which these American born sons of the frontier play a part. The development of the old southwest glows with the heroic legends of Boone, of Sevier, of Robertson. The conquest of the old northwest is the story of Vincennes, of Kaskaskia, of the daring and initiative and resolution of George Rogers Clark. In 1821 the weighty responsibility of legislating for the commonwealth is entrusted, not to an augustly aristocratic Winthrop, or a fanatically zealous Dudley, but to the backwoods bear-hunter, Davy Crockett, the pioneer politician who had never seen a public document "nor knew there was such things," who had "never heard there was such a thing as a judiciary in all nature," but who knew how to win an election by telling funny stories and leading his thirsty constituents on frequent trips to the liquor stand.

In 1822 Jedediah Smith arrives at St. Louis and joins Ashley's trappers in a series of expeditions which cover the unexplored triangle of the trans-Missouri country and open an inland passage to the coveted lands of Oregon and California. A little later, Kit Carson will ride over the trail broken by Jedediah Smith, first as a trapper with Ewing Young, later as the hunter and guide for Fremont, the official "Pathfinder," the dashing soldier of fortune whose "scientific" expedition by strange coincidence is on the spot just as the outbreak of the Mexican war gives the United States a chance to snatch California. Joe Meek, another of Ashley's men, is the escort of the first group of Protestant missionaries to Oregon; his half breed daughter is one of the victims of the massacre in which the missionaries fall eleven years later, and Joe Meek is one of the messengers to carry the news to Washington and demand American protection for American settlers. Soldiers, trappers, hunters, solitary pathfinders and pioneers—a new generation has arisen that knows not Joseph; that gives itself little concern about the Biblical precedents and theological quibbles which were all important on the Puritan frontier. Will they too leave their impress on American literature?

For answer we turn first to that body of writings which if not literature, is at least the raw stuff of literature—the journals, letters, and biographies of these frontiersmen. A new emphasis is at once apparent. In the first place, there is more consciousness of the external world. The battleground of the drama has shifted from the human soul to the geographical environment; a man contends, not against "principalities and powers," but against the treacherous river, which at the very moment of apparent success may fling his hard won treasure of furs over her rapids with a moment's capricious gesture; against the mountain, where a false step may hurl horse and rider to frightful death; against the inhospitable prairie. Human adversaries, too, are not lacking; but in place of Anabaptists, Familists, Quakers, they are the Rees, the Blackfeet, the Crows; the Mexicans, who quite unreasonably consider that they have a right to say who shall or shall not enter their territory; the Hudson's Bay Company trappers, who with criminal perversity conspire to trap the very streams upon which the Americans have designs. The New England frontiersmen, it is true, had their troubles with the Indians; they too had occasional complications with their neighbors, the French. But in the case of King Philip's War, the community appointed a day of fasting and prayer to discover wherein they had displeased the Almighty; in the case of La Tour, Winthrop hunted his Bible for precedents justifying the course of economic advantage.

The younger generation of frontiersmen waste no prayers on the Indians, but sleep with rifle in hand; they do not bother to search in their Bibles for the version of the Golden Rule whereby they do unto the H B C trappers as their rivals would like to do to them.

The chroniclers of the Puritan frontier had their roots deep in the soil of an Old World conflict. They were characters who lived on the frontier by deliberate choice and with a definite motive; they were not frontier characters. When we turn from reading of Winslow and Bradford to read of Boone, of Crockett, of Carson, we feel that we have stepped from the "invisible world" of Cotton Mather's "wonders," to a visible, a realizable world of recognizable political, military, and economic motives, frankly avowed, openly pursued. We read more details of geographical location; we read fewer details of spiritual development; we read more details of fights with the Indians; we have no details of that fight within self which is said to be the ultimate test of manhood. And yet the worthies of Mather's particularized panegyrics flit by us "dream-footed as the shadow of a cloud," while a chance phrase in a letter or a clumsily dictated biography brings Jedediah Smith or Kit Carson before us in his habit as he lived. Here, we feel, or nowhere is our America. Here in these frontiermakers are characters who were themselves made by the frontier. What is the type of character produced under frontier conditions? And what reflections has it found in American literature?

II. JAMES FENIMORE COOPER

Cooper is associated with the frontier Leatherstocking as Hawthorne is associated with the frontier Puritan. In both cases the association has given rise to an oversimplified interpretation which has on the whole, militated against the author. In both cases the limitations of the world which the writer depicts have been accepted as the limitations of the writer. To Hawthorne is ascribed the morbid introspection, the grim austerity of his Puritans; to Cooper is ascribed the kaleidoscopic melodrama which was but a concomitant of the frontier environment. In both cases the author's recreation of his world rather than his commentary on his world have received critical attention.

Cooper's immediate popularity was followed by a reaction of scornful criticism during which it was the fashion to poke fun at every aspect of his method and material. Mark Twain, himself by no means a purist in style, made a savage onslaught upon "Fenimore Cooper's literary offences." Lowell complained of the uniform insipidity of Cooper's "females." Bret Harte devoted one of his *Condensed Novels* to a delightful though decidedly unfair parody in which the fainting Ginivra is rescued in the nick of time by a remarkable shot of Natty Bumppo's which slays five attacking animals with one bullet. Stewart Edward White digresses from his professed intention of writing the life of Boone to make a more serious and mathematically reasoned refutation of some of the shooting feats ascribed to Cooper's hero. Following the fashion, biographers and writers of critical essays meekly admit the many faults of the Leatherstocking Tales. The writers of high school textbooks dutifully echo the opinions of these more distinguished authorities, ridiculing Cooper's stilted style and slipshop English, his tedious moralizing, his artificial dialogue, his stuffed gentlemen and tame females, his blunders in woodcraft—until the student may be pardoned for wondering why he should be bothered at all with the crude stories of such a bungling romancer.

It is a perilous step to go from the reading about books to reading; but the experiment is a rewarding one when tried on Cooper. Forget all that critics have told you about his fainting females and idealized Indians, his pompous platitudes and impossible plots. Read the Leatherstocking Tales—all five of them; read them aloud; better still, read them aloud to a small boy; live with Natty Bumppo from the time when he slays his first Indian and wins for himself the name of Hawkeye to replace the pacific title of Deerslayer, until an old trapper on the prairies he dies among his adopted children the Pawnees and is laid in the same grave with his faithful "pup" Hector. You come back to the glibly critical world of the twentieth century with a start, realizing, Here—here in poor, old-fashioned, much-ridiculed Cooper is, in part at least, that much talked of, elusive *desideratum,* the American epic.

The Leatherstocking Tales are not, as one critic has called them, "the epic of the American Indian." True, Cooper, with an appropriate sense of dramatic values, puts into the mouth of the last of the Mohicans a lament for the vanished greatness of his people. A similar lament taken from the actual speech of an Indian chief is quoted in Sabin's *Kit Carson Days,* but nevertheless Kit Carson and not the Indian is the hero of the narrative. In this connection also should be refuted the oft repeated assertion that Cooper writes of the noble savage with sentimental idealization. Such an assertion must live by the sheer momentum of repetition; the most casual reading of the Leatherstocking Tales should convince a reader that, except in *The Pioneers,* the Indians are invariably the villains—while even in *The Pioneers* Mohegan John is shown disgustingly drunk, a pitiable victim of the white man's vices. I do not forget Uncas and Chingachgook; but even in the chronicles of the Puritan fathers we can find more than two good Indians. Cooper's division of the Indians into good and bad tribes—the Delawares and the Mingoes, the Pawnees and the Sioux, is but the expression of a commonplace familiar to anyone who has taken the trouble to read a few frontier travels. As a "good" child is conventionally understood to be one who does not trouble his elders, so to Cooper or to the frontier trapper, the "good" Indian was one who did not trouble the Americans. Cooper makes it clear that even these "good" Indians are not to be judged by the white man's standards of morality. Hawkeye frequently apologizes for the boasting or the barbarity of his Indian comrades by remarking that these traits are "a red man's gifts." No one holds more dogmatically than Hawkeye that red man and white man are fundamentally different, with the superiority decidedly in favor of the white.

I will pass over another common allegation against Cooper—his alleged inaccuracy in shooting exploits—a point on which I am not qualified to pass judgment. On the one hand, we have the mathematical evidence of Stewart Edward White that the feats ascribed to Natty Bumppo are impossible; on the other, we have the testimony of frontier chronicles that similar exploits were an accepted part of pioneer life. As every woman knows, the mathematically impossible is a part of everyday experience; so we will let the record of Killdeer go at that, and turn to an equally frequent criticism—the lackadaisical ladylikeness of Cooper's heroines.

This accusation, like the idealization of the Indians, is easier to repeat than to verify. Let us look for examples. *The Last of the Mohicans,* conventionally labeled Cooper's best book, furnishes us with one of the few examples of the fainting female: Alice faints after an Indian massacre in which her friends have been tomahawked before her eyes, in which she and her sister have been separated from her father and lover and carried off as captives. We can open any newspaper and read of an automobile or train wreck in which survivors fainted from the shock; yet we do not therefore sneer at the cowardice of twentieth century women. Let us go through the Leatherstocking Tales and see some of the situations in which these frontier women find themselves. Alice and Cora bound to trees and menaced with torments, refuse to buy their safety at the price of life in Indian wigwams. Judith and Hetty think nothing of setting off alone in a canoe to reconnoiter the savage encampment, and if possible to bring aid to Hawkeye. Hetty's repeated visits to the Mingo camp may be explained by the fact that she was feebleminded and proverbially they who know nothing fear nothing; also by the fact that in this case her infirmity gave really less reason for fear, as it was regarded with superstitious respect by the savages. But Judith sets off alone to the enemy camp with no such protection, and appears in full finery, hoping by her negotiations to delay Deerslayer's torture until help may arrive. At the opening of the Indian attack Judith saves the day by pushing the Indian intruder over the edge of the scow into the river. Judith and Hetty return to the ark to find the mangled body of Hutter; there is no time for fainting or hysterics, or even for an expression of grief or horror. They set about bandaging the scalped head, dressing his wounds, making him as comfortable as possible in mind and body during his last hours. Judith is within the space of a few days bereft of her supposed father, her sister, her home, and rejected by the man whom she had come to regard as her only friend, to whom with very un-Victorian initiative, she had offered herself in marriage. But Judith, the most emotional of Cooper's heroines, starts off stoically into the woods on her way to the fort, without making a scene, refusing even the proffered attention of Deerslayer's escort through the woods until she overtakes the soldiers. Elizabeth and Louisa in *The Pioneers* are similarly contemptuous of Oliver's offered protection on their mountain walk. We must admit that Cooper's pages are here again tainted with the mid-Victorianism of a fainting female; but in extenuation let it be mentioned that Louisa faints only when attacked by a panther, and that her fainting serves as the foil for the heroism of Elizabeth who refuses to leave her unconscious friend. And as if that adventure were not enough for the girls, we find them a few days later, in the attempt to keep their promise to Leatherstocking, again ascending the mountain, this time to be trapped by the forest fire.

If we turn to *The Pathfinder,* we find Mabel Dunham, not only braving the terrors of the storm, but when it subsides actually asking to be taken on a pleasure trip in the canoe. Later we find Mabel displaying both heroism and presence of mind in her defense of the blockhouse and unselfish affection in her daring rush from its shelter to seek the wounded body of her father. Is it in *The Prairie* that we are to find the helpless, clinging, fearful female who arouses contemptuous mirth in Cooper's critics? Here is Ellen, a bit of a rowdy, and so indelicately un-Victorian as to steal from the camp at midnight to hold a rendezvous with her lover the bee hunter. Here are Esther and her two daughters who in the absence of the men of the party, defend the rock citadel against attack. "Reared in the hardihood of a migrating life on the skirts of society, where they had become familiarized to the sights and dangers of the wilderness, these girls promised fairly to become at some future day no less distinguished than their mother for daring and for that singular mixture of good and evil which in a wider sphere of action would probably have enabled the wife of the squatter to enroll her name among the remarkable females of her time. Esther had already on one occasion made good the log tenement of Ishmael against an inroad of savages; and on another she had been left for dead by her enemies after a defense that with a more civilized foe would have entitled her to the honors of a liberal capitulation. These facts and others of a similar nature had often been recapitulated with suitable exultation in the presence of her daughters, and the bosoms of the young Amazons were now strangely fluctuating between natural terror and the ambitious wish to do something that might render them worthy of being the children of such a mother." So far from emphasizing the weakness and timidity of his women, Cooper loves to dwell upon their strength and courage—qualities which he expressly attributes to the frontier environment. What he writes of Mabel Dunham applies to all his heroines: "It was one of the peculiarities of the exposure to which those who dwelt on the frontiers of America were liable, to bring out the moral qualities of the women to a degree that they must themselves under other circumstances have believed that they were incapable of manifesting; and Mabel well knew that the borderers loved to dwell in their legends on the presence of mind, fortitude, and spirit that their wives and daughters had displayed under circumstances the most trying. Her emulation had been awakened by what she had heard on such subjects; and it at once struck her that now was the moment for her to show that she was truly Sergeant Dunham's child."

Perhaps it is well to weigh these words of Cooper against the pronouncement of the Cambridge History of American Literature: "Accepting for women the romantic ideals of the day and writing of events in which of necessity ladies could play but a small part, Cooper tended to cast his heroines into a conventional mold of helplessness and decorum." In this commentary on his world, Cooper establishes the connection which he felt between his characters and their environment; he reveals himself as no mere lucky exploiter of a new and melodramatic setting, but as a conscious artist, realizing and rendering the significance of the frontier, making it the basis of an American epic. The frontier affords the setting; it occasions the plot; it offers the theme; it creates the character. And the greatest of these is character. Critics of Cooper agree that he has made a contribution in the creation of Leatherstocking. Lowell says in *The Fable for Critics*:

> He has drawn you one character, though, that is new.
> One wildflower he's plucked that is wet with the dew
> Of this fresh Western world.

Lounsbury calls Leatherstocking "one of the few original characters, perhaps the only great original character that American fiction has added to the literature of the world." Van Doren echoes Lounsbury almost verbatim, in pronouncing Leatherstocking "the most memorable character American fiction has given to the world." But it does not seem to occur to these critics to connect Cooper's creation of this original character with the creation of such characters by the actual frontier.

The frontier setting as used by Cooper may be dismissed with a few words. Critics to the contrary notwithstanding, the isolated descriptions of nature are rare in Cooper and relatively unimportant. Cooper is often called "the American Scott," but while sharing many of Scott's weak as well as strong points, he is more modern than Scott in the matter of descriptions. Description is used by Cooper in two ways: first to create an appropriate atmosphere for some emotion—as when the calm of the evening on the lake above the new made graves prepares Judith for her final understanding with Deerslayer. This use of nature is an essentially modern one, employed at greater length, and of course, with much more psychological finesse by such a writer as Thomas Hardy. A slightly different use of nature in connection with character is found in the comments on the forest which Cooper puts into the mouth of Leatherstocking; these we shall consider later. But the second and far more frequent way in which Cooper makes use of his setting is in a very practical relation to the plot; if we hear of a waterfall, we know that soon Eau-Douce will be shooting the rapids to the terror of the salt water Cap. If a forest thicket is described in detail, it is because the treacherous Magua and his band are lurking there in ambush. If the sentimental Inez is allowed to expatiate at length upon the beauty of the sunrise, the vigilant Bumppo's practiced eye speedily discerns in the rosy glow the menace of a prairie fire.

After Cooper's critics have done their worst, they usually throw in some grudging comments upon the rapid fire ingenuity of Cooper's plots with their breathless interplay of furtherance and hindrance forces, their spectacular reversals of fortune. In my opinion, Cooper deserves less credit for his plots than for any other part of his romances. I do not go so far as to paraphrase Dr. Johnson to the effect that if one reads Cooper merely for the story, one would hang oneself; but if one reads Cooper merely for the story, one might as well read any volume of Thwaites' *Early Western Travels.* All the details are there; ambushments, scalpings, danger, treachery, suspense, surprise, loyalty, courage; at first they take our breath away; after a while they bore us. Why? Because we don't care particularly about the fate of any of the travelers; the fate of a thousand is not tragic; the fate of one may be. The carnage goes on for ten years around Ilium and we remain unmoved; but the beloved Patroclus is slain, and we watch with poignant suspense the combat between the valiant Hector and the avenging Achilles. Plots the frontier offered in abundance; they were sterile until Cooper breathed the breath of life into a frontier character.

Erskine alone of Cooper's critics appears to have recognized the dual parentage of Leatherstocking. He points out in his essay on Cooper in *Leading American Novelists* that: "The restless aspiration of the new age found its image in wanderers and explorers of the frontiers of thought—in the hero of *Alastor* and in *Childe Harold;* and in America it found its expression in these prose parallels of Cooper's." How far is Leatherstocking the child of the frontier? How far is he the child of the romantic movement in European literature? It may seem a mere humorless pedantry even to raise such a question concerning the honest woodsman who himself was content to let his pedigree rest on the assertion: "I come of a humble stock, though we have white gifts and a white nature." But we shall come to the rugged simplicity and sterling beauty of Deerslayer's character with a finer appreciation if we compare him on one hand with the conventional romantic hero of Rousseau's pattern, and on the other, with such flesh and blood sons of the frontier as Boone, Crockett, Clark, Carson, or Jedediah Smith.

The cardinal doctrines of Rousseau's philosophy are, first, the essential goodness of human nature, second, the essential badness of human institutions. On both these points, Deerslayer is heretical. How reconcile the essential goodness of human nature with the fact taught him by repeated experience that treachery, cruelty, arrogant pride, vindictive revenge were "a red man's gifts"; that even among white men there were many like Hurry Harry whose "gifts" were along the line of coarseness, disloyalty, selfishness. So far from holding that private property is wrong, Deerslayer has a scrupulous regard for the rights of private property that would enroll him today among the "Better Americans." He has scruples about opening and ransacking Hutter's chest even in search of articles that might ransom Hutter from the

Indians. Deerslayer's own conduct is regulated by principles of "natural religion" which sound like an echo of eighteenth century Deism; but Deerslayer always speaks respectfully of the teachings of the Moravian missionaries, listens devoutly to Hetty's Bible readings, and when in the settlements is an attendant at the services held by the Episcopal rector. Deerslayer's respect for vested property and organized religion does not extend to a respect for law; his opinions on that point appear to coincide with Rousseau's theory of natural rights. Pressed hard by the increasing population of the settlements and by Judge Temple's game regulations, the old hunter feels that "it's a hard case to a man to have his honest calling for livelihood stopped by laws." The recurrent struggle of the frontier between settlers and hunters is given tragic expression in the farewell of the old hunter as he faces the officers of the law among the ashes of his ruined hut: "You've driven God's creatures from the wilderness where His providence had put them for His own pleasure; and you've brought in the troubles and deviltries of the law where no man was ever known to disturb another." But in *The Prairie* Leatherstocking now still older, asks Ellen:

> 'Did you not know that when you crossed the Big River you left a friend behind you that is always bound to look to the young and feeble like yourself?'
>
> 'Of whom do you speak?'
>
> 'The law! 'tis bad to have it, but I sometimes think it is worse to be entirely without it. Age and weakness have brought me to feel such weakness at times. Yes, yes, the law is needed when such as have not the gifts of strength and wisdom are to be taken care of.'

Leatherstocking then cannot be regarded as an adequate embodiment of the Rousseau philosophy of back to nature. Neither does he conform to the requirements of the romantic hero as depicted by the devotees of

Wertherism. Perhaps the comparison can be made most forcibly by placing Cooper's Leatherstocking besides Chateaubriand's Rene. To Chateaubriand rather than to Cooper are applicable the critic's remarks about noble savages and noble sentiments, lovely ladies and lovely scenery. Let us see what each writer has to offer us by way of a hero.

Rene is a neurotic aristocrat who has sought the American wilderness suffering from a complex which a modern psychoanalyst would probably describe in unpleasant terms. He is sentimental, apathetic, introspective, melancholy; he deliberately turns his back on his people and his country to embrace the life of a savage. Bumppo is a plain commoner, born on the frontier and quite naturally following the frontier calling of a hunter; he is matter-of-fact, energetic, cheerful, healthyminded; his one love affair goes deep, but the wound heals normally; even while it is fresh, we see him forgetting his own disappointment in practical helpfulness to the Indian girl Dew-of-June who has suffered a keener loss. He leaves his home, not from morbid caprice, but from painful necessity; "Othello's occupation gone" he must move on or remain as the pensioner of Elizabeth and her husband. But his roots have gone deep and there is heart-breaking pathos in his cry: "You've driven me that have lived forty long years of my appointed time in this very spot, from my home and the shelter of my head. You've driven me to burn these logs under which I've eaten and drunk for the half of a hundred years; and to mourn the ashes under my feet as a man would weep and mourn the children of his body." Finally, although he dies in the bosom of an Indian tribe, venerated by them as their adopted father, he has steadily refused throughout his career to live as one of the red men. In *The Last of the Mohicans* he invariably refers to himself with pride as "a man without a cross"; in

The Deerslayer he prefers death by slow torture to honored adoption into the tribe as the husband of an Indian squaw.

A comparison of Leatherstocking with historical characters of the frontier will yield a much closer parallel. It would obviously be an interminable task to make a detailed biographical and psychoanalytical study of every frontiersman who has left his record in history, and then a comparison of each with Leatherstocking. The point can be demonstrated with sufficient evidence if we confine ourselves to representative frontiersmen of the various periods and places intervening between the first frontier of the seventeenth century on the Atlantic and the last frontier of 1849 on the Pacific. Let us take George Rogers Clark from the old northwest, Daniel Boone from the old southwest, David Crockett from the new west of Jacksonian democracy, Jedediah Smith, Joe Meek and Kit Carson from the trans-Missouri fur trade.

Diverse as these characters may be from each other and from Leatherstocking in many ways, there are basic resemblances which we may safely consider the common factors in frontier character. Skill in marksmanship and woodcraft, ability to handle Indians both in war and diplomacy, resourcefulness, endurance, daring—without these qualities, not merely distinction, but even survival would be impossible on the frontier. We may, then, accept these traits as marking the type of character inevitably produced by frontier conditions.

But the most confirmed environmentalist realizes that life is not so simple that a man can be explained entirely in terms of his environment. Within the type there is room for individual variation. As we examine these frontier heroes, we find them presenting dominant traits which differentiate them from each other. With George Rogers Clark the distinguishing trait is military ambition, which thwarted, poisons his nature with a corrosive bitterness. With Daniel Boone it is a rugged unassuming honesty and a chronic craving for "more elbow room." David Crockett, like George Rogers Clark, is tormented by ungratified ambitions; but he is a much pettier and cruder man than Clark; his unvarnished egotism, his glaring bad taste, his absurd vanities, his mean resentments, betray the provincialism bred by the isolation of the frontier, the defects which sometimes nearly overbalance the heroic qualities. With Jedediah Smith we return to the serious piety of the Puritan pioneer. Lacking the intolerance, the superstition, the morbidity of Puritanism, Smith preserves its noblest qualities; its unwavering adherence to duty, its sense of immediate responsibility to God. In him we find a recrudescence of the religious motive which made the conquest of the wilderness an adventure in spiritual pioneering: "It is that I may be able to help those who stand in need, that I face every danger. It is for this that I pass over the sandy plains in heat of summer, thirsting for water where I may cool my overheated body. It is for this that I go for days without eating, and am pretty well satisfied if I can gather a few roots, a few snails, or better satisfied if we can afford ourselves a piece of horseflesh or a fine roasted dog; and most of all, it is for this that I deprive myself of the privilege of society and the satisfaction of the converse of my friends." No such noble motives animate Jedediah's companion, the waggish Joe Meek. A big drunk at the rendezvous, a few pretty half-breed girls, a few fights and jokes—these were the things that made life worth living for the happy-go-lucky trapper.

What traits has Leatherstocking that set him apart from any or all frontier characters? He has initiative and courage in devising and executing plans for the safety of the various groups who look to him for guidance; but none of his adventures in strategy compare with the desperate advance of George Rogers Clark upon Kaskaskia. He has the confidence of the "good" and the respect of the "bad" Indians; but testimonials of a similar regard were showered upon Kit Carson. He is marvelously expert with Killdeer; but we have it on the authority of an eye-witness that David Crockett could outdo any feats that Cooper ascribes to Leatherstocking, He is given to sententious moral platitudes; but we find Jedediah Smith, George Rogers Clark, and Kit Carson addicted to similar moralizings. He is modest, deprecating boasting as "agin a white man's gifts," either concealing his meritorious actions, or taking them as a matter of course; a similar pleasing modesty is found in Clark, in Smith, in Carson, most of all, in Boone. He has an innate sense of delicacy; but nothing in his untrained chivalry is finer than Carson's feeling about his Indian wife.

What really sets Leatherstocking apart from these historical frontiersmen is that while he has all their virtues, he has not any of their faults. He lacks entirely the ambition, the desire of self-aggrandizement which motivated the career of Clark, and much more obviously, of Crockett. He lacks the boastfulness and vulgarity of Crockett, and the easygoing unmorality of Joe Meek. Not only does he lack the faults of these characters, but he lacks their group relationships. In each volume of the Leatherstocking Tales we see the hunter in peculiarly intimate relations to a group thrown together by a common danger and relying on him for protection. But the end is always the same; his mission over, he bids farewell to his friends and takes the lone trail. Chingachgook is the one character who remains in intimate relations with him throughout his career; and in the last volume, *The Prairie,* even the Delaware has died, and the old trapper is indeed alone, At the end of *The Pioneers,* the first of the series, and at the beginning of *The Prairie,* the last of the series, we see the solitary trapper, a colossal figure defined against the sunset sky. He stands alone; greater than any frontiersman because he is the symbol of all frontiersmen.

Only one positive trait differentiates Leatherstocking from the actual pathfinders: his intimate and frequently expressed love of nature. This is usually accounted for as a trait borrowed from the romantic school and somewhat incongruously fostered upon a simple backwoodsman. I see no way of proving whether love for and communion with nature was characteristic of the frontiersman. In the first place, such sentiment may be no less genuinely present when inarticulate. Written descriptions of nature are a leisure class amusement chiefly practiced by literary dilettanti who may not be as truly lovers of nature as Daniel Boone who lay singing alone in the wilderness. Then, had such sentiments been cherished and expressed by the frontiersmen, their expression would naturally have been oral. That such campfire descriptions were common and not lacking in poetic imagination, one would gather from Fremont's journals of his expeditions. But such of the frontiersmen as could write employed their ability and opportunity in recording geographical and military data which seemed more important than the feeling of their souls at sunset.

Leatherstocking is the happy product of the romantic movement in literature and the westward movement in history. He incarnates the best qualities of both parents. He has the sentiment of the romantic hero without his mawkishness; he has the heroism of the frontiersman without his vulgarity. He is an idealized frontiersman, not in the sense that any of his qualities are idealized, but in that the combination of these qualities in one individual unmarred by their corresponding defects, is possible only to the conscious selection of art, not to the biological selection of nature. He is a frontiersman, but he is not presented as an inevitable product of frontier conditions. As if to disarm criticism on this point, Cooper has placed beside him undesirable frontier types such as the greedy and unscrupulous Hutter, the boisterous Hurry Harry, Paul the headstrong beehunter, Ishmael the surly n'er do weel.

It is by the creation of this character, not by any cinema-like ingenuity of plot complication, that Cooper's Leatherstocking Tales deserve a place in the history of American literature and in the literature of American history. But the creation of character does not make an epic. What constitutes the peculiar significance of the Leatherstocking Tales is that the frontier furnishes a theme as well as a character.

It is well known that the order in which the Leatherstocking Tales were written does not correspond to the chronological sequence of events in the hero's life. The order of publication is as follows: *The Pioneers* 1823, *The Last of the Mohicans* 1826, *The Prairie* 1827, *The Pathfinder* 1840, *The Deerslayer* 1841. The chronological order is as follows: *The Deerslayer, The Last of the Mohicans, The Pathfinder, The Pioneers, The Prairie.* The first of the series, *The Pioneers,* represents Natty Bumppo and his faithful companion the Mohican, as old men, already out of place and ill at ease as the settlements crowded around them. One of the writers of high school texts comments on this fact with the following ingenuous observation:

> When Cooper published *The Pioneers* he probably had no intention of writing a series of novels recounting the adventures of Natty Bumppo, or Leatherstocking, and his Indian friend Chingachgook; otherwise he would hardly have painted so shabby a picture of these two old heroes, neglected and despised in a land through which they had once moved as masters.

It is hard to conceive of a sentence which could reveal

a more glaring lack of critical insight coupled with a blandly Rotarian worship of SUCCESS. The hero must be successful; Bumppo in *The Pioneers* is not successful; *ergo,* Cooper could not have intended him as a hero. The syllogism is perfect—if we accept the major premise. But as far back as Cooper we find the questioning of the idol of success. Can anyone read *The Pioneers* and not feel that Leatherstocking is a more heroic character than Judge Temple? though Judge Temple is the "successful" man, the landed proprietor, the administrator of the law; and Leatherstocking and his Indian comrade stand before him, symbols of a vanishing type and a vanishing race. Let those who sneer at Cooper read again the scene in which Judge Temple sentences the old hunter for the killing of a deer:

> The Judge waved his hand for silence and proceeded:—'In forming their sentence, the court have been governed as much by the consideration of your ignorance of the laws as by a strict sense of the importance of punishing such outrages as this of which you have been found guilty. They have therefore passed over the obvious punishment of whipping on the bare back, in mercy to your years; but as the dignity of the law requires an open exhibition of the consequences of your crime, it is ordered that you be conveyed from this room to the public stocks, where you are to be confined for one hour; that you pay a fine to the State of one hundred dollars; that you be imprisoned in the jail of this county for one calendar month, and furthermore that your imprisonment do not cease until the said fare shall be paid. I feel it my duty, Natty Bumppo——'
>
> 'And where should I get the money?' interrupted the Leatherstocking eagerly, 'where should I get the money? you'll take away the bounty on the painters because I cut the throat of a deer; and how is an old man to find so much gold or silver in the woods? No, no, Judge; think better of it, and don't talk of shutting me up in a jail for the little time I have to stay!'
>
> 'If you have anything to urge against the passing of the sentence, the court will yet hear you,' said the Judge mildly.

'I have enough to say agin it!' cried Natty, grasping the bar on which his fingers were working with a convulsive motion. 'Where am I to get the money? Let me out into the woods and hills, where I've been used to breathe the clear air, and though I'm threescore and ten, if you've left game enough in the country, I'll travel night and day but I'll make you up the sum afore the season is over. Yes, yes; you see the reason of the thing, and the wickedness of shutting up an old man that has spent his days as one may say, where he could always look into the windows of heaven.'

'I must be governed by the law——'

'Talk not to me of law, Marmaduke Temple,' interrupted the old man with melancholy earnestness. 'Did the beast of the forest mind your laws, when it was thirsty and hungering for the blood of your own child! She was kneeling to her God for a greater favor than I ask, and He heard her; and if you now say no to my prayers, do not think He will be deaf?'

'My private feelings must not enter into——'

'Hear me, Marmaduke Temple, and hear reason. I've traveled these mountains when you was no Judge, but an infant in your mother's arms; and I feel as if I had a right and privilege to travel them agin before I die. Have you forgot the time that you come on to the lake shore when there wasn't even a jail to lodge in; and didn't I give you my own bearskin to sleep on and the fat of a noble buck to satisfy the cravings of your hunger? Yes, yes—you thought it no sin then to slay a deer. And this I did, though I had no reason to love you, for you had never done anything but harm to them that loved and sheltered me. And now will you shut me up in your dungeons to pay me for my kindness? A hundred dollars! Where should I get the money? No, no; there's them that says hard things of you, Marmaduke Temple, but you aint so bad as to wish to see an old man die in a prison because he stood up for the right. Come, friend, let me pass; it's long sin' I've been used to such crowds and I long to be in the woods agin. Don't fear me, Judge—I bid you not to fear me; for if there's beaver enough left on the streams, or the buckskins will sell for a shilling apiece, you shall have the last penny of the fine. Where are ye pups! come away, dogs, come away! we have a grievous toil to do for our years, but it shall be done—yes, yes, I've promised it, and it shall be done.'

One may search American literature for a scene of more gripping dramatic power than this written by Fenimore Cooper whom little critical gentlemen patronize because of his "wooden dialogue" and stilted, slovenly style, and inefficiently unsuccessful hero; Fenimore Cooper, who had the genius, not only to create a living character as the incarnate spirit of the chronic pioneer, but to trace in the life of that character the theme of the receding frontier. At the opening of *The Prairie* Ishmael and his emigrant train have their first view of Leatherstocking, now an old man driven by the pressure of the westward migration to become a trapper on the plains:

> The sun had fallen below the crest of the nearest wave of the prairie, leaving the usual rich and glowing train on its track. In the center of this flood of fiery light, a human form appeared, drawn against the gilded background as distinctly and seeming as palpable as though it would come within the grasp of any extended hand. The figure was colossal; the attitude musing and melancholy; and the situation directly in the route of the travellers.

The mighty hunter has been forced to become a trapper; now the trapper in turn gives way before the advance of the settler and recedes into the sunset glow of a heroic past. The passing of Leatherstocking is identified with the passing of a mighty race; the song of the resistless pressure of "civilization" is sung in a minor key; it is accepted as inevitable, like the Destiny of the *Iliad,* like the Wyrd of *Beowulf;* but it is not made the occasion for cheap jubilation; it is sung, not as a triumph, but as a tragic epic.

III. WASHINGTON IRVING

Fenimore Cooper's fame depends upon his use of frontier materials; Washington Irving's frontier narratives are almost ignored. A recent college text on American literature which devotes a chapter to Washington Irving, spends two pages in comment on *Rip Van Winkle* and one on *The Legend of Sleepy Hollow* while the fact that Irving wrote two volumes on *Astoria* and *The Adventures of Captain Bonneville* (a total output of some six hundred pages) is mentioned only in an appended bibliography, and Irving's account of his own *Tour of the Prairies* is entirely ignored. More remarkable still, an essay ostensibly devoted to the consideration of "Washington Irving's services to American History," makes no mention of *Astoria* or *The Adventures of Captain Bonneville,* but contents itself with the assertion that Irving "did his share in making America historic in giving its past days light, flavor, reality, loveliness." The frontier was without honor in its own country. Now that it has gone, we are becoming aware of its historical and literary significance. Now that American history is being rewritten in terms of the westward movement, it may be well to reconsider Irving's "services to American History" in terms not merely of his revival of legends of the past, but of his interest in the present. *Rip Van Winkle* and *The Legend of Sleepy Hollow* constitute a time-honored part of the "required reading" in all American public schools, till whatever spontaneity of interest these tales may once have possessed has long become exhausted. Why not give the long-suffering Rip another twenty years' sleep, why not let the *Legend of Sleepy Hollow* slumber, and direct the attention of students of American literature to the equally well written, more American, far more interesting narratives of adventures around the Rocky Mountains?

Unlike Cooper, Irving did not use frontier material as a basis for fictitious romance, but developed the inherent romance of the facts which he gathered from journals of exploring expeditions, from interviews with his friends, Mr. Astor and Captain Bonneville, and from his own excursion of a month to the hunting grounds of the Pawnees.

Irving's momentary masquerade as a frontiersman may be dismissed with a casual review. Although literary critics apparently consider *A Tour of the Prairies* of more consequence than *Astoria* and *The Adventures of Captain Bonneville,* the student of Western history cannot but regard it as a bit of *opera bouffe.* The meretricious elements in this self conscious venture into frontier life are evident if one applies as a touchstone the narratives of *bona fide* trappers. Mr. Irving prepares an elaborate stage setting for his near adventures; he goes through all the gestures of deep emotional excitation; but his artificially induced thrills end in anticlimax. His prairie fire is easily extinguished by a few slaps of the blanket; his lost Count is discovered sleeping as peacefully as though he were safe in bed in his native Switzerland; his Pawnee attack turns out to be nothing more momentous than the approach of two of their own rangers.

Irving, proudly bestriding his noble charger and boldly striking into the Pawnee country attended only by a half breed guide, an English botanist, a Swiss Count, a Government Commissioner for Indian affairs, and a corps of riflemen, reminds one of a small lad, caparisoned in khaki bravely setting off for a Boy Scout camp—two miles from his city home! Neither Irving nor the Boy Scout detect any lack of verisimilitude in their adventures as casual frontiersmen. Indeed, the gentlemanly Irving confesses proudly that he finds his "ravenous and sanguinary propensities daily growing stronger upon the prairies" and true to eighteenth century traditions, manifests delight in his return to the pseudo-primitive. He describes his environment with a sophisticated sense of the picturesque. He displays an essentially bookish preference for a state of nature as against a state of civilization. He decorates his pages with charming bits of folk lore, such as the stories of the Flower of the Prairie, of the brave who found the moccasins of the thunder, of the eagle, tutelary spirit of the Delawares, who rescued the Chief in the hour of need. He returns to Fort Gobson "much tattered, travel-stained, and weather-beaten, but in high health and spirits," and with material for a book. And thus ends his "foray into the Pawnee hunting grounds."

In assembling the materials for *Astoria* and *The Adventures of Captain Bonneville,* Irving is dealing not with the accumulated contents of his own portfolio, but with a much larger volume of manuscripts giving the records of genuine trappers. In *Astoria* and *Captain Bonneville* Irving is telling the story not of the pleasure trip of a month but of the grim endeavor of years. The form of these narratives is, as Irving admits in his preface to *Astoria,* "of a rambling and somewhat disjointed nature, comprising various expeditions and adventures by land and sea." The works are not, however, without narrative pattern: "The facts will prove to be linked and bound together by one grand scheme devised and conducted by a master spirit; one set of characters continues throughout—and the whole enterprise winds up by a regular catastrophe."

In spite of this attempt to throw the material into some sort of plot design, Irving's narratives of the frontier are more closely allied to history than to literature; which probably accounts for the fact that we find more frequent references to them in Western History than in American criticism. But to one who believes with G. M. Trevelyan that literature ought to be read in the light of history, and history written as though it were literature, *Astoria* and *Captain Bonneville* are valuable as examples of a successful synthesis of historical material and literary art.

First, we may consider the episodes of romantic charm or dramatic intensity which are scattered through these works, and which, while themselves narrative units, also play a part toward the humanizing and vitalizing of the whole. There is the story of the wreck of the Tonquin, one of the many tragedies furnished by the epic of the fur trade. (Why continue to cumber our "readers" with "The Wreck of the Hesperus," when only the advanced student of history learns the far more significant, far more heroic story of the wreck of the Tonquin?) There is the story of Colter's running the gauntlet and of his marvelous escape naked and alone pursued across the wilderness by his savage foes. (Why go back to the epic of Greece to read of the flight of Hector from Achilles and leave forgotten this heroic race of our own epic?) In more romantic mood is the story of the terrible Wash-ing-guh-sah-ba, the Indian chief who, instructed by an unscrupulous trader in the poisonous qualities of arsenic, prophesied and executed a swift and mysterious death upon all who disputed his commands; who in a transport of rage slew his favorite wife, the beautiful daughter of the Ponca chief, and then starved himself beside her body in an agony of remorse. Chateaubriand's *Atala* reads like cheap sentimentality beside the story of Kosato, the renegade Blackfoot who had eloped from his tribe with the wife of his chief. The experience of Robert Campbell when a guest in the village of the Arapooish proves that there was honor among the Crows. Dashing as the story of young Lochinvar is the audacity with which one of Bonneville's trappers rescues the Indian girl who had been his mistress from the lodge of the Shoshonie brave.

But while these idyllic and tragic fragments abound in *Astoria* and *Captain Bonneville,* they are carefully subordinated to the main thread of the narrative which is concerned with the "grand enterprises of the great fur companies and the hazardous errantry of their associates in the wild parts of our vast continent." *Astoria* deals with Mr. Astor's ill-fated settlement of that name, giving the account of the voyage and fate of the Tonquin, the overland expedition of Mr. Hunt, the return party of Mr. Stuart, and the betrayal (as it seemed to Irving) of Astoria into the hands of the British rivals. In *The Adventures of Captain Bonneville,* Irving takes up the story of the American fur trade from the failure of Astoria, gives a brief résumé of subsequent activities such as the Ashley-Smith expeditions, and then, basing his material on Captain Bonneville's manuscripts, details the travels of that party from their departure from Fort Osage on the first of May, 1832, until their return in the August of 1835.

For our purposes, *Astoria* and *Captain Bonneville* may well be considered, not as separate narratives, but as episodes of the same epic. True, the characters have changed; but the types are the same. In Irving's narratives there is no emergence of one central character who sustains our interest through successive scenes and situations. Neither is the narrative urged forward by the insistence of one dominant narrative question. In leisurely and comfortable fashion, Irving recounts the rapidly shifting ups and downs of the different groups of trappers with whom his narrative is concerned. There are all the elements of plot: conflict, movement, suspense, surprise. Setting comes in for a greater amount of detached attention than is given it in the Leatherstocking Tales. Captain Bonneville, Irving tells us, was a romantic soul with "a susceptibility to the grand and beautiful," and according to the Captain, his enthusiasm for the wild beauties of nature was shared by his men. Characterization deals with type groups—Indians as a class, trappers as a class, rather than with individuals. The individuals who are definitely sketched are usually episodic characters such as the squaw wife of the half breed guide, Pierre Dorien, the suspicious and dogmatic Captain Thorn, the ingratiating Nez Perces patriarch, the prodigal jester, Shee-wee-shee-ouaiter, the treacherous Manuel Lisa, the belligerent M'Lellan.

It is obvious from this analysis that Irving's use of frontier materials lacks the sharply dramatic intensity of Cooper's Leatherstocking Tales. What do *Astoria* and *The Adventures of Captain Bonneville* contribute to the interpretation of the frontier in American literature?

In the first place, they constitute an admirably lucid and readable secondary account of two episodes in the western fur trade. Secondly, their group characterizations, although less dramatically drawn than the characters of the idyllic or comic interludes, are more significant as indicative of the temper of the opposing parties on the historical scene. Irving's comments on the Indians are in the bulk decidedly more favorable than those in the Leatherstocking Tales. The depredations of the "bad" Indians are more often mischievous pranks than brutal barbarities. The massacre on the Tonquin, unlike the massacre in *The Last of the Mohicans,* is represented as directly ascribable to the arrogance of the white man: "Had the deportment of Captain Thorn been properly regulated, the insult so wounding to savage pride would never have been given." On the other hand, wanton outrages of the whites against the Indians are set down without extenuation. Good Indians such as the Nez Perces are depicted (and this on the authority of Captain Bonneville) as possessed of all the virtues with which Cooper endowed the Delawares. The dignity and eloquence of the Indians' speeches may be illustrated by this defiance of the defeated Blackfoot chief:

> So long as we had powder and ball, we fought you in the open field: when those were spent, we retreated here to die with our women and children. You may burn us in our fort;

but stay by our ashes and you who are so hungry for fighting will soon have enough. There are four hundred lodges of our brethren at hand. They will soon be here—their arms are strong—their hearts are big—they will avenge us!

Meeting with the Indians is more often a source of relief than of terror to the trappers; for one time that they are received with open hostility or covert malice, there are many times that they are received with generous and much-needed hospitality.

The other group of actors in the drama of the fur trade, the trappers, are drawn by Irving with equally vivid characterization:

There is perhaps, no class of men on the face of the earth who lead a life of more continued exertion, peril, and excitement, and who are more enamoured of their occupation than the free trappers of the West. No toil, no danger, no privation can turn the trapper from his pursuit. His passionate excitement at times resembles a mania. In vain may the most vigilant and cruel savages beset his path; in vain may rocks and precipices and wintry torrents oppose his progress; let but a single track of a beaver meet his eye and he forgets all danger and defies all difficulties. At times he may be seen with his traps on his shoulder buffeting his way across rapid streams amid floating blocks of ice; at other times he is to be found with his traps swung on his back climbing the most rugged mountains; scaling or descending the most frightful precipices, searching by routes inaccessible to the horse, and never before trodden by white man for springs and lakes unknown to his comrades, and where he may meet with his favorite game. Such is the mountaineer, the hardy trapper of the West; and such is the wild, Robin Hood kind of life, with all its strange and motley populace, now existing in full vigor among the Rocky Mountains.

With the fascination which the man of the study feels for the man of the open, Irving sketches Bonneville's band as they set off on their adventure:

Many of them looked more like Indians than white men in their garbs and accoutrements, and their very horses were caparisoned in barbaric style with fantastic trappings. The outset of a band of adventurers on one of these expeditions is always animated and joyous. The welkin rang with their shouts and yelps after the manner of the savages; and with boisterous jokes and lighthearted laughter. As they passed the straggling hamlets and solitary cabins that fringe the skirts of the frontier, they would startle their inmates by Indian yells and warwhoops, or regale them with grotesque feats of horsemanship well suited to their half savage appearance.

In similar detail Irving shows us the free trappers, "the cavaliers of the mountains," as they dash into Captain Bonneville's camp, and feast, and swagger, and fight with Bonneville's men. He invites us to the wedding of a trapper and an Indian squaw. He takes us to the rendezvous on Green River where the trappers engage in contests of skill in running, jumping, wrestling, shooting, and horseracing, where, "every freak of prodigality was indulged to its fullest extent, and in a little while, most of the trappers having squandered away all their wages and perhaps run knee deep in debt, were ready for another hard campaign in the wilderness."

But for all these graphic and colorful descriptions, the real hero of the American epic as Irving sees it, is not the Indian nor the trapper, but the promoter—the business man who stands in the background scheming, devising, directing; at whose bidding and for whose profit the Stuarts and Hunts and Bonnevilles go forth, before whose advancing mechanistic civilization the Nez Perces and the Blackfeet are doomed. In *Astoria* Irving is playing the Vergil to Mr. Astor's Augustus. At the bidding of the great financier, Irving honeycombs the Astor papers that he may give an account "of the true nature and extent of the enterprise and its national character and importance." This is the real theme of Irving's frontier. The Indians are on the whole, merely picturesque and pathetic specimens of an inferior race. The trappers are merely romantic and venturesome eccentrics of an inferior intelligence—if Irving had enjoyed the recriminative advantages of modern psychology, he would doubtless have called them "morons." The hero whom Irving delights to honor is the shrewd financier who—not for himself—oh, no, but in the sacred name of "service" conceives the project of Astoria. "He was not actuated by mere motives of individual profit. He was already wealthy beyond the ordinary desires of man, but he now aspired to that honorable fame which is awarded men of similar scope of mind, who by their great commercial enterprises have enriched nations, peopled wildernesses, and extended the bounds of empire. He considered his projected settlement at the mouth of the Columbia as the emporium to an immense commerce; as a colony that would form the germ of a wide civilization; that would in fact, carry the American population across the Rocky Mountains and spread it along the shores of the Pacific as it already animated the shores of the Atlantic."

The most important contribution of Washington Irving to the interpretation of the frontier in American literature is, then, the introduction and idealization of a third character—the business man, who, himself remaining at a discreet distance, utilizes for his profit the resources of the frontier and the exploits of the frontiersman. *Astoria* has its starting point in the "enterprise and perseverance of a single merchant," whose efficiency Irving contrasts with the failure of previous attempts by the government, "unsuccessful, as most commercial expedients are prone to be where the dull patronage of government is counted upon to outvie the keen activity of private enterprise." *Astoria* has its catastrophe in the transfer of the post to the British—a catastrophe which Irving implies was due to the negligence of the government in seconding the efforts of the great man. How completely the story of *Astoria* is the story of

Astor may be seen from the superbly unconscious irony of the climax to which Irving mounts in telling of the wreck of the Tonquin. The infuriated savages have succeeded in getting possession of the ship and slaughtering the crew. One of the few survivors, himself mortally wounded, resolves on a fearful revenge; enticing the Indians back to the ship, he sets fire to the powder magazine and hurls them and himself to a spectacular doom, But the crowning instance of heroism as Irving tells the story, is that of John Jacob Astor, who on the evening on which the news of the disaster reached him, "indulged in no weak and vain lamentations . . . but appeared at the theater with his usual serenity of countenance." Irving's *Astoria* presents a frontier dominated by a new type of hero; it marks the beginning of an idealization of the business man which was to be a persistent strain in American literature.

IV. JOHN G. NEIHARDT

Like Washington Irving, Neihardt seeks his characters from the trans-Missouri fur trade; like him he bases his work upon historical facts; like him he sees beyond the intrinsic interest of each adventure the deeper significance of the westering epic.

The contributions of Cooper and Irving have been made sufficiently long ago to permit of their detached valuation. Mr. Neihardt's work is still in the doing. For that reason it is difficult, even impossible, to arrive at any fixed conclusion as to the trend and value of his work; and it is perhaps unfair to pass judgment upon any of his writing when only three parts of his proposed epic cycle have been published. But it would be even more unfair to close a discussion of frontier characters as they appear in American literature without a word in tentative appraisal of a contemporary writer who has dedicated his talent to the literary expression of "the great American epic period, beginning in 1822 and ending in 1890."

Mr. Neihardt's work on the frontier has been of two kinds: though he nowhere appears to feel sharp differentiation between books as similar in theme as *The Splendid Wayfaring, The Song of Three Friends,* and *The Song of Hugh Glass,* these contributions are so diverse in purpose, in method and in value, that they may best be discussed under separate classifications.

The Splendid Wayfaring, as the subtitle informs us, is "the story of the exploits and adventures of Jedediah Smith and his comrades, the Ashley-Henry men, discoverers and explorers of the great central route from the Missouri River to the Pacific Ocean." Mr. Neihardt lists his sources, and a student familiar with the authorities realizes how accurately and intelligently he has followed them throughout his narrative; how he has clarified and vivified them by the careful selection and animated expression of the material; how important a service he has done in the recreation of history, in the rescuing from oblivion of one of those "forgotten brave men" whose hands, as Carlyle says, have made the world for us. Jedediah Smith, as he appears in *The Splendid Wayfaring* is one of the "immortal dead who live again" in the choir invisible of generous heroes.

There is more work to be done in this resurrection of heroes. Mr. Neihardt is admirably fitted to do it and it is to be hoped that he will do it. *The Splendid Wayfaring* (1920) the last of these three books on the frontier, has been followed by another installment of the "epic cycle": *The Song of the Indian Wars.* Evidently Mr. Neihardt instead of following the rich vein which he struck in *The Splendid Wayfaring* intends to follow the less profitable one which he explored in his first books, *The Song of Hugh Glass* and *The Song of Three Friends.*

As the titles of these books imply, they are written in verse while *The Splendid Wayfaring* is written in prose. They are as meretricious as *The Splendid Wayfaring* is meritorious. Mr. Neihardt makes an acceptable Carlyle but a feeble Masefield. Perhaps Mr. Neihardt is a better prose-writer than he is a poet; perhaps prose is the more appropriate medium of expression for the epic of the American frontier. Whatever the cause, certainly the germ stories of the two poems are more dramatic, more moving, more convincing, in the prose form in which they appear in *The Splendid Wayfaring* than they are in the expanded poetic versions.

Take *The Song of Three Friends,* for instance. In *The Splendid Wayfaring* the story is told as follows:

> Fink was a 'wild Irishman,' a famous joker and a terrible fighter, with the body of a Hercules and a face that suggested a bulldog. Men laughed freely at his jokes in those good old days, for it was well known that whoever neglected to laugh must be prepared for instant battle. Carpenter was tall, slenderly but powerfully built and a blond. He smiled much, talked little, and fought well with a show of good nature that was disconcerting. Talbeau was a small man, but one who had once seen the three fight their way through a crowded dance hall on the lower Mississippi, spoke highly of the little man's terrier-like effectiveness in a scrimmage. Fink and Carpenter were expert marksmen, and often each would shoot a whiskey cup from the other's head at a distance of forty yards by way of demonstrating their faith in each other.
>
> These three cronies had joined Henry's expedition of the preceding year, and had spent the winter with nine other men among the Blood Indians at the mouth of the Musselshell. There Fink and Carpenter had fallen out at last over a half-breed girl, and had come to blows despite the desperate efforts of Talbeau to pacify them. The fight that followed was stubborn and long, but Carpenter had won, owing less to his strength and skill perhaps, than to his coolness. Fink was not the man to forgive, and he had never before known defeat.
>
> Spring came, the Musselshell party returned to the fort near the mouth of the Yellowstone, and there the quarrel was

renewed. Once more Talbeau strove to pacify his friends, and with apparent success. At the little man's suggestion, the two big men agreed to join in the old rite of friendship—the shooting of the cup. A coin was tossed for the first shot which fell to Fink. Now calling Talbeau aside, Carpenter willed his gun, flint, powder horn, knife and blankets to the little man, who laughingly accepted the bequest remarking that Fink couldn't miss a target if he tried. Whether or not Fink missed his target was still a question among the tellers of the tale. What he hit was a spot between the eyes of his old friend.[1]

In the poem the story is expanded to one hundred and twenty-five pages. As a result, of course, the frontier is diluted with a good deal of Neihardt. Now Mr. Neihardt's poetry *per se* is neither better nor worse than that of many contemporary versifiers. But when a poet presumes to "approach that body of precious saga stuff which I have called the Western American Epos" (I use Mr. Neihardt's own words), and offer himself as the Homer of the Frontier, the reader has a right to expect that the "precious saga stuff" shall be treated in a style worthy of epic tradition. What has Mr. Neihardt contributed to the raw material?

In the first place, classical allusions.

> The trappers and the singing *voyageurs*
> Are comrades now of Jason and his crew,
> Foregathered in that timeless rendezvous
> Where come at last all seekers of the Fleece.

Carpenter striding into camp at the head of his band, is likened to—

> Some Gothic fighting God——
> Strayed from the dim Hercynian woods of old.

[1] The quotations in this book from the works of John G. Neihardt are used by permission of the Macmillan Company, New York, publishers of "The Splendid Wayfaring," "The Song of the Three Friends," and "The Song of the Indian Wars."

Fink's cast-off mistresses are "blowsy Ariadnes." The tangle of "gray buttes and giddy gulfs" in which Fink and Talbeau find themselves after their escape from the prairie fire, is "a Titan's labyrinth." "Argus-eyed" summits watch the death march of Fink. Now classical allusions may find a place in a literary epic, such as the *Divina Commedia* or *Paradise Lost.* But they have no place in a folk epic such as the *Iliad* or *Beowulf* or (to use Mr. Neihardt' own modest climax) *The Song of Three Friends.*

Secondly, Mr. Neihardt has contributed painfully elaborated figures of speech. The metaphor with its direct audacious identification of the objects of comparison is a mode of expression well adapted to primitive tales; the simile with its detached, deliberate, intellectual parallelizings betrays immediately the sophisticated poet. Such similes abound in these "Songs." The Indian girl is

> like a pasture that is ever green
> Because it feels a mountain's sunny flank.

Mike's song is

> a gently grieving thing like April rain
> That while it wakes old memories of pain,
> Wakes also odors of the violet.

Talbeau's reminiscences of his friend ran

> as t'were the babble of a brook of tears
> Gone groping o'er the ocean of dead years
> Too far away to reach.

The third contribution: lavish descriptions, chiefly of nature. When the band started out, "Girlish April went ahead of them," followed by twenty lines of unrelieved and unmotivated description. The Quarrel is ushered in with sixty-eight lines of coming spring. The three principal characters are introduced by one hundred and sixty-three lines of personal description, varying from dramatic characterization in action, to the banality of such lines as "Behold the splendid creature that was Fink!" Similar padding occurs before The Shooting of the Cup, and in the account of the prairie fire and of Mike's "purgatory." Some of these descriptions have a lyric delicacy, others are forced and incongruous; the bulk of the description in proportion to the bulk of the action falsifies the impression of the whole.

The plot is smothered not only by descriptions but by reflections. Mr. Neihardt is true to epic tradition in his frequent introduction of gnomic passages. He begins with the conventional *ubi sunt*:

> Who now reads clear the roster of that band?
> Alas, Time scribbles with a careless hand
> And often pinchbeck doings from that pen
> Bite deep, where deeds and dooms of mighty men
> Are blotted out beneath a sordid scrawl!

At each turn of the story he tucks in a platitude:

> Ilion held
> Beneath her sixfold cerement of Eld
> Seems not so hoar as bygone joy we prize
> In evil days.

> How may mortals know
> Their gladness, save they sense it by the fear
> That whispers how the very thing held dear
> May pass away?

> Alas the tongue!
> How glibly are its easy guesses flung
> Against the knowing reticence of years,
> To echo laughter in the time of tears,
> Raw gusts of mocking merriment that stings!
> Some logic in the seeming ruck of things
> Inscrutably confutes us!

These philosophizings, unlike the "commonplaces" of the Greeks and the gnomes of the Anglo Saxons, represent external comments, intrusions of the author's own thought into an alien world. When the author of *Beowulf* halts in his narrative to remark:

> Swâ sceal man dôn
> þonne he ät gûðe gegân þenceð
> longsumne lof, nâ ymb his lîf cearað
>
> (so shall man do when he desires to gain lasting glory in battle, nor cares about his life)

he is voicing sentiments which his hero would have understood and echoed, he is epitomizing the *Weltanschauung* of his world. But imagine the bewilderment, the disgust, the ridicule with which Fink or Carpenter would have listened to Neihardt's eloquently phrased reflections on their situation.

The essentially swift and primitive action of the episode is further clogged by detailed and subtle analyses of mental states. Mike's passion for the Long Knife's daughter is sentimentalized into the dawning of a pure romance. The resultant jealousy, the fight, the fatal shooting of the whiskey cup—this catastrophe which Neihardt tells in nineteen lines of prose is dragged out over thirty-seven pages of verse, chiefly telling how Neihardt supposes Fink and Talbeau felt. Entirely of Neihardt's own invention is the closing scene on the fire-swept plain where Talbeau "plays God" and exacts a fearful retribution of one friend for the murder of the other. Chittenden's *American Fur Trade,* Chapter IX, tells the story in practically the form in which it appeared in the *Missouri Intelligencer* for Sept. 4, 1829, This is the ending as given there:

> Talbot who was Carpenter's fast friend, was convinced of Mike's treacherous intent and resolved upon revenge when opportunity should offer. Some months afterward, Mike in a fit of gasconading, declared that he had killed Carpenter on purpose and was glad of it. Talbot instantly drew his pistol,

the same which Carpenter had bequeathed to him, and shot Mike through the heart. Mike fell and expired without a word.

I have nowhere found any explanation given by Mr. Neihardt for his substitution of a Talbeau who "couldn't kill" but could devise and execute a sentence to lingering death.

It is not our purpose here to discuss the merits of the poem as a poem. Parts of it have dramatic power; parts are labored and artificial. It is our purpose to discuss Neihardt's use of frontier materials in the poem; and it is a use which on the whole is regrettable. Let any one read in *The River of the West* of the light-hearted way in which Joe Meek yielded the Indian beauty Umentucken-Tukutsey-Undewatsey to his superior, the Booshway, bided his time, won her from him, and when her day was over, consoled himself with another and yet another—and then read *The Song of Three Friends* with its attempt to represent three redblooded, open air trappers as love sick Byronic heroes. I think such a comparison will convince the reader that if any writer has made a specious idealization of frontier characters, it is Neihardt, not Cooper. The trapper, as we meet him in frontier chronicles, is essentially crude, primitive, healthyminded, given to action rather than to thought or feeling. The trapper as Neihardt presents him in the Songs is credited with a refinement of feeling, a complexity of motives, a power of introspection which would have effectually incapacitated him for fighting Indians, cheating Mexicans, outwitting other trappers, exploring undiscovered country. Neihardt's trappers would serve as the heroes of romantic poetry or psychological fiction, but they are sorry heroes for an epic.

The same analysis applies to *The Song of Hugh Glass*. It is interesting to note that here Neihardt uses a story akin to one included by Irving in *The Adventures of*

Captain Bonneville and also suggestive of the theme of *Roger Malvin's Burial.* Have we "progressed" from Hawthorne to Neihardt only to find the same story? the same use of frontier materials merely to furnish a problem of the individual soul? The emphasis, it is true, is placed differently in the handling of the two situations. Hawthorne is interested in studying the working of remorse in Reuben Bourne; Neihardt is interested in studying the working of revenge in Hugh Glass. But in both cases the emphasis is placed on the moral and psychological rather than the external struggle. The relations of Hugh and Jamie are presented with even greater sentimentality than the relations between the three friends. Now no reader of frontier chronicles can fail to find instances of loyal friendships among the trappers; but it is one thing to recount the acts of heroism and self-sacrifice by which a man proves his willingness to lay down his life for his friend; it is another to emotionalize that friendship in terms more suggestive of Oscar Wilde and Paul Verlaine than of Hugh Glass and Jedediah Smith.

The last, the most elaborate, and the most significant portion of Mr. Neihardt's epic cycle of the West is *The Song of the Indian Wars,* published in 1925. This, in Mr. Neihardt's own words, "deals with the last great fight for the bison pastures of the Plains between the westering white men and the prairie tribes—the struggle for the right of way between the Missouri River and the Pacific Ocean." A large order—and it is hardly to be wondered at that the result is in places confused and sketchy. The confusion is augmented by Mr. Neihardt's inability or reluctance to decide which characters are to play the role of heroes and which of villains. He describes himself in the preface as a "Custer partizan" but his hero-worship fails to vitalize the section of the poem devoted to Custer's last stand. Custer remains throughout the action, elusive and nebulous. In the preface, also, Mr. Neihardt disclaims any intention of sentimentalizing his characters; yet his account of the assassination of "the last great Sioux" Crazy Horse and the reduction of his people to "whining beggars in a feeding pen," reads much like the propagandist pathos of Helen Hunt Jackson's *A Century of Dishonor.* Confusion is inherent in the very nature of Mr. Neihardt's theme. Paradoxically enough, the effect of the book would be less blurred if the confusion were deliberately accentuated. Mr. Neihardt has always been stirred by the pulsating urge of the western migrations. He recognizes in the apparently unscrupulous, coldblooded pushing out of the Indian tribes an inevitable manifestation of this westering:

> Again the bugles of the Race blew west
> That once the Tigris and Euphrates heard.
> In unsuspected deeps of being stirred
> The ancient and compelling Aryan urge:
> A homing of the homeless, surge on surge.

But this belief in the manifest destiny of Aryan stock to inherit the earth does not deaden Mr. Neihardt's sympathies to

> those—and they were also men—
> Who saw the end of sacred things and dear
> In all this wild beginning; saw with fear
> Ancestral pastures gutted by the plow,
> The bison harried ceaselessly, and how
> They dwindled moon by moon; with pious dread
> Beheld the holy places of their dead
> The mock of aliens.

One could wish that this divided sympathy had sharpened the clash of cultures which is the theme of *The Song of the Indian Wars.* But even though weakened by a seesawing between the opposing parties, and by a failure to establish with sufficient clarity the connection between episodes, though disproportioned by an elaborating of the trivial (as in the incident of little Hohay's imaginings) and a neglect of the obligatory (as in the incident of the death of Custer), even though marred by the sententious gnomes, the labored personifications, and the longwinded descriptions which characterize his other Songs, *The Song of the Indian Wars* marks a forward step in Mr. Neihardt's employment of frontier materials. He occasionally sketches situations with a few stark, powerful strokes, as in the description of the despairing wait of the wounded survivors of Beecher's Island:

> The slow sun sank
> The empty prairie gloomed. The horses stank.
> The kiotes sang. The starry dark was cold.

He renders with restraint and dignity the death speech of the betrayed Crazy Horse:

> I had my village and my pony lands
> On Powder where the land was all my own.
> I only wanted to be let alone.
> I did not want to fight. The Gray Fox sent
> His soldiers. We were poorer when they went;
> Our babies died, for many lodges burned
> And it was cold. We hoped again and turned
> Our faces westward. It was just the same.

The most significant feature of *The Song of the Indian Wars* is its perhaps unconscious impersonality. No heroic character such as Leatherstocking or John Jacob Astor dominates Mr. Neihardt's most recent frontier, although many nameless heroes emerge, play their brief parts, and vanish. In spite of Mr. Neihardt's professed admiration for Custer, his evident sympathy with Crazy Horse, neither the General of the Gray Fox nor the brave of the Sioux stands out as a unifying figure of the narrative. Greater than Red Cloud, Roman Nose, or Crazy Horse, greater than Fetterman, Forsyth, or Custer, greater than that "Omniscence in a swivel chair" who "half a continent away" blandly bungles the handling of Indian affairs, is the relentless destiny which makes for the expansion of the Americans and the extermination of the Indians. Mr. Neihardt, unlike Cooper or Irving, writes of the frontier in retrospect. Is not this dwarfing of character in the latest song of the frontier epic an aftermath of the naturalistic philosophy which flourished after the passing of the frontier? Cooper too sensed the defeat of the Indians, the disappearance of the free trappers, but he, at least, imparted to his doomed heroes a tragic grandeur. Neihardt writing after the doom has been fulfilled, finds it scarcely worth his while to elaborate as individual characters combatants already obliterated from the pages of history. Is it too fanciful to see as the real hero-villain of Mr. Neihardt's frontier, the railroad, "the many-footed monster," fit symbol of a mechanistic civilization. To clear its path the thirty-two put up their desperate defense behind the wagon boxes, the eighty are "rubbed out" with Fetterman. Neihardt has here told in verse the story Paxson had previously told in prose: the connection between the advance of the Pacific railroad and the disappearance of the last American frontier. *The Song of the Indian Wars* is essentially a song of the struggle for the right of way of the "iron trail" which "cleft the ancient bison world," until

> at last, the crawling iron snake
> Along the Platte had lengthened to the sea.

V. THE FATE OF FRONTIER CHARACTERS

We have examined at some length the use of frontier characters by Cooper, by Irving, by Neihardt. One suggestive point these writers have in common: they all recognize the frontiersman as a vanishing type. The fate of the historical frontiersman forms a sad anticlimax to the records of frontier heroisms. Boone and Clark were grossly neglected and defrauded by the generation which profited by their pioneering. David Crockett and Jedediah Smith were favored in finding heroic deaths—of Crockett especially it might truly be said that "nothing in his life became him like the leaving of it." Carson and Meek realized before half their span of life was over that times had changed, and they must adjust themselves to an environment in which the trapper no longer held triumphant supremacy. They, like Ewing Young, J. J. Warner, and many other famous trappers, were able to make the adjustment and settle down on ranches. The full burden of the maladjustment fell on the children who born into one generation were required to find their place in an altered world, The story of Carson's eldest son William is not usually included in the various eulogistic biographies of the father; but to see the life of the father in full relation to the changing America, the America which he himself had helped to change, it is necessary to know this pitiful aftermath. Kit Carson dying sent his son, a boy of seventeen, to General Sherman, who had promised to look after him. Let General Sherman tell the rest:

> For three years I paid all his expenses of board, clothing, books etc. amounting to about $300.00 a year. At the end of that time the Priest reported to me that Carson was a good-natured boy, willing enough, but that he had no taste nor appetite for learning. His letters to me confirmed this conclusion, as he could not possibly spell.

Sherman arranged to have the boy sent to Fort Leavenworth where he was employed as a messenger while in training to become a lieutenant of cavalry. When William Carson was twenty-one, Sherman petitioned President Grant to give the boy an appointment as second

Lieutenant in the 9th U. S. Cavalry. The petition was readily granted, contingent, as law required, upon his passing an examination in elementary subjects.

> After careful examination, the board found him deficient in reading, writing, and arithmetic. Of course, he could not be commissioned. I had given him four years of my guardianship, about $1000.00 of my own money, and the benefit of my influence, all in vain. By nature he was not adapted to modern uses. I accordingly wrote him that I had exhausted my ability to provide for him, and advised him to return to his uncle Boggs on the Purgation to assist him in his cattle and sheep ranch.

In later visits to the Purgation, Sherman could learn nothing of his erstwhile protegé, nor of any of the Carson children. He comments on the changed order:

> Since the building of railroads in that region, the whole character of its population is changed, and were Kit Carson to arise from his grave, he could not find a buffalo, elk, or deer, where he used to see millions. He could not even recognize the country with which he used to be so familiar, or find his own children whom he loved and for whose welfare he felt so solicitous. Kit Carson was a good type of a class of men most useful in their day, but now as antiquated as Jason of the Golden Fleece, Ulysses of Troy, the Chevalier La Salle of the Lakes, Daniel Boone of Kentucky—Irvin Bridger and Jim Beckworth of the Rockies—all belonging to the dead past.

The frontiersman of history has had his day and ceased to be. What becomes of the frontiersman of literature? As Cooper saw him in Leatherstocking he embodied three types: a nobleman of nature, a refugee from civilization, a conqueror of the continent. In Leatherstocking these three types mingled in successful fusion as they have never done before or since. Each of the component types has, however, survived and found some sort of literary expression. The ideal of Nature's nobleman, the free, independent, outdoor character, gave us Wister's Virginian and Lin McLean; it survives in the western stories of Zane Grey and Harold Bell Wright; it dwindles down to the hero of the potboiler story of *Adventure.*

The Refugee from Civilization has been deemed less fit to survive in an age which proudly enumerates its "civilization" in terms of bathtubs and motor cars and sees no reason why civilization should be a thing to flee from. When Thoreau made his escape to Walden he was already regarded as a crank who didn't know when he was well off or he would have stayed in the village where he could enjoy the comforts and conveniences of life. When Babbitt bolts to the Maine woods determined to be a real redblooded He-man like the primitive pathfinders, he finds "that he could not escape from Zenith, for he carried Zenith with him." The great open spaces of the Canadian wilderness bring Ralph Prescott only to Mantrap, a manicure girl, and a humiliating realization of his own inadequacy. Nevertheless, the woods, or at least a farm, is still regarded as an orthodox haven of refuge for those fictional characters who have come near shipwreck in a complicated society. The redemption of Dorothy Canfield Fisher's characters is accompanied by a retreat to their Vermont farm. Jadwin, broken by the Pit, goes went to a farm to start life anew. Herrick prescribes back to the farm as the panacea for his characters' ills. Even so realistic a writer as James Oppenheim rescues his "cog" from the wheels of industrial machinery by sending him west to try ranching. The enthusiasm which greeted Ray Stannard Baker's *Adventures in Friendship* and *Adventures in Contentment* proves that the Refugee from Civilization is still a popular character, though his refuge now-a-days has shrunk from a measureless forest to a village farm.

But it is the aspects of the third type, the Conqueror of the Continent, which have become magnified and have produced a new type in American literature. The major contribution of the frontier character was the tradition of the superman, endowed with a more than human measure of prowess and endurance, by divine right victor over nature and his fellowmen. Even in the days of the fur trade, as early as 1812, as we have seen in *Astoria,* the conflict of the frontiersman was quite as much with rival companies as with the forces of nature. The victors became the spoilsmen. Not the man who conquers the wilderness, but the man who controls the wilderness, not the man who explores, but the man who exploits, becomes the hero. The speculator, the profiteer who is the villain of Cooper's frontier becomes the hero of Irving's. The forests and the Indians, the buffaloes and the beavers might pass away, and with them the hunters, the trappers, the heroes of the geographical frontier. The dominant traits of the frontier character survive and find new expression in the heroes of Big Business who take up the work of industrial pioneering.

BIBLIOGRAPHY

I. On James Fenimore Cooper

COOPER, JAMES F.
The Leatherstocking Tales 5 vol.
Boston; Houghton Mifflin Co., 1898

These were originally published as follows:
The Pioneers—1823
The Last of the Mohicans—1826
The Prairie—1827
The Pathfinder—1840
The Deerslayer—1841

For biographical and critical data:
LOUNSBURY, THOMAS R.
James Fenimore Cooper (A.M.L. series)
Boston; Houghton Mifflin Co., 1882

Critical articles in the following:
BOYNTON, PERCY
History of American Literature

BROWNELL, W. C.
American Prose Masters
ERSKINE, JOHN
Leading American Novelists
MACY, JOHN
The Spirit of American Literature
VAN DOREN, CARL
in *The Cambridge History of American Literature* vol. I Bk II ch. VI

II. On Washington Irving
IRVING, WASHINGTON
Astoria
Boston; De Wolfe, Fiske & Co., no date given
The Adventures of Captain Bonneville
Boston; De Wolfe, Fiske and Co. no date
A Tour of the Prairies
Boston; De Wolfe, Fiske and Co. no date
The original dates of publication were:
Astoria—1836
The Adventures of Captain Bonneville—1837
A Tour of the Prairie—1835
For biographical and critical data:
BOYNTON, HENRY W.
Washington Irving
Boston; Houghton Mifflin Co., 1901
IRVING, PIERRE
Life and Letters of Washington Irving
New York; G. P. Putnam's Sons, 1862–64
WARNER, CHARLES D.
IRVING (in A.M.L. series)
Boston; Houghton Mifflin Co., 1881
Critical articles also in the following:
BOYNTON, PERCY
A History of American Literature
BURTON, RICHARD
"Washington Irving's services to American History" in *The New England Magazine*, Aug. 1897, vol. 16, pp. 641–654
MACY, JOHN
The Spirit of American Literature
PAYNE, WILLIAM M.
Leading American Essayists

PUTNAM, GEORGE H.
in *Cambridge History of American Literature* vol. I
Bk. II, ch. IV

III. On John Neihardt
NEIHARDT, JOHN
The River and I
New York; G. P. Putnam's Sons, 1910
The Song of Hugh Glass
New York; Macmillan Co., 1915
The Song of Three Friends
New York; Macmillan Co., 1919
The Splendid Wayfaring
New York; Macmillan Co., 1920
The Song of the Indian Wars
New York; Macmillan Co., 1925
For biographical and critical data:
HOUSE, JULIUS T.
John G. Neihardt, Man and Poet
Wayne, Neb.; F. H. Jones & Co., 1920

IV. On Daniel Boone
BRUCE, H. ADDINGTON
Daniel Boone and the Wilderness Road
New York; Macmillan Co., 1910
ELLIS, EDWARD S.
The Life and Times of Col. Daniel Boone
Philadelphia; Porter & Coates, 1884
FILSON, JOHN
Life and Adventures of Col. Daniel Boone
Brooklyn; printed for C. Wilder, 1823
FLINT, TIMOTHY
The Life and Adventures of Daniel Boone
Cincinnati; U. P. James, 1868
HULBERT, ARCHER B.
Boone's Wilderness Road
Cleveland; Arthur H. Clark Co. 1903
PECK, JOHN M.
Life of Daniel Boone
Boston; Little, Brown & Co., 1848
THWAITES, REUBEN G.
Daniel Boone
New York; D. Appleton & Co., 1903

WHITE, STEWART E.
Daniel Boone, Wilderness Scout
Garden City; Doubleday, Page & Co., 1922

V. On Kit Carson

ABBOTT, JOHN
American Pioneers and Patriots—Kit Carson
New York; Dodd, Mead & Co., 1874

BREWERTON, V.
"A Ride with Kit Carson" in Van Tramp: *Prairie and Rocky Mountain Adventures*
St. Louis; H. Mitter, 1860

BURDETT, CHARLES
Life of Kit Carson
Philadelphia; Porter & Coates, 1869

ELLIS, EDWARD S.
Life of Kit Carson
Chicago; George M. Hall, 1899

FREMONT, JOHN C.
Memoirs of my Life
Chicago and New York; Belford, Clarke & Co. 1887

PETERS, DEWITT C.
The Life and Adventures of Kit Carson
New York; Clark and Meeker, 1858

SABIN, EDWIN S.
Kit Carson Days
Chicago; A. C. McClurg, 1914

VI. On George Rogers Clark

CHURCHILL, WINSTON
The Crossing
New York; Macmillan Co., 1904

ENGLISH, WILLIAM H.
Life of George Rogers Clark (2 vol.)
Indianapolis; Bowen-Merrill Co. 1896

JAMES, JAMES A.: (ed.)
George Rogers Clark Papers
Springfield, Ill. State Hist. Lib. 1912

THWAITES, REUBEN G.
How George Rogers Clark Won the Northwest
Chicago; A. C. McClurg, 1903

VII. On David Crockett

ABBOTT, JOHN S.
David Crockett: His Life and Adventures
New York; Dodd, Mead & Co., 1902

ANONYMOUS
Sketches and Eccentricities of Col. David Crockett
Louisville, Ky.; Morton & Griswold, no date given

CROCKETT, DAVID
Autobiography
New York; Chas. Scribner's Sons, 1923
(First edition) 1834

SPRAGUE, WILLIAM C.
David Crockett
New York; Macmillan Co., 1915

VIII. On Joe Meek

VICTOR, FRANCIS A.
The River of the West
Hartford; Columbian Book Co. 1870

IX. On Jedediah Smith

DALE, HARRISON C.
The Ashley-Smith Explorations
Cleveland; Arthur H. Clark Co. 1918

GUINN, J. M.
"Captain Jedediah S. Smith" in S. Calif. Hist. Soc. Publications, vol. 3

WARNER, J. J.
"Reminiscences of Early California," 1831–1847 in S. Calif. Hist. Soc. Publications, vol. 7

X. On General Historical Background

BRADBURY, JOHN
Travels in the Interior of America
London; Sherwood, Neely and Jones, 1819 (Reprinted in Thwaites' *Early Western Travels* vol. 4)

CHITTENDEN, HIRAM
The American Fur Trade of the Far West
New York; Harper & Bros., 1902

GREGG, JOSIAH
Commerce of the Prairies
Cleveland; Arthur H. Clark, 1905; also in Thwaites' *Early Western Travels* vol. 19–20, original edition 1845

HENDERSON, ARCHIBALD
The Conquest of the Old Southwest
New York; The Century Co. 1920
HILL, JOSEPH J.
"Ewing Young in the Fur Trade of the Far Southwest"
in *Oregon Historical Quarterly* vol. 24, no. 1
OGG, FREDERIC
The Old Northwest
New Haven; Yale Univ. Press, 1919
SKINNER, CONSTANCE L.
Adventurers of Oregon
New Haven; Yale Univ. Press, 1921
Pioneers of the Old Southwest
New Haven; Yale Univ. Press, 1919
WYETH, JOHN B.
Oregon: or the Short History of a Long Journey
Cambridge; printed for J. B. Wyeth, 1833

CHAPTER IV

THE GOLDEN AGE OF TRANSCENDENTALISM

I. THE INFLUENCE OF THE FRONTIER ON TRANSCENDENTALISM

COINCIDENT with the Golden Age of regional pioneering was the Golden Age of transcendental philosophy. Emerson was writing his germinal volume on "Nature" while Captain Bonneville was exploring beyond the Rocky Mountains. While the *Dial* was pursuing its ambitious flights "higher and higher into the empyrean," Kit Carson was guiding Fremont on his "scientific" expeditions through Mexican territory. While Thoreau was philosophizing on his trip down the Concord and Merrimac rivers, Joe Meek was trapping along the river of the west. While Thoreau hoed his beans at Walden, American settlers in California raised the flag of the Bear State Republic and pushed the American frontier to the Golden Gate. When Whitman published the bizarre little group of poems in which he had tried to catch the soul of "these States," the song that was finding most popular response in the hearts of his countrymen was the jubilant ditty of the homesteader, "Uncle Sam is rich enough to give us all a farm."

Perhaps because of the pedagogue's habit of presenting all information in carefully separated, neatly arranged water tight compartments, one seldom reads the history of American literature and the history of western expansion as if they were contemporaneous. One may read extensively in American history and literature without realizing that Ewing Young and Bronson Alcott were each playing a part in American life in 1840; that the United States which sheltered the transcendental movement was the same United States which fostered the northwest fur trade. We read our history in longitudinal strips; what would be the effect, one wonders, if one were to take a cross section of American life, and see if there is a logical connection as well as a fortuitious coincidence between the westward movement which is characteristic of American history and the transcendental movement which is characteristic of American philosophy.

Before attempting to estimate the extent to which the frontier may have been a factor in transcendentalism, it is necessary to admit the indebtedness of transcendentalism to foreign influences. This indebtedness has been so frequently recognized and so capably traced that a brief résumé will here be sufficient. Transcendentalism has been defined as "a system of thought based on the assumption of certain fundamental truths, not derived from experience, not susceptible of proof, which transcend human life and are perceived directly and intuitively by the human mind." Its roots go back as far as Plato's theory of ideas; its issues are the old issues between nominalist and realist, between the schools of sensationalism and intuitionalism, between French rationalism and German idealism. The immediate progenitors of the transcendental movement in New England may be found in Kant's *Critique of Pure Reason,* in Carlyle's interpretation of Novalis, in the early nineteenth century enthusiasm for all that was German.

But there is another line of descent not so frequently traced, not so clearly apparent. Just as we saw in the character of the frontier hero Leatherstocking the product of Rousseauesque romanticism and the frontier environment, so in transcendentalism we see the product of

German idealism and the frontier environment. The indigenous element in the transcendental movement has been recognized though not analyzed by George W. Cook, who takes issue with Frothingham on the exotic nature of transcendentalism: "This is the simple truth about it, that it was a part of the growing individualism that marked the development of democracy. Some of its later phases were undoubtedly due to the influence of Coleridge, Kant, and Cousin, but it had a life of its own long before and gave itself many forms of utterance." Mr. Cooke ascribes transcendentalism to the growing individualism of the American democracy. Mr. Turner ascribes the growing individualism of the American democracy to the continuous rebirth of the frontier, with its offer of cheap land, of opportunity for all. Is it not logical then, to see a very direct and significant connection between the frontier and transcendentalism?

The effort to establish an "influence" easily betrays one into the *post hoc ergo propter hoc* fallacy. Rather than make the fatuous assumption that every similarity is a proof of causal relationship, let us waive all dogmatic assertions about cause and effect, and content ourselves with a search for common factors in the spirit of the frontier and in the spirit of the transcendentalists.

II. FRONTIER ELEMENTS IN TRANSCENDENTALISM

Optimism, as we have seen, is a frontier virtue. The Puritan pioneer was confident that God was for him and nothing could prevail against him; the mere suggestion of possible failure, the mere mention of untoward circumstances, was repelled as treason. The trappers along the river of the west had a superstitious dread of discussing any ill luck that had befallen them. One must go on without a backward glance toward fallen comrades. The life of the trapper, Mrs. Victor tells us, would have been impossible if he had allowed himself to dwell on the hundred and one things that might go wrong. His one chance for success lay in believing that nothing but success was possible.

This incorrigible optimism which was a psychological necessity of frontier life, was given a philosophical rationalization by transcendentalism. Its most familiar literary expression is found in the dogmatic optimism of Emerson's essays. "We learn that God *is;* that He is in me; and that all things are shadows of Him." With such facile premises Emerson establishes the beneficence of the universe. Spiritual laws execute themselves; compensations are meted out unfailingly; nature is an abundant treasure house from which man, the darling of the gods, may take what he will.

The Entente with Omnipotence which tyrannized over the Puritan frontier persists throughout the more urbane and grandiose writings of the transcendentalists. The savagely capricious, the grimly implacable Jehovah of the seventeenth century Puritan becomes the somewhat nebulous but uniformly amiable Oversoul of the nineteenth century transcendentalist. In one significant respect, however, this shadowy Deity resembles his more anthropomorphic predecessor; he approves of the strenuous individual who knows what he wants and goes after it. Is it only an accident that this strenuous individual was the type demanded and produced by frontier conditions?

This sense of co-partnership with Providence gave a religious sanction to the manifest destiny of the westering American. The exaggerated belief in the power of the determined individual is the triumphal motif in the transcendental chorus. Emerson tells us that, "Every man is a channel through which Heaven floweth"; "greater than all the geography and the government of the world."

> Owner of the sphere
> Of the seven stars and the solar year,
> Of Caesar's hand and Plato's brain,
> Of Lord Christ's heart, and Shakespeare's strain.

Whitman sings the glories of the Divine Average. Thoreau challenges the latent divinity and unmeasured capacities of man.

But it may be objected: these are spiritual qualities which the transcendentalists are extolling; their kingdom is not of this world. What have their rhapsodical celebrations of the divine in man to do with such crude successes as those of David Crockett elbowing his way from the backwoods to the legislature, or Ewing Young manoeuvering the Mexicans out of a trapping license? What have they to do with such external manifestations of "progress" as that *coup d'etat* of American exploration and American diplomacy which extended the American frontier to the Pacific?

It is unfashionable in this psycho-analytical age to take an author on his own valuation and admit that he may have known better than anyone else what he was trying to do; but in defiance of fashion we may risk letting Emerson answer this objection. It is not a new one; it is as old as Carlyle's complaint that, "The Dial is all spirit-like, aeriform, aurora borealis like. Will no angel body himself out of that; no stalwart Yankee man with color in the cheeks of him and a coat on his back?" This objection was anticipated by Emerson in the very first issue of the transcendental organ. In "The Editors to the Reader" Emerson announced that the purpose of *The Dial* was to present under varying forms "The spirit of the times felt by every individual." The essence of this *Zeit-Geist* Emerson declared to be "a greater trust in the nature and resources of man"—a motto quite as appropriate for the pioneer as for the transcendentalist. For it was a cardinal point of Emerson's creed that the nature and resources of man were to be made manifest in action. He eulogizes the individual who is "victory-organized." He idealizes the conqueror: "Personal force never goes out of fashion. That is still paramount to-day. The competition is transferred from war to politics and trade, but the personal force appears readily enough in these new arenas. Power first, or no leading class. In politics and in trade bruisers and pirates are of better promise than talkers and clerks." He sings the romance of success, "the transformation of genius into practical power." He anticipates Nietzsche in his worship of the superman. Emerson, like Nietzsche, thinks of the superman as combining spiritual insight with physical energy. Emerson tells us that it is no easy matter to dispense with the world's standards and seek absolution in our own confessional. "If any man think this law is lax, let him try to keep its commandment one day." Nietzsche asks solemnly, "Art thou such a one as canst be a law to thyself?" In practice, however, it is easier to appraise physical energy than spiritual insight; hence the Nietzschean superman like the Carlylean hero tends to degenerate into a blustering bully. But so blandly deceptive has been Emerson's enumeration of his heroic qualities that we innocently set our high school pupils to reading the essay on "Self Reliance" at the same time that we are warning them against the red bogy of Bolshevism.

It is time to decanonize Emerson; to recognize that however truly he may have been "the friend and helper of those who would live in the spirit," he is just as truly the friend and helper of those who want to annex a territory, or corner a market, or spread heretical propaganda. It is time to strip from the Emersonian hero the decorous toga and conventional mask with which rhetoric and philosophy have disguised him, and show that "the American scholar" and Davy Crockett are brothers, that "the heir of Plato's brain" was no mystic recluse, but a man of action well fitted to play a leading part in the drama of pioneering.

III. THE TRANSCENDENTAL IDEALIZATION OF FRONTIER TRAITS

The optimism and individualism which constitute the essence of transcendental philosophy are traits engendered on the frontier. The distinguishing characteristics of the transcendental hero are the characteristics of the pioneer. Transcendentalism, so far from being at variance with its age, a protest against its age, played into its hands by providing a convenient idealization of frontier characteristics.

Let us follow this correspondence through an analysis of the pioneer psychology. Courage was an indispensable quality of the frontiersman; but who more proudly than Emerson has sung "the militant attitude of the soul"? Not only physical endurance, but mental alertness was necessary to guarantee survival in the primitive struggle for existence; but has not Emerson voiced the praises of Prudence as well as of Heroism? Who better than the American pioneer has exemplified the spirit of independence, that self trust in which, according to Emerson, all the virtues are comprehended? The constant contact of man with nature, accompanied by a never-failing belief in the supremacy of man over nature is a basic condition of both transcendental philosophy and frontier life.

So far the analysis is simple, dealing with the more obvious and generally desirable aspects of the pioneer. But it would be misleading to assume, as is sometimes done, that all frontier characteristics are desirable, that the frontier environment was invariably conducive to the production of harmoniously developed personalities. Emerson's own pet doctrine of compensation arises to refute this flattering fallacy. "For everything you lose you have gained something, and for everything you gain, you have lost something." In the year of the Pilgrim tercentenary the eulogistic chorus of ancestor worshipers was given an iconoclastic variation in an article appearing in *The Outlook* under the title "What the Pilgrim Fathers Left Behind Them." What was the precious something which the pioneer lost while he was gaining a continent? What beside the "tyranny" of the Stuarts and the "abominations" of the Established Church did the Pilgrim Fathers leave behind them?

Pioneering involved a break with the past. The pioneer whether as a member of a church seeking "freedom to worship God" after a peculiar fashion of its own, or as a solitary adventurer seeking his own private and material gain, discarded his heirlooms. The story of the Puritan frontier is a story of constantly strengthening Separatist tendencies in church and state until the frail ties that bound the colonies to the mother country were snapped in a moment of exaggerated resentment. The story of the typical frontiersman begins with "When a boy, he ran away from home." The frontier is born in the throes of schisms within schisms, insurrections within insurrections. Churches arise from parent churches and proclaim their own gospel; states arise from parent states and proclaim their own constitutions. It is this aspect of the frontier that has led Professor Paxson to say that the frontier is most significant as a process; the constant rebirth of the frontier constantly necessitating the remaking of human institutions in response to the need of the hour.

The inspiriting influence of this break with the past is sufficiently obvious and has been sufficiently emphasized. It may be salutary to look for a moment on the reverse side and realize the loss involved in this perpetual beginning again. At best it is but a momentary and deceptive gesture. The new church soon subsided into a sterile orthodoxy imperceptibly different from the old; the new state, for all its parade of independence, modeled its constitution on the old. The real advance was infinitesimal; meanwhile what had been lost? The sense of continuity, of permanence, which makes of the present a bridge between a past of revered memories and a future of assured anticipations; the beauty and sentiment which hallow traditions; the tenderness and sympathy which are flowers of slow growth, possible only when man stands in definite and continuous relations to his fellowmen.

Perhaps even to the sturdy, unreflective pioneers the conclusion might have been brought home that the loss counterbalanced the gain. Winthrop's "Great Migration" set sail amid tears at the farewell to the mother church. Even the lighthearted Joe Meek was sobered at the reminder of home associations. But transcendentalism came to the reinforcement of the pioneer to strengthen him against such momentary sentimentality. It confirms the rootlessness of the pioneer by expatiating on the conception of a universe in flux. "In nature every moment is new; the past is always swallowed and forgotten; the coming only is sacred. Nothing is secure but life, transition, the energizing spirit." With such dicta transcendentalism represents the break with the past as a necessary condition of spiritual emancipation. It speaks contemptuously of the past; it directs the energies of the American to the American scene. Even the past which is of one's own choosing and making, even the closest and dearest of personal ties, are to be subordinated to the interest of the individual, to be worn lightly while they last, and dropped unregretfully when they go. Sympathy with one's fellows is a waste of time and energy. The law of self preservation is the first and greatest commandment; let every man help himself and expect his neighbor to do the same.

Mrs. Victor's *River of the West* shows how Emersonian were the frontiersmen in the superb equanimity with which they bore other people's troubles, the self-reliant composure with which they inhibited other's adversities. The imperturbable self-satisfaction of the frontiersman is well illustrated in Joe Meek's attitude when he makes his first appearance in the "settlements" as "Ambassador from the Republic of Oregon to the Government at Washington." "I thought a great deal about it and I finally concluded that as I had never tried to act like anybody but myself, I would not make a fool of myself by beginning to ape other folks now. So I said, 'Joe Meek you always have been, and Joe Meek you shall remain; go ahead, Joe Meek!' " Transcendentalism elevates and prettifies these less desirable characteristics until the very defects have become virtues. The provincialism bred of frontier isolation is idealized into a fine scorn for the hoary past and the effete elsewhere. The crude egotism of a Joe Meek or a Davy Crockett becomes the splendid self-reliance of the Emersonian superman. The primitive selfishness of Keseberg and other starving cannibals of the Donner party is a logical expression of the self-centered emphasis of transcendental philosophy. The conditions of European feudalism bred the comitatus ideal of devoted loyalty: the conditions of American expansion bred the transcendental ideal of self-reliant individualism.

IV. TRANSCENDENTAL RECOGNITION OF REGIONAL PIONEERING

But we need not rest our case on this suggestive though perhaps fortuitious correspondence between the traits engendered by a frontier environment and the traits eulogized by transcendental philosophy. We find in the pages of *The Dial,* in the writings of Emerson, Thoreau, and Whitman abundant evidence that the transcendentalists, so far from living with their heads in the clouds serenely oblivious to what was going on around them, were keenly appreciative of the contemporary drama of regional pioneering. Whitman sings the glad forward song of the pioneers, identifying the physical conquest of the continent with the spread of a better type of civilization:

> Have the elder races halted?
> Do they droop and end their lesson,
> wearied over there beyond the seas?
> We take up the task eternal, and the burden
> and the lesson,
> Pioneers, O pioneers!

As Thoreau floats lazily along the Concord and Merrimac rivers he recalls stories of the Indian wars and the heroic exploits of the New England pioneers. In one of his little known poems he shows his full consciousness of the expansion movement of his own day:

> It is a noble country where we dwell
> Fit for a stalwart race to summer in,
> From Madawaska to Red River Raft,
> From Florida keys to the Missouri forks,
> See the red race with sullen step retreat,
>
> . . . .
>
> Look nearer—know the lineaments of each face
> Learn the far-travelled race, and find here met
> The so-long gathering congress of the world!
> The Afric race, brought here to curse its fate,
> Erin to bless—the patient German too,
> The industrious Swiss, the fickle sanguine Gaul,
> And manly Saxon leading all the rest.
> All things invite this earth's inhabitants
> To rear their lives to an unheard of height
> And meet the expectation of the land;
> To give at length the restless race of man
> A pause in the long westering caravan.[1]

[1] The quotations in this book from the works of Henry D. Thoreau are used by permission of Houghton Mifflin Company, Boston, publishers of Thoreau's works.

This poem, for some reason, was rejected by *The Dial.* The reason, however, cannot have been a prejudice against the westward movement as a subject for verse, for in *The Dial* for October, 1840, we find an even more flamboyantly expansionist poem on "First Crossing the Alleghanies":

Nature vast as thou art, we can unshrinkingly face thee!
Look on thy giant forms with an unfaltering eye;
He who carries within him a spirit conscious and active,
Treasures of well arranged thought gathered from action and life
Has striven, believed and loved—who knows all the worth of the moment
When soul stimulates soul, pulses together beat;
He has a world within to match thine, boastful mother!
He can give to thee more than he can take from thy hand.
Wanderer, tremble not before this grand Panorama,
Let not this mighty scene weary thine heart or thine eye.
Bring the Romance of Life to balance the Romance of Nature,
The Spirit has hopes as vast, the heart has its pictures as fair.

This happy fusion of the pioneer ideal and the transcendental ideal imparts to the slightly chilly pages of Emerson's essays an occasional glow of fervency. With Emerson as with Winthrop there was no incongruity between the ideals of regional and of spiritual pioneering. When he wrote "Hitch your wagon to a star" he was not advising the wrecking of the wagon but its acceleration. Is it too shocking a heresy to suggest that John Winthrop, Ralph Waldo Emerson, and George Follansbee Babbitt stand in logical succession? "If this be treason, make the most of it." Turn to the pages of *The Dial* for April, 1844, and read Emerson's address on "The Young American." This address, like most of the articles in *The Dial,* was printed without signature, and it would be interesting to see how many enthusiastic Emersonians would recognize in it the stigmata of their adored master. Follow it by more familiar addresses, such as "The Fortune of the Republic," for instance, and "Social Aims," and you will have to admit that the matter and method of "The Young American" are genuinely Emersonian—also that they present a very different Emerson from the one who smiles benevolently from the pictures of "Our Poets" and moralizes epigrammatically in the "Selections from American Literature"—an Emerson who is blood brother to the Rotarian. We shall, it is true, miss the "punch" which invigorates the style of Babbitt's memorable speech before the Realtors' Board of Zenith, but the sentiments are impeccable, as may be demonstrated by some extracts from these addresses:

From "The Young American":

> An unlooked for consequence of the railroad is the increased acquaintance it has given the American people with the boundless resources of their own soil.—The bountiful continent is ours, state on state, and territory on territory to the waves of the Pacific Sea.—This great savage country should be furrowed by the plough and combed by the harrow; these rough Alleghanies should know their master; these foaming torrents should be bestridden with proud arches of stone; these wild prairies should be loaded with wheat; the swamps with rice, the hilltops should pasture innumerable sheep and cattle; the interminable forests should become graceful parks for use and for delight.
>
> We cannot look on the freedom of this country in connexion with its youth without a presentiment that here shall laws and institutions exist on some scale of proportion to the majesty of nature.—It seems so easy for America to inspire and express the most expansive and humane spirit; newborn, free, healthful, strong, the land of the laborer, of the democrat, of the philanthropist, of the believer, of the saint, she should speak for the human race. America is the country of the future. From Washington its capital city, proverbially 'the city of magnificent distances,' through all its cities, states, and territories, it is a country of beginnings, of projects, of vast

designs and expectations. It has no past; all has an onward and prospective look.[2]

From "The Progress of Culture":

Was ever such coincidence of advantages in time and place as in America today?—the fusion of races and religions; the hungry cry for men which goes up from the wide continent; the answering facility of immigration, permitting every wanderer to choose his climate and government. Men come hither by nations. Land without price is offered to the settler, cheap education to his children.

From "Resources":

Here in America are all the wealth of soil, of timber, of mines and of the sea put into the possession of a people who wield all those wonderful machines, have the secret of steam, of electricity; and have the power and habit of invention in their brain.—American energy is overriding every venerable maxim of political science. America is such a garden of plenty, such a magazine of power that at her shores all the common rules of political economy utterly fail. Here is bread and wealth and power and education for every man who has the heart to use his opportunity.

From "The Fortune of the Republic":

In proportion to the personal ability of each man he feels the invitation and career which the country opens to him. He is easily fed with wheat and game, with Ohio wine, but his brain is also pampered by finer draughts, by political power and by the power in the railroad board, in the mills, or the banks. This elevates his spirits and gives of course, an easy self-reliance.

From "Social Aims":

The consideration the rich possess in all societies is not without meaning or right. It is the approval given by the human understanding to the act of creating value by knowledge and labor. It is the sense of every human being that

[2] The quotations in this book from the works of Ralph Waldo Emerson are used by permission of Houghton Mifflin Company, Boston, publishers of Emerson's complete works.

man should have this dominion of Nature, should arm himself with tools and force the elements to drudge for him and give him power. Everyone must seek to secure his independence.

Contempt for the old and European as compared with the new and American; pride in "progress" as measured by mechanistic devices; deification of the "prosperous" citizen whose bank account is unquestionably accepted as an index to his character—these were objects of idealism to the reading public of the eighteen forties. It has been reserved for our own day to see in them the objects of satire.

Why is it that the patriotic optimism of Emerson was received—*is* received with respectful homage, while the patriotic optimism of Babbitt has become a synonym for asinine complacence? We must recognize at least two factors which contribute toward a distinction with a difference. In the first place, Emerson addressed a public already intoxicated with the elixir of success. There was no mocking note of irony in his celebration of the vast natural resources of a continent regarded as ours by divine right (the fact that Mexico still held title to a considerable extent of it was a minor detail, habitually disregarded by American transcendentalists as well as by American explorers and statesmen). Emerson had not misstated the case for America. The common people heard him gladly for he told them what they already believed, what they wanted to believe. Furthermore, this gospel of prosperity was presented as a spiritual challenge. It is hard to conceive of even a realtor's missing the essential materialism of Babbitt's speech, however camouflaged it may be with sentiment about the "kiddies" and emotion about the flag. With Emerson, as with the lesser transcendentalists, the basic materialism was so subtly interfused into the very substance of their gospel, that from Carlyle to Macy, critics have denied that transcendentalism had any vital connection with the actual life of the nineteenth century. So nicely does religious idealism accommodate itself to the necessities of its time that the Church of the pacific Jesus bestows its official blessing upon the pugnacious instincts of the crusaders; the Oversoul of the otherworldly transcendentalists smiles upon the greedy activities of the acquisitive pioneers.

V. THE TRANSCENDENTALISTS AS SPIRITUAL PIONEERS

Transcendentalism recognized with approval the contemporary urge to regional and industrial pioneering. Transcendentalism was itself an organized adventure in spiritual pioneering. It is suggestive also to note that in some cases the transcendental zeal for spiritual pioneering was accompanied by an artificial recreation of the conditions of regional pioneering, in a territory "liberated from human ownership" as Alcott wrote of his colony at Fruitlands. Brook Farm, Walden, and Fruitlands were experiments in the simple life which involved a return to conditions similar to those once offered by the frontier. The frontier cannot be discussed solely in terms of rivers and mountains and diplomatic negotiations. The spirit of the frontier is not merely the spirit that leads the pioneer to prefer the wilderness to the settlements, the chance of wealth to the assurance of comfort, "the lure that beckons in the bright eyes of danger" to the probability of dying peacefully in his bed at a ripe old age. The spirit of the frontier is the spirit of beginning again, of building anew, of creating a reality after the pattern of one's dream. New England was born in a passion of spiritual pioneering which almost obscured the aspects of the actual frontier. Virginia was born in a beatific vision of manifest destiny:

> And to the adventurers thus he writes:
> Be not dismayed at all,

For scandall cannot doe us wrong,
God will not let us fall;
Let England know our willingnesse
For that our work is good,
We hope to plant a nation,
Where none before has stood.

The perennial rebirth of this spirit, as Professor Turner has pointed out, constitutes "the significance of the frontier in American history." This spirit, far more than thrilling stories of cowboys and Indians, constitutes the significance of the frontier in American literature. The remodeling of human society, which Hawthorne dreamed of in revulsions of protest against the Puritan world, was boldly proclaimed by the transcendentalists. "What is man born for but to be a Reformer, a Remaker of what man has made?"

Transcendentalism held as its major premise the belief in the constant renewal of life. Thoreau pities the man "who does not believe that each day contains an earlier, more sacred and auroral hour than he has yet profaned." Emerson insisted that man should be independent even of his own past acts and words. "Why drag about this corpse of your memory lest you contradict somewhat you have stated in this or that public place? Suppose you should contradict yourself; what then?" With the same consummate nonchalance, Whitman says:

Do I contradict myself?
Very well then, I contradict myself.

Shall any of us ever be as gloriously free as the transcendentalists were? We too have shaken off the superimposed horrors of Calvinism with its arbitrary predestination and eternal damnation; but we are "cabined, cribbed and circumscribed" by heredity, by environment, by a thousand intangible social pressures, by a foreordained and unalterable intelligence quotient. The transcendentalist lightly dismissed all these limitations on the individual; it left no barrier to the successful exertion of his will power.

This confidence in the endless possibility of new beginnings manifested itself in a contempt for institutions. They were at best man-made; what man has done before, man can do it again—and the chances are that he will do it better. Greater than any institution is the individual. "To educate the wise man the State exists, and with the appearance of the wise man the State expires. The wise man is the State. He needs no army, fort, or navy—he loves men too well;—he needs no library, for he has not done thinking; no church, for he is a prophet; no statute book, for he has the lawgiver; no money, for he is value; no road, for he is at home where he is." If the State with its institutions blindly fails to abdicate upon the appearance of the enlightened individual to whom it is superfluous, he "must not obey the laws too well," he must refuse to be "pursued and pawed by dirty institutions," i.e., those with which he does not find himself in agreement. Emerson, we remember, resigned his pastorate because of his distaste for administering the sacrament of the Lord's Supper, and dismissed the supreme mystery of the Christian Church with what Barrett Wendell calls the "serenely insolent" remark, "It does not interest me." Thoreau calmly announced that he was "better than the state of Massachusetts," and did not wish to share her iniquitous acquiescence in slavery and in the Mexican War, even to the extent of paying his poll tax.

VI. THOREAU, THE INTENSIVE PIONEER

The famous repartee which was occasioned by this private secession of Thoreau's, tells more eloquently than volumes the difference between Thoreau and the other transcendentalists. As Thoreau persisted in going imperturbably about his business and ignoring his tax bill, the embarrassed sheriff was obliged to lodge him in the county jail. Hither the next morning hastened Emerson to the relief of his friend with the reproachful query: "Henry, what are you doing in there?" "Waldo," came the disconcerting rejoinder, "what are you doing out there?"

In writing afterwards of this night in jail, Thoreau said that it seemed to him that his bars shut the outside world into its selfmade prison and left him alone of all men truly free. For all their much vaunted professions of unlimited freedom, Emerson and his circle were lending their moral support to the growing empire of the machine; their very scorn of governmental control, their admiration of individual enterprise, their assertion of absolute *laissez faire,* were destroying the safeguards that might have preserved a world in which the transcendental dream could become a reality. Likewise the pioneer, in the very confidence engendered by abundant natural resources, was doing his utmost to waste them; in the very exuberance of his westering was hastening the day of the passing of the frontier. Thoreau alone of his generation fully recognized the suicidal trend of American pioneering, and in open protest against all that his age held precious, went about his private adventure on an inexhaustible frontier.

It has been the fashion to write of Thoreau's years at Walden either in terms of severe censure or in terms of gentle mockery. It has been reserved for the present generation, conditioned by the mechanistic civilization which Thoreau foresaw, to appreciate the full significance of that withdrawal from America, which took him, it is true, only two miles from Concord, but which, for all that took him into another world. Into this experiment in living, Thoreau put the happiest phases of pioneering: the zest for adventure, the close communion with nature, the independence of social pressure; the worst phases of pioneering, grinding toil, chronic nomadism, sordid lust for acquisition, were deliberately and resolutely banished from his plan of life.

Pioneering was with Thoreau a conscious exploit. He entered in his *Journal* during July, 1845: "I imagine it to be some advantage to live a primitive and frontier life though in the midst of an outward civilization." In *A Week on the Concord and Merrimac Rivers* he makes frequent allusions to stories of the frontier, with the recurrent refrain: We too have a call to pioneering on a new frontier. "We have need to be as sturdy pioneers still as Miles Standish or Church or Lovewell. We are to follow on another trail, it is true, but one as convenient for ambushes. What if the Indians are exterminated, are not savages as grim prowling about the clearing today? "The frontiers are not east or west, north or south, but wherever a man *fronts* a fact. Let him build himself a loghouse with the bark on where he is *fronting* It and wage there an old French war for seven or seventy years, with Indians and rangers or whatever else may come between him and the reality and save his scalp if he can." In *Walden* Thoreau phrases his exhortation to the transcendental mission of self-improvement in terms of the westward migration: "What does the West stand for? Be the Lewis and Clark and Frobisher of your own streams and oceans; explore your own higher latitude—Be a Columbus to whole new continents and worlds within you."

What was the West Thoreau determined to explore, the fact which he determined to front in his sturdy pioneering? Spiritual like regional pioneering must be an expedition into undiscovered country, a departure from the established. We saw the pioneer in Hawthorne most clearly in his dissent from the Puritan conception of woman; we see the pioneer in Thoreau most clearly in his dissent from the American conception of man. In spite of the soulful phrases with which Emerson camouflaged the essential materialism of his superman, his ideal "young American" closely approximated the efficiently acquisitive financier of Irving's panegyric. "He sits secure in the possession of his vast domain rich beyond all experience in resources, sees its inevitable force unlocking itself in elemental order day by day, year by year, looks from his coal-fields, his wheat-bearing prairie, his gold mines, to his two oceans on either side and feels the security that there can be no famine in a country reaching through so many latitudes, no want that cannot be supplied, no danger from any excess of importation of art or learning into a country of such native strength, such immense digestive powers." Thoreau repudiated the standards of an acquisitive society. "The greater part of what my neighbors call good I believe in my soul to be bad." He saw in the rush to the California gold mines, "a touchstone which has betrayed the rottenness, the baseness of mankind. . . . That so many are ready to get their living by the lottery of gold digging without contributing any value to society and that the great majority who stay at home justify them in this both by precept and example!" He saw in the Concord villagers the fruits of the second and third generation after the victory of the pioneers over the forest and the Indians. Farms had been wrung from the wilderness, a settled community had replaced the scattered frontier outposts—with what gain? Instead of the men owning the farms, the farms owned the men; the mass of his fellow townsmen led "lives of quiet desperation," "mean and sneaking lives," from which the pioneer elements of heroism and adventure had departed, in which persisted the pioneer lust for possession, the pioneer drive to incessant toil. Such a life did not seem to Thoreau worth living. He refused to be stampeded by the instincts of the herd. He applied characteristically Yankee shrewdness to a very un-Yankee end. "I went to the woods because I wished to live deliberately, to front only the essential facts of life, and see if I could not learn what it had to teach and not when I came to die, discover that I had not lived."

That was the frontier which Thoreau faced at Walden —"the essential facts of life." And he finds these essential facts to be few and good. Man's actual needs are food, shelter, and clothing; if he confines himself to the providing of these actual necessities and not to the gratifying of a thousand artificially induced desires it is "not a hardship but a pastime" to earn one's living. These necessities provided for, a man is free to live; "to enjoy the friendship of the seasons," "to watch the spring come in," to "rise free from care beyond the dawn and seek adventures."

So thoroughly has the gospel of work been inculcated into the Anglo-Saxon mind that even the Stevenson who apologized for idlers, the Emerson who cherished a philosophy of acquiescence, were scandalized by Thoreau's easy repudiation of the divine duty of making money. Stevenson called Thoreau a skulker; Emerson called him the leader of a huckleberry party. Other critics have followed their lead; granted that Thoreau did manage to enjoy himself after an eccentric fashion of his own; it was at best, a selfish fashion; he was a parasite on the bounty of a competitively strenuous society at the very moment when he denounced it.

Let Thoreau answer this criticism: "I must confess I have felt mean enough when asked how I was to act on society, what errand I had to mankind. Undoubtedly I did not feel mean without a reason, and yet my loitering is not without a defense. I would fain communicate the wealth of my life to men, would really give them what is most precious in my gift. I would sift the sunbeams for the public good. I know of no riches I would keep back. I have no private good unless it be my peculiar ability to serve the public. Each one may thus be innocently rich. I wish to communicate those parts of my life which I would gladly live again myself. If I could help infuse some life and heart into society should I not do a service?"

This was Thoreau's contribution to society—not fine phrases but a genuine life. Well might Alcott call him,

"Friendship's all-adventuring pioneer"

who

"Civility itself would civilize."

Thoreau challenges the two sacred shibboleths of "civility": "progress" and "success." He redefines them in terms which reanimate the fading frontier. In recording a conversation with an immigrant laborer who "rated it a gain in coming to America that here you could get tea and coffee and meat every day," Thoreau punctures the bubble of prosperity. "The only true America is that country where you are at liberty to pursue such a mode of life as may enable you to do without these, and where the state does not endeavor to compel you to sustain the slavery and war and other superfluous expenses which directly or indirectly result from the use of such things. . . . I should be glad if all the meadows on the earth were left in a wild state if that were the consequence of men's beginning to redeem themselves." While Irving celebrates the business acumen of John Jacob Astor, while Emerson identifies a great fortune with "proof of the energy of the spirit," Thoreau gives to acquisitive America a new definition of success: "If the day and the night are such that you greet them with joy, and life emits a fragrance like flowers and sweet-scented herbs, is more elastic, more starry, more immortal—that is your success."

Very insignificant appeared Thoreau's little adventure in regional pioneering on the Walden frontier during the Golden Age of transcendentalism when his fellow transcendentalists were lending their praises to the American energy that swept the continent to open up a garden of plenty. Very foolish appeared Thoreau's adventure in spiritual pioneering, his experiment in a simple and satisfying life, to the ambitious scramblers for the spoils of the Gilded Age when Big Business was capitalizing the resources of a new west. It was not until the passing of the last American frontier, the disappearance of free land and easy fortune, that the American public, beginning to question the traditional concepts of "progress" and "success" read as a new discovery Thoreau's far-sighted strictures against the passion for possession, that it read with new enthusiasm his invitation to build in the heart of the bustling trivialities a Walden of our own where we may pursue our private adventure in intensive pioneering.

And yet the modern reader, for all his admiration of Thoreau, doubts the complete adequacy of his solution. He cannot forget that Thoreau did his pioneering on the free land of Emerson's wood lot; that Thoreau's quarrel with the government was settled by Emerson's paying his poll tax; that the wages of the day labor by which Thoreau earned his living were fixed by men who worked not six weeks but twelve months a year. *Walden* is fascinating as the adventure of a solitary pioneer; it is fallacious as the guidebook for a general migration. An idyl of the golden age of transcendentalism, it is an ineffectual protest against the gilded age of industrialism.

VII. WALT WHITMAN: THE AFTERGLOW OF THE GOLDEN AGE

Transcending the other transcendentalists stands the broad-shouldered son of Manhattan who sought in his life and in the one cumulative book into which he wrote his life, to chant the heroic destiny of these states. Perhaps no American writer has been for better or worse so successful in getting himself accepted at his own valuation. He calls his verse form a "barbaric yawp," and critics have echoed his phrase without suspicion of the cunning craftsmanship of his cadences. He calls himself the poet of the body, and ladylike souls have winced appropriately, without stopping to consider that even the poems in the "Children of Adam" section are decorum itself compared to the Song of Songs which is Solomon's or the dramas which are Shakespeare's. "Solitary, singing in the West," he says, "I strike up for a New World"; "I send you my poems—to define America, her athletic democracy," and condescending critics like Professor Stuart Sherman and Professor Bliss Perry and hero-worshiping critics like Waldo Frank and Van Wyck Brooks alike assume that in Whitman we find the apotheosis of Americanism.

If, as we have intimated, transcendentalism was a frontier philosophy, we should expect to find the closest correspondence between circumstance and creed in the writings of this transcendental panegyrist of the republic. But with the exception of the well known *Pioneers, O Pioneers*, and occasional lines indicative of the frontier environment, as in *The Song of the Broad Axe* and *Song of Occupations*, we find in *Leaves of Grass* and in the prose *Collect* surprisingly little explicit mention of the expansionist urge. Over and over again we find Whitman sonorously cataloging the names of states and citizens of states:

> Land of the Old Thirteen! Massachusetts land,
> land of Vermont and Connecticut,
>
> The Pennsylvanian, the Virginian, the double
> Carolinian,

> Chants of the prairies,
> Chants of the long-running Mississippi, and down
> to the Mexican sea,
> Chants of Ohio, Indiana, Illinois, Iowa, Wiscon-
> sin, and Minnesota.

But of the significant differences between the founding of Massachusetts and the founding of Virginia, of the essential characteristics of the Pennsylvanian as distinguished from the "double Carolinian," of the motives and methods of that frontier push across the prairies, along the Mississippi to the Mexican sea—next to nothing.

The reason for these omissions is obvious: Whitman wrote of the expansion of America as a *fait accompli.* His emphasis was deliberately thrown, not upon the pioneer settlements but upon the welding of these sections into a glorious composite. The ideal of nationality which he had seen imperiled by the Civil War, whose preservation was his supreme cause for pride and thanksgiving, was the ideal which *Leaves of Grass* set itself to foster. Accepting as a matter of course the achievements that lay behind, he pressed America forward to the mark of her high calling in Democracy.

One extremely suggestive circumstance links the life-work of Walt Whitman with the culmination of regional pioneering: the date of his death is also approximately the date of the exhaustion of free land, the disappearance of the frontier. This coincidence may assume a more than fortuitous significance if we think of Whitman, in the words of his own famous phrase, less as an encloser of things to be than as an acme of things accomplished. All unconscious to himself, Whitman, the self-proclaimed prophet of a new era, was in reality singing the swan song of the old.

One signpost that points in this direction is the modification of those less gracious aspects of individualism which we found in the case of the earlier transcendentalists. With Whitman we have already crossed the shadow line that divides the glorification of success from the rationalization of failure. Emerson blandly regrets that so much of hero-worship has been misdirected to the story of "a great defeat," the execution of an unsuccessful youth "at the Tyburn of his nation." Whitman's muse does not disdain to be "the comfortress of unsuccess":

I play not marches for accepted victors only, I play marches for conquered and slain persons.

Have you heard that it is good to gain the day?

I also say it is good to fall, battles are lost in the same spirit in which they are won——

. . . .

Vivas for those who have failed!

Emerson warns us that "a sympathetic person is placed in the dilemma of a swimmer among drowning men who all catch at him, and if he give so much as a leg or a finger they will drown him." Using the same figure, Whitman breathes a spirit of sacrificial devotion:

I seize the descending man and raise him with relentless will
O despairer here is my neck,
By God you shall not go down! hang your whole weight upon me.

At the same time that he parades evidences of material prosperity with the pride of an Emerson or a Carnegie, Whitman sounds the warning that these alone will not suffice. "In the highly artificial and materialistic bases of modern civilization with the corresponding methods and arrangements for living—which now seem with steam engine speed to be everywhere turning out the generations of humanity like uniform iron casings . . . I say of all this tremendous and dominant play of solely materialistic bearings upon current life in the United States . . . that they must either be confronted and met by at least an equally subtle and tremendous force infusion for purposes of spiritualization, for the pure conscience, for genuine esthetics, and for absolute and primal manliness and womanliness—or else our modern civilization with all its improvements is in vain and we are on the road to a destiny, a status equivalent in its real world to that of the fabled damned." In place of the proudly cherished prejudices of Thoreau, Whitman displays indiscriminate and self-contradictory enthusiasms. He liked whate'er he looked on and his looks went everywhere.

If the sterner and more strenuous elements of frontier psychology mellow into an all embracing tenderness, frontier optimism swells into a sweeping paean of praise. Confidence in a destiny commensurate with the size of the continent wide country animates these chants wherein Whitman looks upon his New World and sees that it is very good. But in this beatific satisfaction Whitman is not first but last of a long line of seers who prophesied the glories of the America to be; *Leaves of Grass* are the natural outcroppings from *The Wonder-Working Providence of Sion's Saviour.* The faint but fatal intimations of imminent decline and decay may best be realized if we place Whitman's rhapsodies beside those of Captain Edward Johnson. In unrestrained lyrical outpouring, in passionate faith, in mystical conviction, these celebrations of the New World are very much alike—which means, of course, that both are like the Hebrew Scriptures; that both Whitman and Johnson instinctively fell into Biblical rhythm and phraseology when assuming the role of inspired prophets.

The one point of difference is more significant than the dozen points of resemblance: For all his mystical excitation, Captain Edward Johnson is unmistakably clear on one point: he knows whom he has believed. His New Jerusalem is founded upon a definite dogma—quaintly anthropomorphic, brutally fanatical, if you please, but nevertheless as logically constructed, as impervious a unitary structure as the One Horse Shay to which a later satirist compared the repudiated Calvinism of his forbears. But when, emancipating ourselves perhaps with difficulty from the spell of Walt Whitman's eloquence, we begin to ask ourselves, "What are the articles of the creed on which his New World is founded?" we find Whitman strangely hazy about the specifications of his Divine Democracy. We are inclined to believe that the truest words which fell from his pen were his fustian proclamation, "I do not know what it is, but I know that it is grand."

As we begin to piece together from his apocryphal utterances some definite aspects of this New World in which he is exulting, we find it disappointingly like the old; at one point after another we are amazed by the unconscious antiquity of Walt Whitman. To choose only those pet doctrines which are readily recognized as the cornerstones of his temple. He has very much to say about "the love of comrades,"; one of the distinguishing features of the New World is to be that it has the love of comrades as its cementing bond. But whatever interpretation we assign to that much discussed phrase—whether it refer to phallic perversities, or, as his biographers discreetly assure us, to a purely spiritual but intensely romantic friendship between man and man—in either form it is an essentially Old World relationship—as old as the Oriental vices that corrupted the glory that was Greece and the grandeur that was Rome, as old as the love passing the love of women that was between David and Jonathan, between Amis and Amile.

Another favorite theme of Walt Whitman's is the perfectability of human nature. In so far as it relates to the purification of the soul through endless incarnations it is a commonplace of Hindu philosophy from the Upanishads to Madame Tingley; in so far as it relates to the improvement of human beings by improving their environment, it is a commonplace of all Utopias from Plato's *Republic* to Hudson's *Crystal Age*. As an article of a contemporary political creed, it was the fetish of Godwin and his circle, and had received its baptism of mystic poetry from Blake and Shelley long before Walt Whitman claimed it as a special prerogative of these states.

Most definite of Whitman's dogmas is his superstitious reliance upon the mechanisms of democracy. In a poem entitled *Election Day, November, 1884,* he names the bloodless campaign of the ballot box as the greatest marvel of these states. Here again Walt Whitman reads like an echo from eighteenth century disquisitions on the rights of man; it is a theory not a condition that intrigues him. Far more discerning was De Tocqueville, who years before had pointed out that the good fortune of America lay not in any special merit of her government, but in her abundance of free land.

Accepting Whitman at his own valuation, we have regarded him as fresh, original, daring, the incarnate spirit of the New World. Yet for the regional pioneering of its past, for the spiritual pioneering of its future he has but one shibboleth—Democracy—which he deifies without defining. Whitman's repeated repudiation of Old World feudalism, Old World ecclesiasticism, Old World dilettantism, has prevented us from seeing how much he has in common with Old World liberalism. His acclamation in Europe at a time when he was reviled in America may be less an instance of a prophet without honor in his own country than the recognition of a kindred spirit by a society sophisticated enough to appreciate him. We remember Swinburne hailing as brother Walt Whitman singing overseas. Like Swinburne, Whitman was superciliously hostile to all that was feudal and clerical in the past. Like Swinburne, he reveled in emotional intoxication, caring little how promiscuous the stimulus. Like Swinburne, he breathed languorous lyrics in idealization of death (a theme entirely foreign to pioneer psychology). Like Swinburne, he waxed incoherent in his adoration of "the great God-man which is God." Of Swinburne's *Songs before Sunrise* Chesterton has happily said that they were songs before a sunrise that never came off. In American literature as in English literature, the worship of humanity has proved an anemic cult; perhaps, as Sherwood Anderson has surmised "because man, even the brave and the free man, is somewhat a less worthy object of glorification than God." The thirty odd years since Whitman's death have seen the discrediting of his prophecies. The flowering of "rich, luxuriant, varied personalisms" has been curbed by innumerable legal precautions from the Volstead Act to the Anti-Syndicalism Law. The "bards of democracy" have written her epitaph in a *Spoon River Anthology,* dramatized her workman as a Hairy Ape. Very appropriately did Whitman say that his songs could have been produced at no time other than the last half of the nineteenth century: the fleeting moment when the harvest of the past was still plenteous and the lean years of the future mercifully veiled; the years just before the Armageddon of the agrarian interests under the boy orator of the Platte—the last years of the munificent frontier. Whitman's democratic vistas were in reality a backward glance o'er traveled roads; the songs which he said were "in spirit the poems of the morning," mistook the afterglow of the sunset for the glory of the dawn.

BIBLIOGRAPHY

I. On Transcendentalism

COOKE, GEORGE W.

An Historical and Biographical Introduction to Accompany the Dial. 2 vol.
Cleveland; the Rowfant Club, 1902

Poets of Transcendentalism: An Anthology with Introductory Essay 1903

The Dial: A Magazine for Literature, Philosophy and Religion vol. 1–4, 1840–44

FROTHINGHAM, OCTAVIUS B.

Transcendentalism in New England 1876

GODDARD, HAROLD C.

Studies in New England Transcendentalism 1908

"Transcendentalism" in *Cambridge History of American Literature* vol. I. pp. 546–549

II. On Emerson

Complete Works—The Centenary Edition, 1903–1904, 12 vols.

The original dates of publication of the more important works are as follows:

Nature—1836
The American Scholar—1837
Divinity School Address—1838
Essays, 1st series—1841
Essays, 2nd series—1844
Poems—1847
Nature, Addresses, and Lectures—1849
Letters and Social Aims—1876

For extended biographical and critical data:

FIRKINS, O. W.

Ralph Waldo Emerson—1915

HOLMES, O. W.

Ralph Waldo Emerson (A.M.L. series) 1885

MICHAUD, REGIS

Autour D'Emerson—1924

WOODBERRY, G. E.

Ralph Waldo Emerson (E.M.L. series) 1907

Also critical articles in:

BOYNTON, PERCY
A History of American Literature
BROWNELL, W. C.
American Prose Masters
MACY, JOHN
The Spirit of American Literature
MORE, PAUL ELMER
in *Cambridge History of American Literature* vol. I, ch. IX.
PAYNE, WILLIAM M.
Leading American Essayists

III. On Thoreau
The complete works are published in the Riverside edition, 1894, ten volumes, and in the Walden edition, 1906, 20 volumes. The last fourteen volumes of this edition are devoted to the complete journal. The works originally appeared in book form as follows:
A Week on the Concord and Merrimac Rivers—1849
Walden—1854
Excursions—1863
The Maine Woods—1864
Cape Cod—1865
A Yankee in Canada—1866
Anti-Slavery and Reform Papers—1890
For extended biographical and critical data:
SANBORN, FRANK B.
Life of Thoreau (A.M.L. series) 1882
VAN DOREN, MARK
Henry David Thoreau, a Critical Study—1916
Also critical articles in:
BOYNTON, PERCY
A History of American Literature
LOWELL, J. R.
My Study Windows
MACMECHAN, ARCHIBALD
in *The Cambridge History of American Literature*, vol. II, ch. X
MACY, JOHN
The Spirit of American Literature
MICHAUD, REGIS
Autour D'Emerson

STEVENSON, R. L.
Familiar Studies of Men and Books
For an enthusiastic appreciation:
BAZALGETTE, LEON
Henry Thoreau, Bachelor of Nature—1924

IV. On Walt Whitman

BAZALGETTE, LEON
Walt Whitman, the Man and His Work
New York; Doubleday, Page & Co., 1920
BROOKS, VAN WYCK
"Whitman the Precipitate"
in *America's Coming of Age*
New York; B. W. Huebsch, 1915
CARPENTER, GEORGE RICE
Walt Whitman
New York; Macmillan Co., 1909
FRANK, WALDO
"The Multitudes in Whitman"
in *Our America*
New York; Boni & Liveright, 1919
OVERTON, GRANT
The Answerer
New York; Harcourt, Brace & Co., 1921
PERRY, BLISS
Walt Whitman
New York; Houghton Mifflin Co., 1906
ROGERS, CAMERON
The Magnificent Idler,
Garden City; Doubleday, Page & Co., 1926
STEVENSON, ROBERT LOUIS
"Walt Whitman"
in *Familiar Studies of Men and Books*
New York; Chas. Scribner's Sons, 1898
WHITMAN, WALT
Complete Prose Works
Boston; Small Maynard & Co., 1907
Leaves of Grass
Boston; Small Maynard & Co., 1907

CHAPTER V

THE FRONTIER OF '49

I. LITERARY FRONTIERS

EVEN a casual comparison of the successive frontiers in American history with the frontiers represented in American literature, betrays a discrepancy. By what uncharted principle of psychological selection, one wonders, have writers flocked around certain frontiers to the neglect of others? Inherent dramatic value appears to have little or nothing to do with the choice of a specific frontier as a favorite among American authors. One might search the records of world history for a migration more grandiloquently prompted, for a settlement more dramatically directed than that which established the Mormon frontier. Yet, so far as I know, it has been employed as a setting only in the distorted dénouement of *A Study in Scarlet* (and that by an English writer!) and in one of the coarsest and most forced of Mark Twain's chapter in *Roughing It*. The homesteader, the fur-trapper, the gold-miner have found patrons among the aristocracy of letters, while the cowboy, equally heir apparent of the American frontier, has, in the phrase of Carl Van Doren, "regularly moved on the plane of the sub-literary, in dime novels and latterly in moving-pictures." Two frontiers and two types of frontier character geographically and psychologically remote have been leading favorites in American literature; the New England frontier of the seventeenth century Puritan and the California frontier of the fortyniner are the ones about which imagination has played most freely.

It is easy to see the aspects of the California frontier which offered a rich lode for literary prospectors. It was the outpost of advancing frontiers, acquired in the heat of jingo patriotism and the flush of easy victory; it was vivified by contact with foreign peoples: with the Spanish whose missions and presidios and ranches still give a romantic glamour to the land; with Chinese, with Russians, and of course, as always, with Indians. The discovery of gold offered fabulous inducements of wealth. Popular tribunals established their own swift means of meting out justice. Complications over land titles added to the belligerent alignments arising out of conflicting mine claims and conflicting civilizations. Individualism always rampant in the frontiersman, manifested itself with keenest verve in its last flame-up on the last frontier.

The brilliant debut of California in American literature may be explained as a mere fortunate coincidence of the time, the place, and the men, or it may be explained as the inevitable response of genius to the stimulus of the hour. Such speculations are interesting but irrelevant; the point of moment is that within a year Mark Twain jumped into a not altogether welcome celebrity with "The Jumping Frog of Calaveras County" and Bret Harte struck a lucky vein in "The Luck of Roaring Camp." These two famous short stories initiated the Wild West movement in American literature. This movement has met rather incongruous receptions. On one hand, it has been either ignored or patronized by such "highbrow" critics of American literature as George Edward Woodberry and Barrett Wendell. Barrett Wendell devotes fourteen pages of the five hundred and thirty in his *Literary History of America* to his chapter on the west, which resembles the famous one on snakes in Iceland: There is no literature in the west. Woodberry like Turner recognizes the reaction of the frontier upon the more conservative sections, but is much less flattering in his estimate of the value of the influence. He speaks of "the first irruption of Western roughness like a back water wash upon the more staid and respectable communities of the East." While regretting this contaminating influence of West on East, he denies that the West has produced anything worth calling literature. "The ideal imagination, the power to recast truth and remake the world had not arrived in the West, nor, indeed, has it ever arrived there." On the other hand, in seeming contradiction to this heroic stand of the Old Guard of culture was the enthusiastic reception given these western stories in the very citadels of the Brahmins, in the East and in Europe. It is well known that the fame of such essentially western writers as Bret Harte and Joaquin Miller was greater in proportion to the distance from the locality which they described. They were lionized in London while patronized in Boston; patronized in Boston while anathematized in Oakland. This vogue of the wild westerner may indicate a reversion to the primitive which is a frequent affectation of the hyper-civilized; it may indicate that desire for something afar which finds somewhere else and never here the land of true romance; it may indicate that, as is often alleged, the west as depicted in frontier fiction was a distorted picture, not recognizable, or recognized only to be deeply resented, by contemporary Westerners.

II. THE HISTORICAL FIDELITY OF WESTERN LITERATURE

It is difficult to decide that question so often interestingly debated: are the literary pictures of the California frontier, as given by Bret Harte, for instance, valid historical documentations? The difficulty of deciding this question arises largely from the fact that we have no representative journal literature of the California fortyniners such as the pen-minded Puritans left us in their minutely detailed chronicles of old New England. We have, certainly, authentic diaries of California frontiersmen from the unabashedly personal narrative of James Ohio Pattie to the consciously literary letters of "Shirley." But these differ as much among themselves as they differ from Bret Harte or Joaquin Miller. Who shall say which record is truly representative of the California frontier — Nelson Kingsley's or Walter Colton's, Delano's or Dana's, Larkin's or Bryant's? Royce points out the fallacy of relying on pioneer testimony for our impressions of the essentially unstable, heterogeneous California society of the mid nineteenth century. "Many pioneers seem to assume that save their own anecdotes, no sound records of the early days are extant. Yet the fact is that valuable as the honest man's memory must be to retain and convey the coloring of the minds and moods of individuals and parties, this individual memory cannot be trusted in general either for the details of any complex transaction, or for an account of the whole state of any large and mixed community. One finds this especially true when one reads some of the more personal reminiscences of the more forgetful California pioneers. . . . The boastful and reckless old pioneer who imagines himself to have seen all the heights and depths of the early life, who knows more about it in consequence than human speech can express—he, when he begins to tell you of it is commonly simply incoherent. He boasts on occasion and with equal earnestness of the piety and of the viciousness, of the gayety and of the seriousness, of the brutality and of the peacefulness of the early days."

In a scholarly study of *La Société Californienne de 1850 d'àpres Bret Harte,* Dr. Reau has reached the conclusion that Bret Harte gives a well rounded and essentially accurate picture of the pioneer community in California and that his works present "un véritable caractère de documentation historique." For purposes of this chapter it is sufficient to accept Dr. Reau's verdict without reopening the case. With however much earnestness we attempt to approach the problem from an objectively historical basis, we find Bret Harte like Joaquin Miller's "lawyer who never lost a case": when debarred as a lawyer, he gets in as a witness. As Erskine says: "Whether the picture he drew was accurate or colored by a sentimental temperament, must remain a conjecture, for he has taught his admirers to see the rough mining life through his eyes, and his critics when they would contravert him, are embarrassed by the lack of other accounts than his." Writers who start out to estimate the credibility of Bret Harte's picture of California, generally end by using Harte's preface to *The Tales of the Argonauts* as the touchstone by which to try his stories. To avoid any danger of this intellectual somersault, let us waive any attempt to make meticulous comparisons of Bret Harte's California with the California reflected in contemporary journals; let us base our judgment of his California frontier not upon the test of historical accuracy but upon the test of literary power.

III. BRET HARTE, MELODRAMATIST

This method of procedure places Bret Harte at a disadvantage. From the first, his prestige has rested on his employment of a new and picturesque setting. His immunity from puncturing criticism is due to the fact, often alleged as his unique claim to fame, that he localized the short story. To think of Bret Harte is to think of Red Gulch, Roaring Camp, Poker Flat, uncouth miners with hearts of gold, melancholy gamblers with a fine sense of honor, women who were fair and frail, life that was vivid and vigorous—in short, to think of the California of the fortyniners. Even Erskine, evidently an admirer of Bret Harte, admits that: "One reason why Bret Harte's fame rests on California is that he was strangely incapable of drawing any other life. Only when he wrote of California was he possessed of the magic of genius." Well even a flash of genius is much to be grateful for; and if that flash illuminates California, we should not complain if it does not illuminate a continent. But that brings us back to the disputed question: Has Bret Harte illuminated the California of his day? Was he capable even of drawing California? The repudiation of Harte's portrayal of California by contemporary Californians is generally known and generally accepted as proof of the all too unflattering accuracy of the stories. Pattee suggests another reason for California's rejection of Harte's California: "It is not fair to picture an era simply by dwelling on its exceptions and its grotesque possibilities. Art must rest upon the whole truth, not upon half truths."

It is this emphasis of half truths that makes Bret Harte's fiction melodramatic rather than dramatic. The setting on which his fame depends is treated merely as a picturesque background. Harte approaches nature, not with a reverent sense of something far more deeply interfused, but with a showman's appreciation of effective stage property. The spirit of the mountains does not surround and sustain the tales of the Argonauts as the spirit of the forests surrounds and sustains the tales of the Leatherstocking. Both Harte and Cooper wish to suggest the power of nature as an educator. With delicacy and artistic restraint Cooper suggests by repeated touches the molding of Deerslayer's character through the pervasive influence of the Great Mother. Bret Harte briskly introduces Nature as part of the cast in *The Luck of Roaring Camp:*

> Whether creeping over the pine boughs or lying lazily on his back blinking at the leaves above him, to him the birds sang, the squirrels chattered and the flowers bloomed. Nature was his nurse and playfellow. For him she would let slip between the leaves golden shafts of sunlight that fell just within his grasp; she would send wandering breezes to visit him with the balm of bay and resinous gum; to him the tall redwoods nodded familiarly and sleepily, the bumblebee buzzed and the rooks cawed a slumbrous accompaniment.[1]

Harte's character effects are equally specious. Our complaint is not so much that he peoples California with grotesque exceptions like Colonel Starbottle and Cherokee Sal and Yuba Bill, but that in handling these exceptions he fails to show a discriminating sense of proportion. Again and again we find his work marred by the amateurish tendency to elaborate a part at the expense of the whole. We have all seen plays in which a minor character insisted on thrusting himself into the spotlight. How much less excusable is it for an author to insist on thrusting a subordinate character, or one that should be subordinate, into the spotlight. In Bret Harte's stories we are constantly distracted by false leads. Who would not predict after reading the opening pages of "The Man on the Beach" that Cousin Maria was to be the leading lady? Miss Nelly Arnot in "The Fool of Five Forks" is elaborated at far greater length than is necessary to establish the Fool's unfaltering fidelity. Hermit Gray in "Princess Bob and Her Friends" comes perilously close to supplanting the Princess in our interest. The chronically smiling and retreating Mrs. Tennessee's Partner, the suspected and sensitive bride of the Old Man of

[1] The quotations in this book from the works of Bret Harte are used by permission of Houghton Mifflin Company, Boston, publishers of Bret Harte's complete works.

Simpson's Bar, are allowed to hold center stage regardless of the fact that theirs is another story.

Furthermore, those characters which are legitimate leads are unreal because of over simplification of character. We realize, of course, that within the scope of the short story it is impossible to give a picture of life at its full complexity; that the short story writer must assume that each man is governed "by a ruling passion, the very pulse of the machine," and proceeding on this assumption, must interpret incidents in relation to this dominant character trait. It is a difficult matter to draw the line between the simplification of experience necessary for literary interpretation, and the mutilation of experience which makes possible the high lights of melodrama. But in even the ablest of Bret Harte's stories the ruling passion is carried to the point of obsession. Surely it is a perverted view of life which narrows it to the range of one emotion concentrated on one individual, whether the emotion be the ennobling one of devotion, as in "Miggles," "Tennessee's Partner," "The Fool of Five Forks," and "The Luck of Roaring Camp"; or the corroding one of revenge as in "Mrs. Skaggs' Husbands," and "The Iliad of Sandy Bar."

At this point the admirers of Bret Harte will spring to his defense. Who so much as Harte, they exclaim, has portrayed the contradictory characteristics so incongruously blended in human nature? Who has delighted so much as Harte in the paradoxes that make up the spectacle of life?

Bret Harte indeed realized that there is "much of good in the worst of us and much of ill in the best of us," but he does not agree with the conclusion, "It hardly behooves any of us to talk about any of the rest of us." The discovery of the mingled potentialities of human nature, instead of furnishing food for sober reflection, is news for vociferous trumpeting. "Life is a paradox," he shouts through his megaphone; "People are queer. I, Bret Harte, have discovered it. Look here and see what I have found." And with the easy assurance of a showman exhibiting freaks, he displays the incongruities of his characters. He says of the inhabitants of Roaring Camp:

> The assemblage numbered about a hundred men. One or two of these were actual fugitives from justice, some were criminals, and all were reckless. Physically they exhibited no indications of their past lives and character. The greatest scamp had a Raphael face with a profusion of blond hair; Oakhurst the gambler, had the melancholy air and intellectual abstraction of a Hamlet; the coolest and most courageous man was scarcely over five feet in height, with a soft voice and an embarrassed, timid manner.

Equally deceptive in appearance are the house guests of the Maecenas of the Pacific Slope:

> The very gentle clerical looking stranger, mildest of a noisy disputing crowd at the other table, was a notorious duellist and dead shot; the only gentleman at the table who retained a flannel shirt and high boots was not a late coming mountaineer but a well known English baronet on his travels; the man who told a somewhat florid and emphatic anecdote was a popular English clergyman; the one querulous, discontented face in the laughing group was the famous humorist who had just convulsed it; a pale handsome young fellow who ate and drank sparingly, and regarded the coquettish advances of the prettiest Diva with the cold abstraction of a student, was a notorious roue and gambler.

Of course, Bret Harte discovers more deep lying discrepancies between what people are and what they appear to be. The unamiability of good people is brought out repeatedly. The mother of the Chatelaine of Burnt Ridge is a malevolent shrew "nursing her resentment and a large Bible which she held clasped against her shawled bosom at the same moment." The Rev. Joshua McSnagley and his worthy parishioners make life intolerable for M'Liss. The virtuous ladies who enjoy Miggles' hospitality refuse to share her bedroom. On the other hand, gamblers and philanderers like Oakhurst and Hamlin are delineated as scrupulous on points of honor, quixotic in deeds of kindness; social outcasts like Mother Shipton and Miggles are capable of touching self-sacrifice.

The best deserved portion of Bret Harte's popularity rests upon his sympathetic portrayal of the essential goodness that shines in even the most tarnished specimen of humanity. But even in his revelation of the nobleness that lies sleeping but never dead in the most sordid, Harte is the melodramatist. It is true that he avoids the naive simplicity of painting characters either all black or all white; but he puts them in an equally crude motley of sharply contrasted black and white; his art is not sufficiently subtle to paint in shades of gray. Compare Edwin Arlington Robinson's Flammonde with Harte's Oakhurst, and Oakhurst falls into the category of stage villains with redeeming traits.

An author has a right to be judged by his best rather than his worst; if we tear to pieces Bret Harte's plots in an attempt to prove him a melodramatist, we should avoid dependence upon such obvious claptrap as "Gabriel Conroy," "Mrs. Skaggs' Husbands," "Tompson's Prodigal," "The Man on the Beach," and "The Rose of Tuolome," and seek evidence rather in the stories generally ranked as his greatest. I shall base my criticism, then as far as possible on five stories generally classed a his best work: "The Luck of Roaring Camp," "Tennessee's Partner," "The Outcasts of Poker Flat," "The Idyll of Red Gulch," and "Miggles."

If we examine the most famous of Bret Harte's situations, we find that the situations like the characters are composed of violent contrasts. A baby born and reared among miners; a beautiful daughter of joy devoting her life to the care of a helpless paralytic; a simple-hearted man in all innocence offering his pile as a bribe to the jury to release his friend—how much of the appeal of these striking situations depends on the revelation of character in a crisis? How much upon startling incongruity? One such contrast which is a favorite device of Harte's is the setting of purity against stain. In "The Idyll of Red Gulch": "The young girl reached out her arms and caught the sinful woman to her own pure breast for one brief moment." In "The Outcasts of Poker Flat": "The Duchess putting her head on Piney's shoulder, spoke no more. And so reclining, the younger and purer pillowing the head of her soiled sister upon her virgin breast, they fell asleep."

Seldom can Harte resist the temptation to add an extra touch of meretricious ornamentation. One such instance is the procession of miners to view the hour-old child, the deliberately ridiculous assortment of gifts included in the donation from Roaring Camp: teaspoons, Bibles and surgeon's lancets. The incongruity of the group caught in the storm must be accentuated by having the outcasts of Poker Flat join Piney and her lover in a gospel hymn. Probability must be still further violated in the interests of incongruity when the company are entertained by the story of the Iliad rendered in the common vernacular of Sandy Bar. Another picturesque tableau is afforded by posing Miggles in the moonlight as she retails her history to a company of strange men. All these scenes are theatrically effective—but are they convincing? Do we feel it probable or even possible that on the frontier or anywhere else given people under the given circumstances would act in this way?

Not only does the showman assemble his tableaux but he exhibits them at length. Harte gives himself away by his hesitancy to let his situations make their own appeal. "The Outcasts of Poker Flat" is his strongest story largely because there he is, in the main, satisfied to let his characters speak for themselves. But even here he cannot refrain from overexhibiting the final tableau. He has already pointed out the pathetic contrast afforded by having a prostitute die in the arms of a virgin. Not content, he has to rub it in. "All human stain, all trace of earthly travail was hidden beneath the spotless mantle mercifully flung from above. When pitying fingers brushed the snow from their wan faces, you could scarcely have told from the equal peace that dwelt upon them, which was she that had sinned." The regenerating influence of the baby upon the men of Roaring Camp is repeatedly insisted upon, rather than dramatically portrayed. Miggles' position is played up by touches which we resent as meretricious. She had been, she tells us, a rich woman; she had friends. Then why the necessity of her living in a room papered with illustrated magazines, with furniture "extemporized and adapted from candle boxes and packing cases"? why the necessity of the bear and the magpie to companion her loneliness? Surely the tragedy of her position is only cheapened by such spurious appeals to pathos. Here again the central tableau is overexhibited, in this case, with flagrant bad taste: "The moon touched the lonely figure in the chair with infinite compassion and seemed to baptize with a shining flood the lowly head of the woman whose hair, as in the sweet old story, bathed the feet of him she loved." And when we take leave of Miggles, Harte is still afraid the point is not sufficiently clear, and so drives it home once more in the judge's toast, "Here's to Miggles; God bless her." In all these situations we have the taint of conscious showing off, characteristic of all Bret Harte's stories, reaching its most glaring expression in his apostrophe in "How Santa Claus came to Simpson's Bar":

Sing, O Muse, the ride of Richard Bullen. Sing, O Muse, of chivalrous men, the sacred quest, the doughty deeds, the fearsome ride, and gruesome peril of the Flower of Simpson's Bar!

Sentiment is a precious thing; and like other precious things, it should be used sparingly. If a writer deliberately plays upon our emotions, we have a right to demand that he do so for the sake of arousing the ennobling pity and terror evoked by the deepest truths of human experience; we have the right to resent the solicitation of our emotions under false pretenses. The author who plays upon emotion as an end in itself, may be an expert in sob stuff; he is not a master of drama.

We have a right to test every emotional appeal by the question of little Peterkin, "What good came of it at last?" The attitude of the men of Roaring Camp toward the Luck will not meet this test. They act against the child's interests in refusing to send it to a camp where it could have a woman's care. They are animated by a motive of superstition combined with a desire to "have something on" other camps. Miggles' devotion to Jim need not have been accompanied by isolation and neglect of convention. The story attempts to enlist our sympathy for a heroine who is deliberately courting martyrdom, and who evidently enjoys it so much that it is difficult to see why we should be expected to pity her. Tennessee's Partner and the Fool of Five Forks display quixotic devotion carried to a ridiculous extreme, to the annoyance rather than the advantage of the objects of that devotion. The mother of the anonymous pupil in "The Idyll of Red Gulch" rises to heights of renunciation which have a purifying effect upon her grammar. She begins the conversation by remarking, "I heerd tell that you were goin' down to the Bay" and says of her son, "There aint a sweeter, dearer, better boy lives than him." But a minute later under the emotional excitation of self-sacrifice, she utters this impassioned outburst:

> Do with him what you like. The worst you can do will be kindness to what he will learn with me. Only take him out of this wicked life, this cruel place, this home of shame and sorrow. You will. I know you will. You must not, you cannot say No. You will make him as pure, as gentle as yourself, and when he has grown up you will tell him his father's name, the name that hasn't passed my lips for years —the name of Alexander Morton whom they call here Sandy. Miss Mary—do not take your hand away. Miss Mary, speak to me! You will take my boy. Do not turn your face from me. I know it ought not to look on such as me—Miss Mary! My God, be merciful! she is leaving me.

Evidently we are expected to admire the mother thus tragically parting forever from her child; we are expected to admire Miss Mary thus cruelly disillusioned and bravely accepting responsibility for her lover's illegitimate child. But if we have kept our heads we will do no such thing. We will reflect that a mother who really cared for her child would have made her life such that she could keep him with her and teach him all that she had learned from the scarlet letter. We will reflect that a Miss Mary who really cared for Sandy's regeneration would have seen the supreme opportunity for Sandy in assuming his rightful responsibility for his son. But, of course, it is much more romantic to have both women torture themselves as cruelly and as futilely as possible, regardless of the welfare of Son or Sandy.

Just as we see behind each effective grouping of puppets the hand of the showman, so we hear behind each fairly mouthed speech the voice of the ventriloquist. Where character and situation have been falsified, we cannot expect dialogue to ring true. We must be satisfied if the melodramatist gives us highflown expressions of the romantic sentiments in which he delights. No one can seriously believe that Miggles would have told her story after this fashion:

They advised me to send him to Frisco to the hospital for he was no good to anyone and would be a baby all his life. Perhaps it was something in Jim's eye, perhaps it was that I never had a baby, but I said "No." I was rich then, for I was popular with everyone—gentlemen like yourself, sir, came to see me—and I sold out my business and bought this place and I brought my baby here.

The doctor would ask to see Miggles' baby, as he called Jim and when he'd go away he'd say, "Miggles, you're a trump—God bless you," and it didn't seem so lonely after that. But the last time he was here he said as he opened the door to go, "Do you know, Miggles, your baby will grow up to be a man yet and an honor to his mother; but not here, Miggles, not here!"

Background instead of atmosphere, tableaux instead of situations, declamations instead of dialogue—all show how consistently Bret Harte, in the words of Pattee, "Sought for the startling and the dramatic and elaborated the outside of it with care." But the writer who elaborates outsides may seek the dramatic, but he will never find it; the springs of drama lie too deep for him; what he gives us is melodrama.

IV. THE HEART OF THE WEST

We have tried Bret Harte by the test of literary power and found him wanting. And yet the stubborn fact remains: Bret Harte more than any other writer has fixed in imperishable outlines the fleeting film of the California frontier, till the places of which he wrote are known as "the Bret Harte country." When a writer has succeeded in stamping his interpretation upon a region, it is futile to scrutinize suspiciously every detail of his stories, demanding that they be matched with authenticated incidents from *bona fide* narratives. The significance of the frontier of '49 in American literature lies not so much in what it was as in what people wished to believe it was.

Of course, influences quite aside from the frontier played their part in determining the bent of Harte's talent. It would be fallacious to attempt to interpret the development of a literature in relation to the development of its contemporary history without recognizing that the immediate social and economic environment is only one of many influences which determine a writer's choice and treatment of his subjects. It is a commonplace of critical research that literature has always to be interpreted in the light of other literature. The fact that the tracing of an "influence" has been solemnly pursued to a *reductio ad absurdum* does not absolve us from taking it into account as a factor in our analysis. To understand Cooper's Leatherstocking we had to take into account not only the frontier hero but the romantic philosophy; to understand Emerson's transcendentalism we had to take into account not only the impetus of the westward expansion, but the vaulting idealism of Kant and Cousin. To understand Bret Harte's Argonauts we have to take into account not only the actual frontier of '49, but the Dr. Sentiment of contemporary London—Charles Dickens.

The influence of Dickens upon Bret Harte is so obvious as to amount sometimes to almost a verbatim echo. This is particularly apt to be true in the deathbed scenes for which both are famous. Mrs. Dombey dies holding little Florence in her arms:

> Clinging fast to that slight spar within her arms the mother drifted out upon the dark and unknown sea that rolls round all the world.
>
> Kentuck "clinging to the frail babe as a drowning man is said to cling to a straw drifted away into the shadowy river that flows forever to the unknown sea."

The influence of Dickens is also apparent in the display of the body of Wan Lee:

> Dead, my reverend friends, dead. Stoned to death in the streets of San Francisco, in the year of grace 1869 by a mob of half grown boys and Christian school children.

This parallels closely the peroration of Dickens over the body of little Joe:

> Dead, your Majesty. Dead, my lords and gentlemen, dead, Right Reverends and Wrong Reverends of every order. Dead, men and women born with heavenly compassion in your hearts. And dying thus around us every day.

We mention the influence of Dickens because it is in terms of that influence that any staginess or sentimentality in Bret Harte is frequently explained. Now the influence of Dickens may or may not explain why Harte was a melodramatist; but it fails to explain why O. Henry's *Heart of the West* is melodrama. O. Henry and Dickens stand at opposite poles in the effects they sought and the methods they employed; but *The Heart of the West* continues the conventions of the western story as established by Bret Harte. A month on a ranch is guaranteed to make a "plumb white" character out of "the low-downest passel of inhumanity"—witness "The Higher Abdication" and "Hygeia at the Solito." Scarcely less efficacious is the power of a good woman: a few words of affectionate trust from his old mother achieve the reformation of the town terror Calliope; an appeal from a little girl transforms a hold-up man into a chaparral prince. The bond of loyalty between partners is almost as much of a fetich as in "Tennessee's Partner." In "Telemachus Friend" it passes the love of woman; in "A Call Loan" it defies a bank examination between friends. A benevolent *Deus ex Machina* has his hangar in the west. Cherokee sentimentally yearning for a

Christmas with children, finds in the one child that Yellowhammer is able to produce, his long lost son. Calliope's mother arrives just at the crucial moment. Ed returns from the sale of the steers in the nick of time to meet the call loan. And so we might trace the descent of the western story from Bret Harte to Bill Hart, from O. Henry to Harold Bell Wright; always in the heart of the west a man's a man, goodness is easily acquired, sentiment is easily touched, the right things happen to the right people at the right time.

V. MARK TWAIN: "WILD WEST HUMORIST OF THE PACIFIC SLOPE"

If the frontier of Bret Harte is melodrama, the frontier of Mark Twain is farce. Strictly speaking, of course, Mark Twain represents the silver mines of Nevada rather than the gold mines of California. But the distinguishing features of the gold rush of the forties were repeated in the silver rush of the sixties: the characters, the motives, the situations, the tragi-comic interplay of lights and shadows on the screen of the magic interlude.

In Mark Twain's account of Roughing It he displays the same triple personality which so distressed his mentors and so intrigues his biographers. He is a scathing satirist, a delightful boy and a crude comedian, simultaneously, or in inexplicably swift succession. We shall consider later the penetrating satire with which Mark Twain touched the tragical depths under the hilarious surfaces. Here we shall think only of those parts of *Roughing It* which people chuckled over and thrilled over in the simpleminded days before psychoanalysis and sociology complicated the study of literature.

Mark Twain writes of the silver mining fever in Nevada with his customary deliberate accentuation of high lights. If he wishes to show how the improvised folk drama of the practical joke filled the place of more vicarious and refined entertainments, he develops at chapter length the fantastic yarn of the famous case of Hyde vs. Morgan in which the pretentious tenderfoot, General Buncombe, United States attorney, was inveigled unsuspectingly into defending the interests of the plaintiff in a fictitious landslide suit. If he wishes to show the effect of the law of supply and demand in creating an interest in women and children, he gives such extravagant examples of adulation as the offer of one hundred and fifty dollars' worth of gold dust for the privilege of kissing a child, and the making up of a purse of twenty-five hundred dollars for the sight of a sickly emigrant woman. "Once in Star City in the Humboldt Mountains I took my place in a sort of long, postoffice single file of miners to patiently wait my chance to peep through a crack in the cabin and get a sight of the splendid new sensation—a genuine live Woman! And at the end of half an hour my turn came, and I put my eye to the crack and there she was with one arm akimbo, and tossing flapjacks in a frying pan with the other. And she was one hundred and sixty-five years old and hadn't a tooth in her head."

It would be a *reductio ad absurdum* of historical method to refute these exuberant exaggerations with earnestly offered selections from Royce's *California* or from the *Shirley Letters*. Obviously, Mark Twain is not trying to give an exact historical picture, obviously he does not expect to be taken literally—indeed, he adds in a note on the woman's age: "Being in calmer mood now, I voluntarily knock off a hundred from that." With no intention of being fettered by the letter, he gives himself up to the infectious spirit of that unique community "of two hundred thousand *young* men—not simpering, dainty, kid-gloved weaklings, but stalwart, muscular, dauntless young braves, brimful of push and energy, and royally endowed with every attribute that goes to make up a peerless and magnificent manhood—the very pick and choice of the world's glorious ones. No women, no children, no gray and stooping veterans —none but erect, brighteyed, quick-moving, strong-handed young giants—the strangest population, the finest population, the most gallant host that ever trooped down the startled solitudes of an unspoiled land." He delights in the comic incongruities of this interlude of youth and luck: the lofty indifference to wealth mingled with the feverish greed for wealth; the romantic desperadoes with their illogical but exacting code of honor; the sensibly simple judicial procedure which proposes hanging a man first and trying him afterwards; the melodramatic reversals of fortune which keep life at fever pitch.

VI. THE PSYCHIC WEST

The wild west, as it is customarily presented, not only by its first exploiters, Bret Harte and Mark Twain, but by the myriad lesser lights of story and screen, is a world made up of these very dramatic incongruities, a world where anything might happen. Now of course, in matter of fact, the world always is a place where anything may happen. But in the golden age of transcendentalism, the age of the frontier heroes, it was habitual to speak as if what happened were contingent almost entirely, if not entirely upon the will of the determined individual. During the recent vogue of naturalism it has been customary to speak as if what happened were contingent almost entirely, if not entirely upon the blind workings of impersonal forces. During the magic interlude of gold-hunting, youth had a respite from the oversoulful seriousness of transcendentalism, a reprieve from the unnatural seriousness of naturalism. It was not unduly depressed by being told either how much or how little it could do. And so, for a brief enchanted period, the American knew gay irresponsibility. For once—perhaps partly because of intimate contact with Latin peoples?—the American frontier laid aside its tense determination for joyous abandon. Quite characteristic is the jubilee of Mark Twain's emigration: "Ham and eggs, and after these a pipe—an old, rank, delicious pipe—ham and eggs and scenery, a 'down grade,' a flying coach, a fragrant pipe, and a contented heart—these make happiness. It is what all the ages have struggled for."

With characteristic humorlessness, Mr. Brooks in his *Ordeal of Mark Twain* interprets this "down grade" as a symptom of moral deterioration—a curiously anachronistic echo from the Puritan frontier where happiness was sin. Without taking too seriously Mr. Brooks' solemn diagnosis of the ham and eggs, the scenery and the down grade, it is significant to notice how happily Mark Twain has here caught the motive of letting go, Now Mark Twain himself is the first to recognize that there are established conventions of unconventionality, that the intolerance of radicalism is fiercer than the intolerance of conservatism. But even while recognizing that freedom from convention generally means freedom to change an old convention for a new one, Mark Twain creates throughout his hilarious sketches of California and Nevada, a psychic West, an illusion of freedom, of irresponsibility, of buoyancy, which has become as much a part of the traditional west of literature as the miners and gamblers and lynchings and lucky strikes. Not here where Mrs. Grundy is watching and whispering, but out in the great open spaces, out where the west begins, the lover of life may find outlet for moods taboo in a more sophisticated society. It may very well be true, as Chesterton surmises, that these moods are apt to be softer, not harder than those enjoined by the Ten Commandments and the Book of Etiquette. But whether more sentimental or more stern, whether tending toward bathos or brutality, the range of moods was greater on the western frontier than in more formalized communities. Not only was the range of moods within the individual, but the range of types in the community more elastic on the frontier than on Main Street. Criminals who would land in jail in Spoon River are heroes of the frontier. If the hand of justice overtakes them, it is in the theatrical form of the lynching posse or vigilance committee and their end is invested with a picaresque piquancy. Incompetents, chronically handicapped by an inferiority complex in organized occupations, might by sheer fool luck, strike it rich on the mining frontier.

The transforming power of the psychic west finds a favorite expression in stories of how Yankees became Californians. Canfield's spurious *Diary of a Forty-Niner* centers around such a metamorphosis. With narrative finesse which in itself should warn the reader of a literary hoax in the supposed diary, Mr. Canfield tells how the staid New Englander who came to California wanting only to make money enough to return to his farm and his girl, falls under the spell of the passionately seductive climate, the unmoral, vagabond life of his associates; how his loneliness is tempered by the finding of a pal with a mystery in his past, and a French sweetheart who runs a gambling hall; how finally he realizes that he has become quite another man than the simpleminded chap who would have been content to vegetate all his days on a New England farm.

Canfield's made-up diary is suggestive testimony from the standpoint of literature, though an imposture as history. There was no Alfred Jackson, it is true; but there must have been many Alfred Jacksons to have created the legend of the psychic west which is the *leitmotif* of Canfield's invention. Alfred Jackson is more significant as a type than he would have been as an individual. Nor is it difficult to find individuals whose authentic diaries record a similar weaning. Russ in *The Log of a Forty-Niner* entitles one section: "The Yankee becomes the Californian." Disappointed in his hopes of easy fortune in the new country, he yet felt amply repaid in the broadened outlook upon life. "My experiences had been as valuable to me as the bag of gold I had come home without." Nelson Kingsley's account of his voyage to California reminds one of the memoirs of his Puritan forbears in its record of pious pleasures: "We had a prayer meeting in the evening which seemed much like enjoying nature in her true light once more, for since we abandoned it on the other side of the Continent we have had bad weather, but whether from this piece of negligence or not, I will not pretend to say, but it is truly interesting to have a meeting of this kind, as it gives one new interest, as well as remind him of days gone by which has been spent in a land where the gospel in its true light is known and felt and besides this it alleviates the dull feeling which is prevalent among us all." But the devout Nelson slips from grace after a few months in California, and we find him entering in his diary that he spent a Sunday retorting and dividing gold: "I find that one does many things here that in Connecticut would be termed sabbath breaking, but custom guides conscience in this country as well as others." In *Argonauts of '49* Howe describes the New England exodus to California as a sort of religious crusade "Bibles in one hand and good New England civilization in the other," and then goes on to detail the change that came over these worthies upon arrival at the diggings: "The discovery of gold in California and the exodus from the east which followed had a profound and lasting effect on the commercial, social and political life of the country. It had also a profound effect on the social and religious life of New England. Those who returned from California came back with a broader catholicity and less restricted views."

Bret Harte is fond of using this reorientation of the easterner as the pivot for his stories. One of the most effective examples is "Snowbound at Eagle's," in which the easterner's passion for law and order leads him on a wild goose chase after hold-up men. His experiences with a legally constituted minion of the law during his search, his discovery of the motives of the hold-up, of the legal outrage of justice which had provoked it, throw new light on the redefinition of law and order required on the frontier; he returns to find that during his absence the highwaymen whom he has been pursuing have been entertained with mutual enjoyment by his wife and his sister.

Another effect of the psychic west has already been mentioned. Strangely enough the far western frontier was conducive alike to the relaxing and to the reinforcing of inhibitions, In the sunburnt west the bad get better as the good get livelier. Sherwood Anderson in his intellectual autobiography, *A Story Teller's Story,* comments with gentle irony on this familiar device of western fiction: "A man went into the redwood forests or into the deserts and took up land. He had been rather a mean, second-rate chap in civilization, but in the new place a great change comes over him. Well, the writer had got him out where there was no one looking and could do as he pleased with the fellow. Never mind what he had been. The forests or the deserts had changed him completely. The writer could make a regular angel of him, have him rescue downtrodden women, catch horse thieves, exhibit any kind of bravery required to keep the reader excited and happy."

VII. THE FRONTIER AND LOCAL COLOR

It may be surmised that just as the material west was looted before Americans discovered the value of their dissipated heritage, so the psychic west vanished before Americans realized the real significance of the magic interlude of '49. The history of California in literature from *The Splendid Idle Forties* to *The Octopus* is the history of the transition from romance to naturalism. With the fading of the last frontier went the last opportunity for the moral holiday. Royce writing of the emergence of California from the turbulent lawlessness of frontier mining camps to the orthodox regulations of municipalities, condemns the "social irresponsibility" of the days of '49 and rejoices that the welfare of the community now prevails over the unbridled vagaries and violences of the individual. But Royce's *California* should be read in the light of his *Philosophy of Loyalty*. Royce invariably holds a brief for the sanctity of the social order. Cherishing its interests as always paramount, he is unduly severe upon the happy-go-lucky, demoralized life of the Argonauts.

Well, in our day we have lived to see the spiritual appeal of the philosophy of loyalty cheapened into one-hundred-per-cent-ism. In the days of the frontier there were drives—of buffaloes on the plains or rabbits on the ranches; now there are drives of the employed and the impressionable for everything from Liberty Loans to Community Chests. Like the frightened rabbits of whose wholesale dispatching Norris writes in *The Octopus*, employees scuttle into the round-up; instead of submitting to occasional hold-ups from gallant desperadoes, they submit to systematic hold-ups from philanthropic citizens.

The figures of speech will not, I admit, bear pressing too far; but let them serve for what they are worth to illustrate a definite and crucial difference between the spirit of the California Argonauts and the spirit of Californians Incorporated. Perhaps the very immoralities which historical philosophers deplore, the very melodramatic incongruities which make western stories seem crude and meretricious when judged by abstract standards of narrative art, represent a safety valve once offered by the frontier and now withdrawn. The modern reaction against Bret Harte, Carl Van Doren tells us, is a reaction against the school of local color. He tells us that the school of local colorists is going out of vogue; may not the reason be that local color itself is going out of existence? Waldo Frank complains that Our America is "a land of buried cultures"; that in our zeal for Americanization we rob ourselves of the grace and beauty that Chinaman and Mexican and Indian would have offered us; that America has no local colors but a universal drab. Chesterton is surprised that Americans care so little for local traditions, that St. Louis, and Philadelphia, and San Francisco care so little for the associations of their founding, make so little poetry out of their history; that in Minneapolis "the factory chimneys might have been Pittsburgh, the sky signs might have been New York." But Mr. Chesterton is only a casual visitor, an English lecturer and journalist; the up-to-date American welcomes the standardization which Mr. Chesterton deplores. You remember Babbitt's favorite poem the column contribution of Chum Frink. In his travels he goes from one American city to another; he has moments when he is tempted to be homesick—but when he enters the "swell hotel" he finds the same magazines, the same menus, the same line of talk from representative Rotarians. And his soul is comforted by this obliteration of sectional variations: "For in these States where'er I roam, I'm always in my home, sweet home."

It is only logical that Professor Turner should follow

his monograph on "The Significance of the Frontier" by one on "The Significance of the Section." The sectionalism produced by frontier isolation, the eccentricity permitted by frontier independence, furnished the distinctive settings and the distinctive characters for the local color stories which had their inception on the frontier of '49. These picturesque variations are ironed out by the regimentations which rule Main Street, which bring the rebellious Babbitt back to norm. The triumph of standardization is possible only after the passing of the frontier.

BIBLIOGRAPHY

I. On the Period

CANFIELD, CHAUNCEY
The Diary of a Forty Niner
Boston; Houghton Mifflin Co., 1920

CLAPP, LOUISE A. (Dame Shirley)
The Shirley Letters from California Mines in 1851–52
San Francisco; T. C. Russell, 1922
(Originally printed in *Pioneer Magazine* of 1854–55)

DELANO, A.
Life on the Plains and Among the Diggings
New York; Miller, Orton & Co., 1857

HASKINS, C. W.
The Argonauts of California
New York; Fords, Howard & Hulburt, 1890

HOWE, OCTAVIUS T.
Argonauts of '49
Cambridge; Harvard Univ. Press, 1923

KNOWER, DANIEL
Adventures of a Forty Niner
Albany; Weed-Parsons Printing Co., 1894

KINGSLEY, NELSON
Diary [edited by Frederick J. Teggert]
in publications of the Academy of Pacific Coast History, vol. 3, no. 3

ROYCE, JOSIAH
California
Boston and New York; Houghton Mifflin Co., 1886

RUSS, CAROLYN H.
The Log of a Forty Niner
Boston; B. J. Brimmer Co., 1923
SHINN, CHARLES H.
Mining Camps: A Study in American Frontier Government
New York; Chas. Scribner's Sons, 1885
WHITE, STEWART E.
The Forty Niners
New Haven; Yale Univ. Press, 1921

II. On Bret Harte
Works: Standard Library Edition, 20 vol. During his lifetime his works were issued in forty-nine successive volumes between 1867 and 1902. His best known tales of California are included in *The Luck of Roaring Camp and other sketches* and in *The Tales of the Argonauts.*
Critical and biographical material:
MERWIN, HENRY C.
The Life of Bret Harte
Boston and New York; Houghton Mifflin Co., 1911
REAU, A. CECILE
La Société Californienne de 1850 d'après Bret Harte
Paris; Ollier-Henry, 1921
Critical articles in:
ERSKINE, JOHN
Leading American Novelists
PATTEE, FRED L.
History of American Literature since 1870

III. On Mark Twain
See bibliography to chapter VI.

CHAPTER VI

THE GILDED AGE OF INDUSTRIAL PIONEERING

I. EXPLOITATION OF NATURAL RESOURCES: THE MASTERS OF CAPITAL

"LAND" in the technical jargon of economists is understood to include all natural resources. This connotation of the word should be emphasized when we speak of the frontier as affording "free land." This free land included not only the surface of the earth over which the trapper could hunt his furs, on which the settler could establish his home, but gold mines, coal beds, and oil wells, timber claims, water power. Albert Shaw writing in the *South Atlantic Quarterly* of "Our Legacy from a Century of Pioneers" discusses this legacy in terms of exploitation of natural resources by the masters of capital, and pronounces the greatest triumph of the pioneering period in America to be "the creation of a great body of capitalized wealth." The decade before the Civil War saw the extension of the American frontier to the Pacific. The decade after the Civil War saw the capitalization of the national domain on a scale unprecedented in human history. The newly acquired territories were spanned by railroads, the railroads were followed by mushroom growths of boom towns. The disbanded veterans of the grand army were speedily absorbed by the western lands. The "irrepressible conflict" was succeeded by an era of irrepressible confidence. The aftermath of Appomattox is written in terms of grandiose schemes floated on preposterously inflated credits; of financial panics and political scandals; of gold conspiracies, Credit Mobiliers, and Tweed rings; of millionaires who began as messenger boys; of inventions that transform the egalitarian democracy of Jefferson into the mechanistic plutocracy of Jay Cooke; of wizards of finance who juggle with the resources and enterprises of the continent. Regional pioneering gives place to industrial pioneering; the age of discovery and occupation and annexation is succeeded by the age of Big Business.

The era of Big Business was, it is true, the child of the Industrial Revolution; but it was also the child of the frontier. The transformation which the Industrial Revolution wrought in England, in Europe, was modified by the presence of a hereditary aristocracy, by more or less paternalistic governments, by limitation of natural resources. The United States remained almost untouched by the Industrial Revolution until nearly a half century after the Victorian Compromise; but when in the decade of the seventies the United States took her place among industrial nations there was no suggestion of compromise. It was an era, says Van Wyck Brooks, "when presidents were business men, and generals were business men, and preachers were business men." In other words, the "higher classes" were not leisure classes—they would have spurned the imputation with contempt; writers, and clergy, and statesmen aimed at business methods, business "efficiency." It was but a step from a genuine admiration of the business man to a grateful reliance upon his favors, which at its worst, was unblushing corruption, which at its best, made the political and intellectual leaders of the country mere henchmen of the triumphant bourgeoisie. As for the "lower classes," the organization of labor, then in its infancy, was retarded and handicapped by the tradition that every industrious workman could rise to be a capitalist. Anything like solidarity of the labor cause was impossible as long as the cult of the self-made millionaire inspired the workman to rise out of his class rather than redress the wrongs of his class.

Thanks to the frontier, industrialism had in America a triumphal progress unhampered by effectual protest from above or below. First of all, the frontier contributed the essential physical conditions: abundant natural resources afforded prizes well worth striving for; while they enlisted the energies of the supermen, the captains of industry, they contented the average man with a modest measure of prosperity. Secondly, the frontier contributed the essential philosophical conditions. Frontier democracy necessarily fortified itself with pragmatic rationalizations. The test of a measure was "Will it work?" The test of an individual was "Can he make good? Can he deliver the goods?" In a new country, freed from inhibiting precedents and traditions, no stratifications of class, no meddlesome interference of government checked the career of the aggressive individual. On the contrary, social judgments encouraged a rampant individualism. If a section grew conservative, tended to rigidify along class lines, there was always a new field for opportunity springing up somewhere farther west where ambitious young men could make a future for themselves; the reaction of this new progressive center upon the old tended, as Professor Turner has shown, to dissolve conservatism before it had time to harden. American idealisms, as we have seen in the case of the transcendentalists, followed the frontier pattern, bestowed the accolade upon the frontier character.

The age of Big Business contributed new elements to American literature: a new setting—the secret chambers of the masters of capital where the resources of the newly developed country were shuffled and staked in the game of high finance; a new plot—the rise from poverty and obscurity to wealth and notoriety by shrewd manipulation of speculative values; a new character—the alchemist of capitalism whose daring touch transmutes the potentialities of the frontier into gold; a new philosophy—the glorification of success. These by-products of the frontier colored American literature after 1865 as they dominated American life. It is as we seek in American literature successive portraits of titanic financiers that we find the most significant revelation of the Gilded Age, from the grandiose proclamations of its inception to the ominous "Mene, Mene, Tekel, Upharsin" of its decay,

II. ANDREW CARNEGIE: TRIUMPHANT DEMOCRACY

We are fortunate in being able to derive our first impressions of the Gilded Age from an author who was also an actor, who writes in soaring superlatives of an age in which he had played a great part, who reduces to unctuous platitudes for the benefit of young aspirants the Gospel of Wealth which had made him the steel king of the world. With unconscious irony, this uncrowned monarch ascribed his success to the lavish largesse of "Triumphant Democracy."

In the life of Andrew Carnegie we have that most popular of all themes—the Dick Whittington motif of the poor boy rising by worth and perseverance (and lucky chance) to a position of wealth and honor. The American frontier with its unstratified society, with its bountiful opportunities, translated this pleasing theme of fiction into actual fact. The frontier gave us our Lincoln—and a half century later we still hug the flattering delusion that a boy may be born in a log cabin and rise to the White House. The frontier gave us our Carnegie—and a half century later we still hug the flattering delusion that a boy may begin at $1.20 a week and die a multi-millionaire.

The Industrial Revolution which brought Carnegie to poverty in Scotland brought him to wealth in America. Andrew's father, a master weaver at one time owner of four damask looms and employer of apprentices, was driven out of business by the advent of steam looms. Indelibly stamped on Andrew's youthful consciousness was the terrible day when his father came home to say: "Andy, I have no more work." Like thousands before and since who have found themselves in a similar situation, the Carnegies turned to America. The marching song of the Carnegies, like the marching song of the Garlands, catches the specious lure of the sunset regions:

> To the West, to the West, to the land of the free
> Where the mighty Missouri rolls down to the sea;
> Where a man is a man even though he must toil
> And the poorest may gather the fruits of the soil.

The Carnegies' migration led them as far west as Pittsburgh where Andrew, then a boy of thirteen, started his business career as a bobbin boy working from dawn till dark, with only an interval of forty minutes for dinner, and receiving $1.20 a week. His first promotion was in the form of added responsibility rather than added prosperity. He was employed to fire the boiler and run the steam engine which drove the machinery of a small factory—a heavy responsibility for a lad of thirteen, since, as he well knew, one false move on his part might cause the whole place to be blown to atoms. Even in his hours of sleep, the pressure of anxiety weighed upon the boy, who in troubled dreams would reach out his hand to test the water gauge.

A year later we find Andrew working as telegraph boy at $3.00 a week, pooling the earnings of the telegraph boys from specials, dividing his spare time between practicing telegraphy and patronizing the free library provided by the generosity of a Mr. Anderson. Then we follow him through his service as telegraph operator on the railroad; we see him with characteristic audacity plunging in and giving orders on his own responsibility for straightening out the movement of trains. We see him making his first modest investment, jumping at the chance offered him by his superior to buy ten shares of Adams Express though it involved putting a mortgage on their humble home. With equally unflinching promptness of decision, he accepts Mr. Scott's offer to accompany him to Altoona where in 1856 Mr. Scott had been promoted to be general superintendent of the Pennsylvania railroad. Here as always with Andrew Carnegie, it was Business First. "This breaking up of associations in Pittsburgh was a sore trial, but nothing could be allowed to interfere for a moment with my business career." This decision was rewarded by eventual promotion to be superintendent of the Pittsburgh division. Indefatigable in his labors—he boasted that "snatches of half an hour's sleep at intervals during the night in a dirty freight car were sufficient"—instant in his recognition of opportunity—as in the immediate closure of the Woodruff sleeping car proposition—his rise continues at a constantly accelerating rate, until we find him no longer an employee of the railroad, but owning his own transportation facilities, possessed of seven great iron and steel works, owning thousands of acres of coal lands, controlling the destinies of thousands of workmen, finally naming his own price for the disposal of his properties in the greatest sale in history, and determined to avoid the disgrace of dying rich, deliberately devoting his closing years to authorship, philanthropy, and—crowning irony of the steelmaster!—to the promotion of world peace.

In Scotland in 1848 the Industrial Revolution made of the boy Andrew Carnegie a Chartist whose dearest pride was the insurgent flag which his father and uncle cherished as a secret emblem of their protest against a world in which they were no longer able to make a living. In America in 1892 the Industrial Revolution made of the man Andrew Carnegie a capitalist who was discreetly absent, inaccessible to the intervention of benevolent mediators while his colleagues put down the Homestead strike with the aid of Pinkertons and electrically wired ramparts. The Chartist of the Old World has become the capitalist of the New. He ascribes the transformation to Triumphant Democracy; we may be more inclined to ascribe it to the Benevolent Frontier.

Triumphant Democracy was published in 1886, inspired by Carnegie's desire to stagger the land of his birth by showing the strides that had been made in fifty years' march by the land of his adoption. The opening paragraph strikes the theme which is harped upon as Carnegie considers every phase of American life, which is demonstrated with imposing arrays of statistics, which is celebrated with ludicrously fulsome rhapsodies:

> The old nations of the earth creep on at a snail's pace; the Republic thunders past with the rush of the express. The United States, the growth of a single century, has already reached the foremost rank among nations, and is destined soon to outdistance all others in the race. In population, in wealth, in annual savings, and in public credit; in freedom from debt, in agriculture, and in manufactures, America already leads the civilized world.

Mr. Carnegie then proceeds to proclaim the superiority of America in every aspect: her government with its senate, "the most august assembly in the world"—"marvelous in efficiency and strength"; its constitution, "the most perfect piece of work ever struck off at one time by the mind and purpose of man"; its presidents, "uniformly poor and pure"; its universal suffrage, leveling all distinctions, giving the "vote of a Lincoln or an Emerson no more weight than that of the poorest negro";

her manufactures, from Bessemer steel to thread; her agriculture—sometimes, he admits so unremunerative to the farmer that he is driven to burn the corn for which he can find no market, but nevertheless a stable factor in the national wealth; her literature—as evidence of whose excellence Mr. Carnegie cites the facts that eighty tons of paper were used in printing Scribner's "Statistical Atlas of the United States," and that General Grant made $250,000 from the sale of his *Personal Memoirs* while the less efficient Englishman John Milton disposed of *Paradise Lost* for five pounds. The paean of praise swells to its highest when Mr. Carnegie takes up the subject of America's natural resources. On the one hand, he records with pride the rapid advance from frontier settlements to commercial cities, the improvement of facilities for transportation, the phenomenal utilization of mines and timber. On the other hand, he refuses to admit the possibility that these resources may not be inexhaustible and that with their exhaustion will come a modification of the benefits which he attributes to triumphant democracy. In Mr. Carnegie's conception, these resources are self-renewing, perennial, infinite. They are accepted without analysis or forethought as part of God's beneficently bountiful provision for the United States.

In his life and in his writings Carnegie exemplified the *Weltanschauung* which marked the inception of the Gilded Age. He embodied the finest characteristics of the first masters of capital. He rose from poverty and obscurity by his own industry and intelligence. He was conscientiously opposed to speculation on the Stock Exchange and acquired his fortune by conservative and legitimate investments. He held in all sincerity a trustee theory of wealth, early conceiving and consistently executing a plan for stopping the amassing of a fortune and devoting his closing years to its intelligent and systematic distribution. He was a Puritan in conduct, though not in theology, tenderly affectionate in his personal, scrupulously honorable in his public relationships.

When this benevolent capitalist writes of "The Gospel of Wealth" and "The Empire of Business" he gives us the first version of the creed of the industrial pioneer. His enthusiasm for the country, his faith in the resources and future of the country, are unbounded. Amid such opportunities, if a man fails to make good it is *prima facie* evidence that there is something wrong with him. A career is open to talents. He is fond of quoting Emerson: "No young man can be cheated out of an honorable career in life, unless he cheats himself." Success is not merely an opportunity but an obligation. "It becomes the duty of the millionaire to increase his revenues. .The struggle for more is completely freed from selfish or ambitious taint and becomes a noble pursuit." This noble pursuit calls for a dedication as exacting as was ever demanded from a squire determined to win his spurs, from a novice eager to make his profession. The candidate for business success must "concentrate his attention, his efforts upon the performance of his duties to his employer. All other studies, occupations, and all amusements are subordinate to the business which holds paramount sway." By a similar process of simplification and concentration, Carnegie achieves a philosophy. With unconscious blasphemy, he attaches a "new meaning" to the words of Christ, "The kingdom of Heaven is within you." Translated into the pragmatic language of the industrial frontier, this becomes: "All our duties lie in this world and in the present, and trying impatiently to peer into that which lies beyond is as vain as fruitless."

But even to a mind as remote from philosophical complexities as Andrew Carnegie's there is apparent a slight discrepancy between the Gospel of Wealth which he enthusiastically preaches and the law of competition which he recognizes as inevitable. His formula for success is, "Conduct your business with just a little more ability than the average man in your line." But one cannot escape from the converse of this proposition which implies that the other fellow must be conducting his business with a little less ability than you; your margin of superiority is his margin of inferiority, your proportion of success, his proportion of failure. Hence even the Gospel according to St. Andrew is forced to qualify its religion of energetic optimism by reluctant recognition of the men who are not successful; who remain wage workers, or at best, salaried employees, while the superman of industry piles up his profits.

This class is constitutionally distasteful to the benevolent despot of steel. True, he is fond of talking about the dignity of labor, of eulogizing the traditional laborer who recapitulates Carnegie's own career, beginning by sweeping out the office and ending as a financial magnate. But labor, from Carnegie's point of view, is honorable only as a transition stage. It's all very well to begin by sweeping out the office—but how despicable to end there! Or even to be so spineless as to stop half way up. Carnegie speaks with pitying contempt of those "doomed to a salaried life." The genius of industry is the man who can control the labor of others. "The supremely great managers, such as you have these days never do any work themselves worth speaking about; their point is that they make others work while they think."

But sometimes the great Carnegie thinks of his workmen—those low-grade citizens whose labor is the connecting link between the resources of the ravished continent and the master mind that transforms these raw materials into finished products and fabulous profits; those unsuccessful, unimaginative toilers who depend upon his plants for their daily wage, who, when that wage is cut, humbly address him as their "Kind Master"

—supreme irony of "triumphant democracy" . . . "Kind Master, tell us what you want us to do, and we will do it." And even the sanguinely successful Carnegie is unable to glorify the condition of these serfs in his empire of business. Returning to Pittsburgh after his trip around the world, he observed that "the Americans were the saddest looking race we had ever seen." Nor can he escape from the conclusion that this sadness is directly due to the demands of his very Gospel of Wealth. "Life is so terribly earnest here. Ambition urges us all on, from him who handles a spade to him who employs thousands. We know no rest. . . . Extra work is forced by the tremendous drive and pressure of the American system. The men are bent upon earning high wages and the masters are determined to beat all competition. Progress, the accumulation of wealth, complete supremacy over all competitors, these are the paramount considerations and everything else is disregarded."

But Carnegie never falters in his faith that his adored Juggernaut deserves the homage of human sacrifices. He is dumbfounded by the incomprehensible indifference of Matthew Arnold to the offered treat of a visit to the slaughter houses of Chicago "with new machines so perfected that the hog driven in at one end came out in hams at the other before its squeal was out of one's ears." "Why should one go to slaughter houses, why should one hear pigs squeal?" asked the apostle of sweetness and light. And the apostle of the gospel of wealth could find no answer. What could one say to a man who, for some strange reason, failed to realize that the ingenious mechanisms of Big Business were objects of veneration? But Carnegie, high priest of the Gilded Age, is unwavering in his devotion to its idols, in proclamation of its dual creed of SUCCESS and SERVICE. For the superman of industry whom he embodied in his life and described in his writings is axiomatically assumed to be not only a shining example but a practical support to his less able countrymen. If rabid radicals couple "progress and poverty," Carnegie comes back with: "I know that my 'progress' has inevitably carried with it, not the growing 'poverty' but the growing riches of my fellow countrymen, as the progress of every employer of labor must necessarily carry with it the enrichment of the country and of the laborer." Carnegie anticipates Upton Sinclair in pointing out that, "It is to business men following business careers that we chiefly owe our universities, colleges, libraries, and educational institutions." Addressing an audience of potential millionaires he says: "I assume that you save and long for wealth only as a means of enabling you the better to do some good in your day and generation." The riches amassed by the genius of the industrial pioneer are "to be regarded as a sacred trust to be administered by its possessor into whose hands it flows for the highest good of the people." Thus on the frontier of finance, we find an echo of the casuistry of the Puritan frontier, the persistent American myth which glorifies the success of the strong by Divine sanction, which rationalizes it by benevolent result.

III. MARK TWAIN: SON AND SATIRIST OF THE GILDED AGE

Like Andrew Carnegie, Samuel Clemens rose in a meteoric career from a humble origin to a spectacular fame. A friend and admirer of Carnegie, Clemens like him was both a capitalist and an author, both actor and analyst of the Gilded Age. But unlike the steelmaster, Mark Twain, while profiting from the Gilded Age, wrote of it with a fierce undercurrent of savage criticism. The extent to which this criticism was suppressed or modified, the reasons for its suppression and modification, and the effect of this censorship on the genius of Mark Twain, have been brilliantly suggested by Van Wyck Brooks in *The Ordeal of Mark Twain.* Like most theses, this book suffers from its attempt to prove too much; intrigued by a Freudian curiosity concerning Mark Twain's wife and mother, Mr. Brooks is diverted from a consideration of Mark Twain's social purposes to an investigation of his personal complexes. The newest of critical methods results in the old *Cherchez la femme:* the women in the case are found responsible for the alleged miscarriage of Mark Twain's genius. Absorbed in the decanonization of "Livy," Mr. Brooks loses sight of the larger social group whose standards, motives, and activities made up the *Zeitgeist* of the sensational seventies; he underestimates the extent to which Mark Twain was himself a product of the Gilded Age, like Hawthorne impotently critical of the forces which had entered into the very fiber of his being.

In the career of Mark Twain we have the recapitulation of the successive stages of American pioneering. He was born into a family sustained by the hope of ultimate riches from the Tennessee land. His childhood was passed in squalid, straggling hamlets of the southwestern frontier. Following his short-lived profession as a pilot, his travels took him to the far western frontier, where he roughed it as a pocket miner, sometimes becoming "a millionaire for ten days," sometimes slinking through back streets to avoid his creditors, finally emerging as newspaper writer and lecturer. The early life of Mark Twain is, then, one conditioned by the environment of regional pioneering. This life passes by imperceptible degrees into that of industrial pioneering. He soon tires of the actual work involved in mining; it is much more fun, much more profitable to trade stock. "We had learned the real secret of success in silver mining which was, not to mine the silver ourselves by the sweat of our brows and the labor of our hands, but to *sell* the ledges to the dull slaves of toil and let them do the mining!" At this period comes his meeting with Anson Burlingame and the memorable advice, "Never affiliate with inferiors, Climb!" Mark Twain enters upon a literary career, not so much as an end in itself, but as a means to an end, a capitalizing of his brains by which he may achieve the Open Sesame into the world of his admiration. Throughout his life we find him involved in one speculative scheme after another. He was always quite as much the speculator as the author—often an author only that he might finance the latest pet speculation or retrieve the breach it had made in his fortunes. The Page type setting machine is the symbol of his implication in the hazards of industrial pioneering as the Tennessee land is the symbol of his implication in the hazards of regional pioneering. But the Page machine was only one of many fantastic projects, neither the first nor the last of his stakes in the game of Big Business.

So far Clemens like Carnegie, is the son of the Gilded Age. But he lacks Carnegie's implicit filial loyalty. He sides as instinctively with the underdog as Carnegie does with the superman. His sympathy with labor unions was strong in the days when labor unions were new and consequently even more suspect than they are today. While Carnegie prides himself on a clever maneuver by which he outwits the union representatives and preserves the principle of individual bargaining, Mark Twain writes with glee of the success of the Pilots' Protective Organization in bringing their employers to terms. He refuses to report an insolent brakeman, restrained by the thought that it is hardly fair to expect the manners of a Sydney from an employee who is paid only twenty dollars a month.

This compassion for failure prevents Mark Twain from paying unreserved homage to success. The fatal cleavage which Mr. Brooks has traced in his nature represents not so much superimposed inhibitions of Howells, of *The Atlantic Monthly,* of Mrs. Clemens, as a divided self which, on the one hand, admires the gentility, the ease, the power, which are the rewards of success, and on the other, has a tenderness for the pathetic fools of fortune, a fierce contempt for the hypocrisy and greed and cruelty underlying the social conspiracy which assures the success of the successful. Hence even in his gayest writings about the Gilded Age there is a note of satire.

We have already discussed *Roughing It* as a picture of a frontier community. We shall mention it here as an example of the Get-Rich-Quick spirit which animated the Gilded Age. The picturesque and picaresque aspects of the days of '49 are played up by Mark Twain as by Bret Harte for all they are worth. But the tragic significance of this picturesque community with its picaresque heroes haunts Mark Twain and creeps in among his most exuberant pieces of horseplay. Thus after a description of early days in the Sacramento Valley couched in superlatives worthy of a Californiac, Mark Twain asks: "And where are they now? Scattered to the ends of the earth—or prematurely aged and decrepit, or shot or stabbed in street affrays—or dead of disappointed hopes and broken hearts—all gone or nearly all—victims devoted upon the altar of the golden calf—the noblest holocaust that ever wafted its sacrificial incense heavenward. It is pitiful to think upon."

Life on the mining frontier was a beggar's revel of potential millionaires without the price of a square meal. Great expectations furnished a joy in life undampened by any discrepancy with actual fulfillment. "Every man believed that his little wild cat claim was as good as any on the 'main lead' and would infallibly be worth a thousand dollars a foot when 'he got down where it came in solid.' Poor fellow, he was blessedly blind to the fact that he never would see that day. So the thousand wild cat shafts burrowed deeper and deeper into the earth day by day, and all men were beside themselves with hope and happiness. How they labored, prophesied, exulted! Surely nothing like it was ever seen before since the world began. . . . One would suppose that when month after month went by and still not a wild cat mine yielded a ton of rock worth crushing, the people would begin to wonder if they were not putting too much faith in their prospective riches; but there was not a thought of such a thing. They burrowed away, bought and sold and were happy."

The many whose mines brought little, if any, return were eclipsed in the popular mind by the few who made fabulous fortunes overnight. Mark Twain devotes a chapter to Nevada nabobs created by lucky strikes. Two teamsters, obliged to take a share in a silver mine in lieu of wages for hauling, a year later were receiving an income of one hundred thousand dollars a year apiece from the property that had been forced upon them. A humble hay farmer traded a few acres of his ranch for a small undeveloped silver mine; eighteen months afterwards, he retired from the hay business with an income of thirty to sixty thousand dollars a month. A few instances of this sort obscured many failures and produced an atmosphere of unreasoning optimism. In these boom days, wrote Mark Twain: "Joy sat on every countenance, and there was a glad, almost fierce intensity in every eye that told of the money getting schemes that were seething in every brain and the high hope that held sway in every heart. Money was as plenty as dust; every individual considered himself wealthy, and a melancholy countenance was nowhere to be seen." Those were the days when money was so plentiful that the problem was not how to get it but how to spend it, when men gave each other presents of feet in mines as nonchalantly as they would offer each other a cigar; when the flour sack put up for sale for the benefit of the U. S. Sanitary Commission sold for the grand total of a hundred and fifty thousand dollars. The hectic stimulation of these boom days measured the depth of the depression that followed a general collapse, when the bottom dropped out of Gould and Curry, for instance, "and everything and everybody went to ruin and destruction." Never was the shifting society of the frontier more dramatically exemplified than in the mining communities where "every sun that rose in the morning went down on paupers enriched and rich men beggared."

The uproarious fun of *Roughing It* is interspersed with pity and irony for the frenzies of speculation. But for a fully developed picture of the temper of industrial pioneering we must turn to the novel which Mark Twain wrote in collaboration with Charles Dudley Warner, to which he gave the title that best characterizes the era he is depicting—*The Gilded Age*. In this novel Mark Twain utilized the family tragedy of the Tennessee land; he drew the portrait of Colonel Sellers from his mother's cousin James Lampton, the portraits of Squire Hawkins and Washington Hawkins from the chronically unsuccessful pioneers, his father and his brother Orion. He staged his farcical melodrama against a background of the scandals of the seventies: the Tweed ring, the Salary Grab Act, the travesty of Congressional "investigations" as practiced in the Credit Mobilier affair, the lobbying and bribery by which measures were put through Congress for the benefit of the ingenious financier. But the novel is historical in a deeper sense than the mere employment of actual persons and events. Vitiated as it is from the literary point of view by two flimsy plots, it is significant from the historical point of view as a portrayal of the gambling spirit of the financial frontier; the spectacular reversals of fortune, the alternations of hope and despair in the devotees of quick profits. This spirit is crystallized in two characters: Colonel Sellers and Senator Dillworthy. Reference to the division of labor between Clemens and Warner as indicated in the Paine biography of Mark Twain, will show that Mark Twain was responsible for the chapters featuring Sellers and Dillworthy, while Warner was responsible for the sub-plot concerning Philip Sterling and Ruth Bolton. With this in mind, it appears singular that Van Wyck Brooks, the one critic to estimate the relation of Mark Twain to the Gilded Age, limits his discussion of the novel almost entirely to the story of Philip's search for the coal mine. Mr. Brooks devotes a few casual and superficial sentences to Colonel Sellers and makes no mention at all of Senator Dillworthy. Yet it is these two who form a composite picture of the character produced by the Gilded Age as seen by one who regarded it with both fascination and contempt.

In the inimitable Eschol Sellers Mark Twain portrayed the chronic pioneer of industrialism in his most lovable guise. Even Sellers' victims can hold no grudge against him, he is so palpably self-deceived. He lives in a world of splendid illusions; the wealth and fame which are always just around the corner are more real to him than the turnips and water on which he feeds, the candle-lit stove which makes a brave pretense of warmth in his shabby house. His exuberant optimism is born of a passionate faith in the future of the country. "The whole country is opening up; all we want is capital to develop it. Slap down the rails and bring the land into market. The richest land on God Almighty's footstool is lying right out there. If I had my capital free I could plant it for millions."

Of all Sellers' grotesque projects, the most significant is his boosting of Stone's Landing; with true insight, Mark Twain develops this, making it pivotal to the plot.

The religious fervor of pioneering glorifies Sellers' vision of this town; he sees it, not as it is—a mere matter of a dozen miserable cabins on the prairie beside a crooked, sluggish stream—but as it will be when the "Columbus River" by means of the government appropriation has been widened and deepened and straightened and the "city of Napoleon" is a flourishing metropolis on the new railroad. Not lightly does he couple the name of the Almighty with his schemes for boosting and developing this embryo municipality. He is as sure as the Puritan pioneers that he is a partner in the Divine purposes—if the methods used to carry out these purposes appear at times questionable, he exonerates himself by the old maxim of religious fanaticism, that the end justifies the means. In his spontaneous enthusiasm, his touching trustfulness, his persistent hopefulness, his resourceful ingenuity, his openhearted generosity, he epitomizes the irresistible, lighthearted buoyancy of the era of crazy schemes. Mrs. Hawkins sums him up in a happy phrase, "It's always sunrise with that man."

But if Mark Twain draws the figure of Eschol Sellers with affectionate raillery, he compensates for it by the savage contempt with which he delineates Senator Dillworthy. Like Colonel Sellers, Senator Dillworthy gambles on the future of the undeveloped country; like Colonel Sellers he glibly links the name of the Almighty with his purposes. But we feel that Senator Dillworthy is an unctuous hypocrite while Colonel Sellers is a sincere fanatic. The Senator lends himself facilely as a partner in Colonel Sellers' scheme for getting the government to improve Columbus River; in Washington Hawkins' scheme of getting the government to buy the Tennessee land for a negro university. He makes inflated speeches before Sunday Schools, holding himself up as a glorious example of a poor boy who rose from a humble home to the Senate—thanks to the Sunday

School and Sunday School morality. Finally detected in bribery, he asks for a "suspension of public opinion" and later for an "investigation" which develops, as such investigations have been known to do in more recent times, into an indignant investigation of the informer.

The significant addition which Mark Twain makes to the interpretation of the business man in American literature is the relation of Big Business to the government. The Triumphant Democracy of Andrew Carnegie's effusive eulogy is here shown for the first time as the soiled plaything of a little group of greedy men. Not only in the main plot, but in incidental comments, Mark Twain flays the prostitution of government by the lust of self-aggrandizing profiteers. The sketch of the rise of O'Reilly who "furnished shingle nails to the new Court House at three thousand dollars a keg, and eighteen gross of 60-cent thermometers at fifteen hundred dollars a dozen," the remarks on the career of Balloon as Indian agent, are written, not in admiration of the cleverness and energy displayed by these shrewd manipulators of public funds, but in passionate disgust at the fraud and chicanery by which the successful arrive at their success. He pierces the flimsy structure of "prosperity" and shows the rotten foundation on which it rests, the cheap pretense of its success, the squalid misery of its failures, the waste of energy and talents in the pursuit of its glittering delusions.

Gifted with a fatal insight into the hollowness of the Gilded Age, Mark Twain takes refuge in a philosophy of fatalism. It is, of course, mere evidence of the curious gaps in his culture that he should for a moment have imagined that his conception of man as the victim of his temperament and environment was a new one. But it was, at least, new in American philosophy and marks the first ominous sign of the disintegration in the frontier morale, in the cult of the strongwilled individual which prevailed in the Golden Age of regional pioneering. The conquering hero of Irving's history, of Emerson's philosophy, of Carnegie's autobiography and addresses, disappears. Throughout Mark Twain's writings the heroic myth of the frontier is treated with cynical contempt. His frontier towns are not democratic communities of fraternity and equality, but crude, squalid villages. His frontier characters are desperadoes or fools. In *Life on the Mississippi* he gives a suggestive variant on Turner's procession of the frontier:

> How solemn and beautiful is the thought that the earliest pioneer of civilization, the vanleader of civilization, is never the steamboat, never the railroad, never the newspapers, never the Sabbath School, never the missionary—but always whiskey! Such is the case. Look history over; you will see. The missionary comes after the whiskey—I mean, he arrives after the whiskey has arrived; next comes the poor immigrant with axe and hoe and rifle; next, the trader; next the miscellaneous rush; next the gambler, the desperado, the highwayman, and all their kindred in sin of both sexes; and next, the smart chap who has bought up an old grant that covers all the land; this brings in the lawyer tribe; the vigilance committee brings the undertaker. All these interests bring the newspaper; the newspaper starts up politics and a railroad; all hands turn to and build a church and a jail—and behold, civilization is established forever in the land.[1]

Mark Twain finds himself confronted by the spectacle of a world where the strong use their strength in brutal and unscrupulous domination, where the shrewd achieve their purposes by contemptible trickery, where the weak struggle in vain. He is too intelligent to join in the blind adulation of the successful, he is too tenderhearted to join in the superior scorn of the unsuccessful, he is too deeply involved in the hazards and triumphs of the Gilded Age to extricate himself from it and launch such

[1] The quotations in this book from the works of Mark Twain are used by permission of Harper and Brothers, New York, publishers of "Roughing It," and "Life on the Mississippi."

an unqualified invective as was poured forth a generation later by the muckrakers. He takes refuge in a philosophy of fatalism which transfers the responsibility from the individual to the universal.

What is Man? he asks, and answers the eternal question to his own satisfaction: Man is a chameleon, the creature of his environment; man is an automaton, the victim of his temperament, a mere pawn of inscrutable forces over which he has no control, for which he has no responsibility. Not blind enough to be the idolater of the Gilded Age, not brave enough to be its iconoclast, Mark Twain evolves this ingenious compromise. He portrays the Gilded Age as a spectacle for scornful laughter. He reveals the paltriness of its heroes, the pitifulness of its victims. He demolishes forever two solacing myths of triumphant democracy: that the success of the strong is a benefit to their less gifted fellows, and that the successful deserve credit for their success. The critic who would trace the apparently strange development of American literature from easy optimism to bitter naturalism, must go back to the high hopes and tragic disillusionments of the Gilded Age and to the fatalistic formula by which Mark Twain attempted to endure an irrational universe.

IV. ROBERT HERRICK: THE STORY OF A SELF-MADE SENATOR

Herrick's *Memoirs of an American Citizen* is apparently built on the timehonored model of records of success. Edward Harrington, like the typical frontiersman, begins his career by running away from home. He reaches Chicago with only a few cents in his pocket and starts his life in that city as a vagrant tramping by night along the railroad tracks to keep from freezing, tramping by day through the business district asking for a job.

He finally finds an opening as a clerk at a small meat market at ten dollars a week. By following the conventional formula of docility and industry he gets two raises in pay. Presently the chance comes to buy out the business from the unsuccessful proprietors—to marry a fellow employee and settle down in "that plain, ordinary happiness which our unambitious fathers and mothers took out of life." But by this time Harrington is infected with the spirit of the city; he has more ambitious plans than settling down as the proprietor of a retail market. He has caught on to the methods by which the men higher up run the game; he determines to get in on it. As the Enterprise Market crumbled rapidly to its end, he kept his eyes open for a landing when he should have to jump. When the wholesale dealer Dround refused to continue credit to the Enterprise, Harrington went over to the packer, beginning again by driving a wagon at fifteen a week. He had the pioneer gift of imagination—the vision of the possibilities of things. His employment might seem to an outsider humble and prosaic enough, but it stirred his blood with a sense of latent power:

I liked it all. Something told me that here was my field—this square plot of prairie, where is carried on the largest commissariat business of the world. In spite of its filth and its ugly look, it fired my blood to be a part of it. There's something pretty close to the earth, in all of us, if we have the stomach to do the world's work; men of bone and sinew and rich blood—the strong men who do their deeds at the heads of the ranks, feed close to the earth. The lowing cattle in the pens, the squealing hogs in the cars, the smell of the fat carcasses in the heavy wagons—it all made me think of the soft fertile fields from which we take the grain—the blood and flesh that enter into our being.

The bigness of it all! The one sure fact before every son and daughter of woman is the need of daily bread and meat. To feed the people of the earth—that is a man's business.

My part was to drive a wagon for Dround at fifteen a week, but I walked out of the Yards with the swagger of a packer![1]

Unlike Carnegie's model youth, Harrington, impatient with the slow accumulation of capital from his savings, takes a flyer on the stock exchange. He clears four thousand dollars on his first speculation in pork, and buying out a small sausage and kosher business, becomes a packer on a small scale. He sells the business which cost him seven thousand for seventy thousand. From that point his rise is rapid; he assumes control of the business which was stagnating under the squeamish management of Henry Dround and with high handed audacity, squeezes out competitors, bids for rebates and franchises, bribes judges and legislators, and ends as creator of the American Meat Products Company, the meat king of Chicago. From that it is an easy step to the millionaires' club, the senate, and the triumph of his career is complete.

Yet not quite complete. Something is lacking in this picture—something of the wholehearted faith that glorified Carnegie's emperor of business. A disturbing note creeps in among the major chords, a recurrent suggestion of the price paid for wealth and fame, of elusive values which not all the millions of the sausage sovereign are able to buy. Harrington's wife is humiliated and broken by the attacks of press and pulpit upon her husband's business methods. His brother and his brother's wife refuse to have any relations with him, preferring to struggle on in their poverty rather than to accept help from one who had outraged their moral sense. The gentleman of the old school who was Harrington's first financial backer is the first to withdraw in grieved displeasure from an association which he considers dishon-

[1] The quotations in this book from "Memoirs of an American Citizen" by Robert Herrick, are used by permission of the Macmillan Company, New York, publishers.

orable. Harrington's earliest and best friends, his confederates in the shady transactions by which he fortified his business position, are morally degraded or professionally ostracized. All this the self-made senator is forced to set down on the debit side. "I was senator of these United States, from the great state of Illinois; but there were Hostetter, and the old banker Farson, and my best friend Slocum, and my brother Will and May and their little children, who stood to one side and turned away."

In self-defense, Harrington formulates a philosophy. It is a curious combination of the frontier philosophy of the superman and the emerging naturalistic philosophy of irresponsibility. On the one hand, he reiterates his belief that the world is for the strong and that he is one of the strong. On the other, he exonerates himself by the plea of necessity. Trapped in his factory by a vindictive anarchist, the capitalist reads his would-be assassin his gospel of inevitable competition: "I showed him how I was more bound than he, bound hand and foot, for he could run away and I couldn't." Mingled with this plea of necessity is an incongruous survival of the old excuse of "service." Harrington relies upon the old argument that he is a benefit not only to his investors but to his employees: "For thousands of such workers as live from day to day, depending on men like me to give them their chance to earn bread for their wives and children, I had made the world better rather than worse. Unthinking thousands lived and had children and got what good there was in life because of me and my will." Once in a moment of discouragement, Harrington, hard hit by the Spanish War panic, emotionally disturbed by the excitement of war psychology, considers running away, throwing up his interests, enlisting, starting over again on a selfless career. At the moment of this noble resolve he is approached by the very minister who had denounced him from his pulpit. The Reverend Mr. Hardman had invested his little all under Harrington's advice, and now worried by the panic, appeals to Harrington to take the bonds off his hands. Hard upon his heels follows a young doctor who has intrusted his savings to the financier. After he too had gone away reassured, Harrington sat down to think. "There were a good many others like these two—little people, or well-to-do who had put their faith in me and had trusted their money to my enterprises. Not much, each one; but in every case, a cruel sum to lose. They had brought me their savings, their legacies, because they knew me or had heard that I made money rapidly. Could I leave them now?"

So Harrington reinforces his position with the pleas of necessity and duty. He insists that his career be judged pragmatically, not according to the exacting requirements of some abstract system of ethics. He lived in a great age. "The greatest period of prosperity this country had ever seen was just starting. It was the time when two or three good gamblers could pick up any kind of property, give it a fine name, print a lot of pretty stock certificates, and sell their gold brick to the first comer. The people were crazy to spend their money. It was a great time!" In this strenuous time it was, according to his favorite phrase, a case of "Eat or be eaten." It was futile to judge the industrial pioneers of this Gilded Age by the simple axioms of more leisurely days. "No business in this large modern world could be done on her plan of life. That beautiful scheme of things which the fathers of the country drew up in the stagecoach days had proved itself inadequate in a short century. We had to get along with it the best we could. But we men who did the work of the world, who developed the country, who were the life and force of the times, could not be held back by the swaddling clothes of any political or moral theory. Results we must have: good results; and we worked with the tools we found at hand."

V. THEODORE DREISER: COWPERWOOD, THE CREATURE OF CHEMISTRY

The culminating portrait of the industrial pioneer is given us in Dreiser's *The Titan* and *The Financier,* novels directly based upon the notorious career of Charles Yerkes, the Chicago railroad king. Dreiser's interpretation, like those of preceding chroniclers of the Gilded Age, is colored by his own experiences and the outlook upon life which they have formed.

Dreiser is haunted by the realization of the complexity of life. Never able to reduce it to a simple formula which he finds adequate and satisfying, he contents himself with sketches of its wonder and mystery, its beauty and terror. In *A Book About Myself* he gives with more than the usual frankness of autobiography, his impressions as an unsuccessful spectator of life. He tosses helpless and bewildered in the maelstrom of the Gilded Age. "At that time, as I see it," he writes in 1892, "America was just entering upon the most lurid phase of that vast, splendid, most lawless and most savage period in which the great financiers were plotting and conniving at the enslavement of the people and belaboring each other." He contrasts with this maddened rush of industrialism, the peaceful, domestic idealism of the agricultural period. He visits his fiancée on the family farm in the backwoods of Missouri and wistfully appreciates a heritage lost to him. "To me it seemed that all the spirit of rural America, its idealism, its dreams, the passion of a Brown, the courage and patience and sadness of a Lincoln, the dreams and courage of a Lee or a Jackson were all here. The very soil smacked of

American idealism and faith, a fixedness in sentimental and purely imaginative American tradition in which I, alas, could not share—I had seen Pittsburgh."

One of the things he had seen at Pittsburgh was the Carnegie plant. As a newspaper reporter, he had studied conditions among the steel workers, had interviewed the steel master. He gives a graphic description of the homes of the Homestead laborers "who worked and lived in order that Mr. Carnegie might give the world one or two extra libraries with his name plastered on the front. It seemed astonishing to me that some men could thus rise and soar about the heavens like eagles while others, drab sparrows all, could only pick among the offal of the hot ways below. What were these things called democracy and equality about which men prated?"

This inability to reconcile or accept the tragic contrasts of the industrial regime underlies Dreiser's approach to the Gilded Age. He can never forget "the forgotten man" who plods along in patient, unremunerative toil, while the superman gambles with the profits of his labor. "I could never think of the work being done in any factory or institution without passing from that work to the lives behind it, the crowds of commonplace workers, the great streets which they filled, the bare homes, and the separate and distinct dramas of their individual lives. I was tremendously interested by the rise of various captains of industry then already bestriding America, their opportunities and pleasures, the ease and skill with which they organized trusts and combinations, their manipulation of the great railroads, oil and coal fields, their control of the telegraph and telephone, their sharp and watchful domination of American politics; but only as drama . . . it was the underdog who interested me more than the upper one, his needs, his woes, his simplicities."

Dreiser is constantly haunted by the question: What

constitutes the difference between the superman and the failures. Why do some men win fame and fortune from the same conditions that bring others to poverty and despair? Carnegie had a simple answer: Hard work, plus the conventional moralities, plus the manifold opportunities of triumphant democracy constituted the invariable formula for success. It had worked in his case, and in all sincerity he passed on the talisman to other candidates for industrial renown. Dreiser's observation of life fails to substantiate the simple philosophy. As Dreiser sees it: "Neither sobriety, nor virtue, nor continence nor incontinence was either a compelling or preventing cause of either success or failure . . . rather, men succeeded by virtue of something that was not intimately related to any of these."

So Dreiser gives us his picture of the financier who is, in the Emersonian phrase, "victory-organized." Frank Cowperwood is presented to us, not as a self-made superman, but as a creature of chemistry; a brilliant personality, a powerful intellect, it is true, but a man not responsible for his superior endowments of brain and will, a man impelled by the law of his being along a meteoric path of ruthless ambition and gratification. Occasionally we find in the analysis of Cowperwood a survival of the old rationalizing hypocrisy of "service": "He seemed a kind of superman, and yet also a bad boy . . . impelled by some blazing, internal force which harried him on and on, believing that men like himself were sent into the world to better perfect its mechanism and habitable order." But the consideration of improving the world—the Gospel of Wealth theory of trusteeship, plays a very minor role in Cowperwood's purposes. Whether in sexual or financial intrigues, his motto is "I satisfy myself."

Dreiser presents the titanic role of his financier against the background of American expansion. The challenge of the country enters into Cowperwood's earliest conception of life:

> Since his birth in 1837 he had seen the nation reach that physical perfection which it finally retained. Not so much earlier than his youth Florida had been added to the Union by purchase from Spain; Mexico after the unjust war of 1848 had ceded Texas and the territory to the West. The boundary disputes between England and the United States in the far Northwest had been finally adjusted. To a man with great social and financial imagination, these facts could not help but be significant; and if they did nothing more, they gave him sense of the boundless commercial possibilities which existed potentially in so vast a realm. He was not of that order of speculative financial enthusiasm which in the type known as the promoter sees endless possibilities for gain in every unexplored rivulet and prairie reach; but the very vastness of the country suggested possibilities which he hoped might remain undisturbed.[1]

To the exploitation of these possibilities Cowperwood brings a philosophy of misapplied Darwinism. As a boy he is fascinated by the contest between a squid and a lobster in a tank at the fishmarket. Day after day as he passes by he watches the pursuit of the squid by the lobster. Little by little, the squid's one means of defense, his ink-bag becomes empty; little by little, pieces of his body are torn off by his relentless foe. This tiny tragedy becomes for Cowperwood an allegory of life. The weak are inevitably destined to perish; the strong as inevitably destined to satisfy themselves at the expense of their less capable associates.

Cowperwood never doubts that he is one of the strong. In the beginning of his business career he silently sizes up his employers, learns from their limitations, determines to play with brilliant audacity the game they play

[1] The quotations in this book from the works of Theodore Dreiser are used by permission of Boni and Liveright, New York, publishers of the works of Theodore Dreiser.

with timorous conventionality. When in the full swing of his deals he is caught by the panic, is unable to cover his city loans and sentenced to a term in the penitentiary he accepts the failure as a temporary set-back—inconvenient, no doubt, but in no way reflecting on him, in no way prejudicing his future career. Upon receiving a pardon, he goes to Chicago, then a young city with dazzling opportunities for the daring. The industrial like the regional pioneer can go west and begin again in a more youthful and progressive community. The past is unknown or ignored. The future beckons, radiant, enchanting. One panic ruined him—a second brought him a second fortune. The dynamic urge of Chicago "that singing flame of a city" finds a response in the driving power of the Titan who becomes its master.

What is Dreiser's interpretation of this superman of finance? What role does he play in the drama of the Gilded Age? Neither that of hero, as in Carnegie's Empire of Business; nor that of villain as in the diatribes of the later muckrakers. Cowperwood and Cowperwood's victims alike are puppets directed by invisible wires. If the underdog with whom Dreiser sympathizes is not to blame for his failure, neither is the superman to be praised for his success. If the virtuous are not to be lauded for their conventional morality, neither are the unscrupulous to be condemned for seeking their own satisfaction. With Dreiser we find completed, intensified the philosophy of naturalism so far at variance from the frontier philosophy of free will, of a career open to talents. The apotheosis of the assertive individual has been reached—and the hour of its triumph is also the hour of its decay. Few can succeed where many must fail; the glorification of success is swiftly followed by the rationalization of failure. The gilded veneer of a gold-greedy age is chipped and broken revealing the baser metal. The superman of industry is a superman no longer, but at best a super-puppet, a master marionette.

BIBLIOGRAPHY

The Gilded Age of Industrial Pioneering

I. On the Period

HENDRICK, BURTON J.
The Age of Big Business
New Haven; Yale Univ. Press, 1919

MOODY, JOHN
The Masters of Capital
New Haven; Yale Univ. Press, 1919

NOYES, ALEXANDER
Thirty Years of American Finance
New York; G. P. Putnam's Sons, 1898

ORTH, SAMUEL P.
The Armies of Labor
New Haven; Yale Univ. Press, 1919

SHAW, ALBERT
"Our Legacy from a Century of Pioneers" in South Atlantic Quarterly, vol. 4, pp. 311–333, Oct. 1906

II. On Andrew Carnegie

ALDERSON, BERNARD
Andrew Carnegie: The Man and His Work
New York; Doubleday, Page & Co., 1905

CARNEGIE, ANDREW
Autobiography
Boston; Houghton Mifflin Co., 1920
The Empire of Business
New York; Doubleday, Page & Co., 1902
The Gospel of Wealth and other Timely Essays
New York; The Century Co., 1901
Triumphant Democracy
New York; 1886

III. On Mark Twain

MARK TWAIN: *Works*: The dates given are of the first edition:
The Jumping Frog—1867
Roughing It—1872

The Gilded Age (with Charles Dudley Warner) 1873
Tom Sawyer—1876
Life on the Mississippi—1883
Huckleberry Finn—1884
A Connecticut Yankee at the Court of King Arthur —1889
The American Claimant—1891
Pudd'nhead Wilson—1894
What is Man?—1906 (privately printed)
The Mysterious Stranger—1916
Autobiography—1925

The complete works were published in twenty-five volumes in 1910.

For biographical data:

PAINE, ALBERT B.
Mark Twain: A Biography
New York; Harper & Bros., 1912
Mark Twain's Letters
New York; Harper & Bros., 1917

For critical comment:

BROOKS, VAN WYCK
The Ordeal of Mark Twain—1920

HOWELLS, WILLIAM D.
My Mark Twain—1910

Also articles on Mark Twain in the following:

BOYNTON, PERCY
A History of American Literature—1919

PATTEE, FRED. L.
American Literature since 1870—1915

PHELPS, WILLIAM L.
Essays on Modern Novelists—1910

SHERMAN, STUART
On Contemporary Literature—1918

IV. On Robert Herrick

The only novel directly pertinent to this chapter is:
Memoirs of an American Citizen
New York; Macmillan Co., 1905

Other novels dealing with the problems of industrial America are:
Homely Lilla
New York; Harcourt, Brace & Co., 1923

The Common Lot
New York; Macmillan Co., 1919
The Web of Life
New York; Macmillan Co., 1908
Waste
New York; Harcourt, Brace & Co., 1924
Critical comment in:
Van Doren, Carl
Contemporary American Novelists

V. On Theodore Dreiser
Dreiser, Theodore
A Book About Myself
New York; Boni & Liveright, 1922
Hey-Rub-a-Dub-Dub
New York; Boni & Liveright, 1920
The Financier
New York; Harper & Bros., 1912
The Titan
New York; John Lane, 1914
Critical comment in Carl Van Doren's *Contemporary American Novelists*

CHAPTER VII

THE FRONTIER AND THE NESTER

I. FRONTIER AND FARM

THE Pathfinder of romantic adventure, the Profiteer of brilliant financiering may be the outstanding characters produced by the drama of westward expansion. But more important in mass if less conspicuous as individuals are the nameless, unremembered thousands whom love of home, hope of economic independence lured to the cheap lands of the frontier. Wherever we study the march of the frontier, from Cooper's family estate in New York to Norris's wheat ranches of California, we find the settlers in constant association and antagonism with the other persistent characters in the drama of pioneering, the trapper and the speculator. It rests with the prejudices of the author which of these characters plays the role of villain and which of hero. As Emerson Hough tells the story of *The Passing of the Frontier* the heroic figures of miner, hunter, and cowboy vanish before the advance of the insignificant and commonplace "nester." As Crèvecoeur tells the story, the undesirable characters of the extreme frontier are fortunately displaced by industrious and progressive husbandsmen. From the Yazoo land frauds in Florida and the difficulties of the Henderson land company in Kentucky and the Symmes land company in Ohio, to the war between cattle kings and homesteaders in Nevada, the settlement of the public lands has been attended by controversy between those who wanted land for speculation and those who wanted land for settlement. Because it is easier to write history in terms of diplomatic treaties, official explorations, and legal statutes than in terms of that unobtrusive individual, the average citizen, the records of western expansion often appear to overlook the fundamental factor—the settler who, sometimes at the urging of the government, sometimes in defiance of the government, went west and settled not only the untamed land, but many ticklish questions of diplomatic and economic procedure on the simple principle that possession is nine-tenths of the law. Study the acquisition of Florida, of Texas, of Oregon, of California, and amid the complicated details of diplomatic and military strategy, you find a casual mention of the fact that American settlers were already in actual occupation of much of the disputed territory. The political importance of the "nester" is evident when we recognize that the diplomat with his fine phrases only confirms what the settler has done with his hard work. The economic importance of the settler is evident when we recognize that the history of the public domain is the history of land legislation framed to accommodate his changing necessities, that the value of the land is a value chiefly contributed by his occupation, that its products are the products of his labor. The importance of the settler as a factor in our social history is ably traced by Hill in his study of *The Public Domain and Democracy,* in which he shows that it is the frontier settlements with their rough equality, their aggressive individualism which have determined the characteristic features of American democracy.

It is human nature to accept what we have as a matter of course, a permanent possession of negligible importance, to awaken to its value only when we are on the point of losing it. But this old commonplace of human nature is always manifesting itself in new forms; in recent writings on American history it manifests itself most ironically in a sudden concern about the disappearance of the frontier. Professor Turner hardly deserves the full credit for having made the discovery that whereas from the beginning of American history we had had a frontier with its concomitants of free land and open opportunities, we now have one no longer. Henry George had anticipated Turner's thesis in his paradoxical grouping of *Progress and Poverty:*

> The public domain—the vast extent of land yet to be reduced to private possession, the enormous common to which the faces of the energetic were always turned, has been the great fact that since the days when the first settlements began to infringe the Atlantic coast, has formed our national character and colored our national thought. . . . The general intelligence, the general comfort, the active invention, the power of adaptation and assimilation, the free independent spirit, the energy and helpfulness that have marked our people, are not causes but results—they have sprung from unfenced land. This public domain has been the transmuting force which has turned the thriftless, unambitious European peasant into the self-reliant Western farmer; it has given a consciousness of freedom even to the dweller in crowded cities and has been a well-spring of hope even to those who have never thought of taking refuge on it. . . . In America there has always been the consciousness that the public domain lay behind him; and the knowledge of that fact acting and reacting has penetrated our whole national life, giving to it generosity and independence, elasticity and ambition. All that we are proud of in the American character; all that makes our conditions and institutions better than those of older countries, we may trace to the fact that land has been cheap in the United States because new soil has been open to the emigrant.
>
> The republic has entered upon a new era, an era in which the monopoly of the land will tell with accelerating effect. . . . California figures on the books of the land department as the greatest land state of the union, containing nearly one hundred million acres of public land. Yet so much of this is covered by railroad grants . . . so much consists of untillable mountains or plains which require irrigation, so much is

monopolized by locations which command the water, that as a matter of fact it is difficult to point the immigrant to any part of the state where he can take up a farm on which he can settle and maintain a family.

Henry George's analysis of the frontier was accompanied by his propaganda for the single tax as the solution for the evils arising from the disappearance of cheap land; so Henry George was dismissed as a crack-brained radical with an alarmist interpretation of the present and a demagogic prescription for the future. It was not until a group of eminently respectable university professors listened to a paper read by one of the most eminent of their number before the American Historical Association that it became not merely safe and sane, but quite the thing, to analyze the American spirit in terms of agrarian opportunity; to talk glibly and regretfully about the disappearance of the frontier. Since Professor Turner's epoch-making monograph of 1893, the frontier has been a term to conjure with. Frederic Paxson writes of *The Last American Frontier,* and more recently and in more detail a *History of the Frontier from 1763–1893.* Emerson Hough writes of *The Passing of the Frontier.* Carl Becker writes of Kansas as an example of the frontier spirit. Solon Buck writes of *The Granger Movement,* and in more popular form of *The Agrarian Crusade,* showing that "the disappearance of the frontier closed a door of opportunity which had previously been open to the oppressed and discontented," that whereas "In earlier times farmers would have struck their tents and moved farther west, taking up desirable land on the frontier and starting out in a fresh field of opportunity," as early as the decade of the seventies. "The era of the self-sufficing pioneer was drawing to a close, and the farmer on the frontier, forced by natural conditions over which he had no control to engage in the production of staples, was fully as dependent on the market and on transportation facilities as was his competitor in the East." Payson Treat studies *The National Land System* showing the interaction of settlers and speculators in accelerating the exhaustion of the public domain. Romanzo Adams, limiting his consideration of the problem to the public range lands of Nevada, decides that here at least, the speculator has got the best of the settler. "By far the greatest part of the privately owned land, including most of the irrigated land, is in the hands of a few great corporations which through this ownership secure the control of the public pasture lands of the state. . . . The existence of these great holdings of irrigated land effectively prevents the growth of a farm population to which the natural resources of the state entitle it, and which it needs to give economic and social prosperity." Otto Cartwright in a study of *The Middle West Side of New York* traces its development "from forest land to city lots," and shows how "the farm purchased by the Astors in 1803 for twenty-five thousand would now sell for twenty-five million"—except that it is not for sale, but leased for tenement buildings on which quick profits must be realized before the lease expires and the ramshackle buildings are pulled down. Herbert Quick tells us that "agriculture is in its agony," and that *The Real Trouble with the Farmers* is that they need a return to cheap land prices such as prevailed in the days of the frontier. "We have had faith in our democratic form of government; but was it our government which has given us our undoubted national comfort and happiness in the past? I do not believe it. I believe it has been the fact that we have had a vast area of cheap land over which our people could live and dwell in freedom. . . . This condition of our farmers seems to me the inevitable result of our passage from the status of a nation with a frontier of free land to that of a great people with the frontier gone." Arthur Bentley, basing his judgment of *The Condition of the Western Farmer* on an intensive study of conditions in Harrison township, Nebraska, declares that "though the available free government land has been practically exhausted, yet the tradition of cheap farms easily obtainable still lingers in the minds of the people, and so the homeseeker still turns his thoughts toward the West." Mr. Bentley makes a dispassionate economic analysis of the difficulties under which such a homeseeker labors, and reaches the conclusion that:

> The would-be purchaser, at least the one whose means are not sufficient to pay entirely for his farm and then tide him over all subsequent periods of hard times, had almost better throw his money away than invest it in farming operations in Nebraska at the current prices of land and under the present agricultural conditions.—Any man who undertakes farming in Nebraska at the present day requires in order to be assured of success at least three things: first, that he have some little capital, second that he possess good business qualifications, and third, that he escape any extraordinary misfortunes—in short, if the farmer of today expects to achieve the same success as the pioneer achieved, he must, except where good fortune and the possession of unusual personal qualities are combined, have capital in sufficient amount to offset the free land and the low cost of living of the pioneer period.

We saw early in the nineteenth century the disappearance of the initial figure of Mr. Turner's procession, the trapper, from the epic of the frontier. Now, in turn, the succeeding figure, the settler, the pioneer homesteader has vanished. The trapper was a divergence from norm, an exceptional individual, a solitary; his occupation, however remunerative, was not an indispensable one. In the disappearance of the trapper from the stage of American life, we have lost a picturesque figure, a romantic variation on the humdrum theme of the work-a-day world. But in the disappearance of the independent farmer we are losing, not a pleasing deviation from normality, but the very quintessence of normality; not an inspiriting romance, but a fundamental reality. The pioneer farmer was the incarnation of the domestic and bourgeois virtues; his labors were the basis of the much vaunted American "prosperity." But he too, our historians and economists tell us, has had his day and ceased to be. And American history is being rewritten in terms of his winning fight against the niggardliness of nature and his losing fight against the greed of speculators and exploiters, in terms of his heroic hara-kiri on the last American frontier.

II. THE FARM IN AMERICAN LITERATURE

Has this theme so vital in American history found no echo in American literature? One might be tempted to answer that up to the disturbing *fin de siècle* American literature was nothing but a reverberation of agrarian prosperity, a purring of content. To revert to the old commonplace, up to the *fin de siècle* American literature said comparatively little about the frontier with its cheap land and abundant opportunity, because it was there; it had always been there; one never stopped to consider that it might not always be there any more than one wastes time worrying about the ultimate extinction of solar heat. It is impossible to say to what extent the pervading optimism of American literature, its exaltation of home and home virtues, its genial sense of friendliness with nature, are conditioned by the presence of cheap land on which any industrious citizen could establish a home and pursue the normal career of earning a living and raising a family. The frontier, it is true, called for and brought forth, exceptional men—the Pathfinders who broke the trails, the Profiteers who exploited the natural resources. But even under the stimulus of frontier opportunities, exceptional men *are* the exception.

The average man is neither a Jedediah Smith, impelled by inspired curiosity to seek a new route through the South Pass, nor a John Jacob Astor shrewdly perceiving and "prosecuting a grand scheme of commerce and colonization." The average man wants a family and a home; in the task of providing for them he has not advanced very far from the primitive injunction laid upon Adam to till the earth and subdue it, to earn his bread by the sweat of his brow. The significance of the frontier in American life was that it provided outlets for the energies not only of the Pathfinders and the Profiteers, but of that larger and more important class, the Peasants.

If we discard the mass of American literature which is mere imitation of European models, we find that the distinctly indigenous American authors may be aligned either with Emerson or with Whittier. The tradition of Emerson and his circle was, as we have seen, a tradition which, starting by the exaltation of the Pathfinder, easily shaded into the deification of the Profiteer. The tradition of Whittier and his circle, of those writers whom Boynton has aptly called "fireside poets," was a tradition which glorified the Peasant. The essential goodness of labor, the simple joys of the normal biological career, occasionally sung even by the "highbrows" of American literature, are the main stock in trade of a school of less pretentious poets from Whittier to James Whitcomb Riley, from James Whitcomb Riley to Edgar A. Guest. The order is hardly felt to be one of increasing literary merit; perhaps because of the increasing meretriciousness of the theme. When Whittier sang his "Songs of Labor" no industrial unrest belied his wellmeaning attempt

> to show
> The orchard bloom and tasseled maize
> That skirt and gladden duty's ways
> The unsung beauty hid life's common things below,

no "agrarian crusade" belied the exultation of his

> Heap high the farmer's wintry hoard!
> Heap high the golden corn!
> No richer gift has Autumn poured
> From out her lavish horn.

But a contemporary versifier who wishes to sing the praises of the homesteader is obliged to admit that while he is "one part hero" he is "three parts fool." As Elliott Lincoln sees him he is,

> Buried up to his ears in debt,
> Fighting the heat, and cold, and wet,
> His chances worse than an even bet——
> You'll find the homesteader.

Paradoxical as it may seem, the rootedness of the peasant as well as the restlessness of the pathfinder had their origin in the frontier. For as Hill points out in his study of *The Public Domain and Democracy:* "The term 'frontier' is not only applicable to outer fringes of sporadic settlement, but also to social life far removed from these conditions of hardship usually associated with an absolutely new country. The effects of the frontier persist long after the first pioneer line has moved on. In this sense pioneer influences in America have affected our local and national life long after the first settlers with their canvas-topped wagons disappeared over the western horizon." The frontier meant abundant undeveloped land. Land meant security for the peasant as it meant adventure for the pathfinder. From this security developed the bucolic satisfactions which are idealized by Whittier. *Snowbound* is the idyl of the winter of American content. The fury of the storm without only added to the cosiness of the family circle who

> Sat the clean-winged hearth about,
> Content to let the north wind roar
> In baffled rage at pane and door.

Their domestic felicity, their simple piety, their unquestioning assurance that their industry will be rewarded by a comfortable measure of prosperity, typify the traditional American *Weltanschauung* which has illogically persisted long after the conditions which justified it have changed.

This latent sense of security and the optimistic view of life which it occasioned are perhaps the most important contributions of the frontier to American literature. But in proportion as these influences are important, they are indirect; they are taken for granted, accepted as a matter of course. This implicit influence of the "nester" on American literature may, then, be suggested, but by its very nature is not susceptible of proof. For direct and explicit recognition of the frontier "nester" in American literature, we have to go back to a time when the novelty of abundant land had not worn off, we have to go back to a writer who, coming from the old world to the new, is never tired of drawing a contrast in favor of his adopted country.

III. HECTOR ST. JOHN CREVECOEUR

Crèvecoeur's *Letters from an American Farmer* is a record of success explicitly attributed to abundance of free land. His definition of an American is couched in terms which combine the activities of regional and spiritual pioneering:

> He is an American who leaving behind him all his ancient prejudices and manners, receives new ones from the new mode of life he has embraced, the new government he obeys, and the new rank he holds.—Here the rewards of his industry follow with equal steps the progress of his labor; his labor is founded on the basis of nature, *self-interest;* can it want a stronger allurement? Wives (sic) and children who before in vain demanded of him a morsel of bread, now fat and frolicsome, gladly help their father to clear those fields whence

exuberant crops are to arise to feed and clothe them all.—The American is a new man who acts upon new principles; he must therefore entertain new ideas and form new opinions. From involuntary idleness, servile dependence, penury, and useless labor, he has passed to toils of a very different nature, rewarded by ample subsistence.—This is an American.

Crèvecoeur initiates the practice which continues through Emerson and Whitman to Andrew Carnegie and George F. Babbitt, of comparing the American with the European in terms odious to the latter. He wonders why people should waste their time going to Italy where they "trace the vestiges of a once flourishing people, now extinct" and "amuse themselves in viewing the ruins of temples and other buildings which have very little affinity with the present age," when they might be better employed "in observing among us the humble rudiments and embryos of societies spreading everywhere, the recent foundation of our towns, and the settlement of so many rural districts." In Italy "all the objects of contemplation, all the reveries of the traveler must have a reference to ancient generations, and to very distant periods clouded with the mist of ages. Here, on the contrary, everything is modern, peaceful, and benign. Here we have no war to desolate our fields: our religion does not oppress the cultivators: we are strangers to those feudal institutions which have enslaved so many. Here nature opens her broad lap to receive the perpetual accession of newcomers and to supply them with food. . . . Here we have in some measure regained the ancient dignity of our species; our laws are simple and just, we are a race of cultivators, our cultivation is unrestrained, and therefore everything is prosperous and flourishing." European society is composed "of great lords who possess everything and of a herd of people who have nothing," while in America "the rich and the poor are not so far separate from each other," "we are all tillers of the soil," "we are all animated with the spirit of an industry which is unfettered and unrestrained because each person works for himself." If the European travels through America "he views not the hostile castle and the haughty mansion contrasted with the claybuilt hut and the miserable cabin" but finds that "a pleasing uniformity of decent competence appears throughout our habitations. The meanest of our log houses is a dry and comfortable habitation." "Europe contains hardly any other distinction but lords and tenants; this fair country alone is settled by freeholders, the possessors of the soil they cultivate." America is run on a larger scale than Europe: "A European when he first arrives, seems limited in his intentions, as well as in his views; but . . . he no sooner breathes our air than he forms schemes and embarks in designs he would never have thought of in his own country." "The means of procuring subsistence in Europe are limited; the army may be full, the navy may abound with seamen, the land perhaps wants no additional laborers, the manufacturer is overcharged with supernumerary hands; what then must become of the unemployed? Here, on the contrary, human industry has acquired a boundless field to exert itself in a field which will not be fully cultivated in many ages." After enumerating all these grounds for thankfulness that we are not as other men of other nations, Crèvecoeur bestows a pitying exordium upon the benighted inhabitants of the old world:

Ye poor Europeans, ye who sweat and work for the great —ye who are obliged to give so many sheaves to the church, so many to your lords, so many to your government, and have hardly any left for yourselves—ye who are held in less estimation than favorite hunters or useless lapdogs—ye who only breathe the air of nature because it cannot be withheld from you; it is here that ye can conceive the possibility of these feelings which I have been describing; it is here the laws of naturalization invite everyone to partake of our great labors and felicity, to till unrented, untaxed lands.

Crèvecoeur delights in making the contrast concrete by telling the stories of emigrants who have risen from depressing poverty in the old world to gratifying prosperity in the new. The newcomer without resources becomes a hired man. "Instead of being employed by a haughty person, he finds himself with his equal, placed at the substantial table of the farmer," he "becomes, as it were, a member of the family." Improved material conditions raise his self-respect. "He begins to feel the effects of a sort of resurrection; hitherto he had not lived, but merely vegetated; he now feels himself a man because he is treated as such." He sees around him others who from as humble beginnings have by their own exertions acquired a comfortable competence. Encouraged by their success, "he purchases some land; he gives all the money he has brought over, as well as what he has earned, and trusts to the God of harvests for the discharge of the rest. . . . He is now possessed of the deed conveying to him and to his posterity the fee simple and absolute property of two hundred acres of land situated on such a river."

There is something sacred about private property as the glow of this moment is described by Crèvecoeur. The possession of land is bound up with the assertion of manhood. The title deed is a symbol of consecrated endeavor, a pledge of ultimate reward. The American Farmer frankly says that he likes to visit and talk with prosperous families. Their prosperity is a token of character, their success a proof that all is right with a world in which "sobriety and industry never fail to meet with the most ample rewards."

Crèvecoeur tells in detail the story of Andrew the Hebridean to illustrate "the progressive steps of a poor man advancing from indigence to ease, from oppression to freedom, from obscurity and contumely to some degree of consequence—not by virtue of any freaks of fortune, but by the gradual operation of sobriety, honesty and emigration." While on a visit to Philadelphia in 1770 Crèvecoeur witnesses the arrival of a vessel of Scotch emigrants, among them the simple Andrew from the island of Barra with his wife and fourteen-year-old son. Andrew is beginning life in America on a capital of eleven and a half guineas, the remainder of a legacy from his uncle. Crèvecoeur becomes interested in him, and offers to take him into his house for two or three weeks until he has learned something of American ways. Then Crèvecoeur finds a place for him with a friend who pays him four dollars a month for the first six months and five thereafter. The wife is placed in another house where she earns half a dollar a week by spinning; the son earns a dollar a month by driving a team. These wages besides "good victuals to eat and good beds to lie on" appear munificent to Andrew. At the end of a year, the combined earnings of the family amount to eighty-four dollars, and Andrew consults Crèvecoeur about buying land. Crèvecoeur presents Andrew's desire to his friend, Mr. A. V. who proposes the following terms:

> 'I will let you have a hundred acres of good arable land that shall be laid out along a new road; there is a bridge already erected on the creek that passes through the land, and a fine swamp of about twenty acres. These are my terms: I cannot sell, but I will lease you the quantity that Mr. James your friend has asked; the first seven years you shall pay no rent; whatever you sow and reap and plant and gather shall be entirely your own—the remaining part of the time you must give me twelve dollars and a half a year.—Within the first three years you must plant fifty apple trees, and clear seven acres of swamp—whatever you do more within that time I will pay you for it at the common rate cf the country.'

Andrew, ignorant of legal technicalities, voices a fear lest after he has made his improvements, he should be disturbed in the possession of the land.

'No, no,' said Mr. A. V. 'There is no such danger; the king and his ministers are too just to take the labor of a poor settler; here we have no great men, but what are subordinate to the laws; but to calm all your fears, I will give you a lease, so that none can make you afraid. If ever you are dissatisfied with the land, a jury of your own neighborhood shall value all your improvements, and you shall be paid agreeably to their verdict.'

Thus encouraged Andrew begins clearing his land and planting his crops. Then comes the great day of the houseraising, made a communal festival according to the pioneer custom of "changing works":

Mr. P. R. his old friend came at the time appointed with all his hands and brought victuals in plenty: I did the same. About forty people repaired to the spot; the songs and merry stories went around the woods from cluster to cluster, as the people had gathered to their different work; trees fell on all sides, bushes were cut up and heaped; and while many were thus employed, others with their teams hauled the big logs to the spot which Andrew had pitched upon for the erection of his new dwelling. We all dined in the woods; in the afternoon the logs were placed with skids and the usual contrivances: thus the rude house was raised, and above two acres of land cut up, cleared and heaped.

Crèvecoeur goes on to tell the further improvements Andrew made on his property, the size of his crops, the gradual growth of a settlement around him, his elevation to civic responsibilities in jury service and in the capacity of overseer of the road, and closes with an itemized statement of his assets amounting to the grand total of $640.00. "By the literal account hereunto annexed, you will easily be made acquainted with the happy effects which constantly flow in this country from sobriety and industry when united with good land and freedom."

Crèvecoeur draws a sharp distinction between American farmers like honest Andrew and himself, and those whom he calls "back settlers," men "no better than carnivorous animals of a superior rank," "a mongrel breed," whose "actions are regulated by the wildness of the neighborhood," whose time is "divided between the toil of the chase, the idleness of repose, or the indulgence of inebriation," the worst of whom have "degenerated altogether into the hunting state." In these pages we have a contemporary's contemptuous differentiation of the chronic and the creative pioneers. The chronic pioneers are the advance guard of the civilization which disowns them. Even Crèvecoeur admits their usefulness in clearing the way for their more exemplary successors: "Thus are our first steps trod, thus are our first trees felled, by the most vicious of our people; and thus the path is opened for the arrival of a second and better class, the true American freeholders; the most respectable set of people in this part of the world." Crèvecoeur anticipates Turner in pointing out the social significance of this continuous purgation made possible by the frontier:

> He who would wish to see America in its proper light, and have a true idea of its feeble beginnings and barbarous rudiments, must visit our extended line of frontiers where the last settlers dwell and where he may see the first labors of settlement, the mode of clearing the earth in all their different appearances.—There, remote from the power of example and check of shame, many families exhibit the most hideous parts of our society. They are a kind of forlorn hope, preceding by ten or twelve years the most respectable army of veterans who come after them. In that space prosperity will polish some, vice and the law will drive off the rest, who uniting again with others like themselves will recede still farther; making room for more industrious people, who will finish their improvements, convert the loghouse into a convenient habitation, and rejoicing that the first heavy labors are finished, will change in a few years that hitherto barbarous country into a fine fertile, well-regulated district. Such is our progress,

such is the march of the Europeans toward the interior parts of this continent. In all societies there are off-casts; this impure part serves as our precursors or pioneers.

Free land is, then, according to Crèvecoeur, the basis of social prosperity: it affords to the "respectable" class of creative pioneers a chance to achieve a competence by their own industry; it relieves these worthy farmers of the problem of the social derelicts, the chronic pioneers, who can always move on, and incidentally clear the way for the subsequent advance of the staid settlers. But Crèvecoeur finds the land the source not only of social prosperity but of personal delight. When he attempted to imagine himself divested of his farm he "found the world so wide and every place so full that I began to fear lest there would be no room for me." After his son is born he ceases even to imagine a world beyond the bounds of the three hundred and seventy-three acres which his father had cleared, improved, and left to him, and which he, in his turn, hopes to develop, enlarge, and pass on to his children. He likes the epithet of "farmer of feelings" and indulges in a sensuous ecstasy over all the petty routine of farm duties, over the commonplace incidents of domestic life. "When I contemplate my wife by my fireside while she either spins, knits, darns, or suckles our child, I cannot describe the various emotions of love, of gratitude, of conscious pride, which thrill in my heart." "When I see my table surrounded with my blooming offspring all united in the bonds of the strongest affection, it kindles in my paternal heart a variety of tumultuous sentiments which none but a father and a husband in my situation can feel or describe." This "Mother, Home, and Heaven" motif, so familiar in American literature and near literature, is closely linked with satisfaction in the soil. Both are primitive possessive instincts, occasions for a pride in ownership. "The instant I enter upon my own land, the bright idea of property, of exclusive right, of independence, exalts my mind. Precious soil, I say to myself, by what singular custom of law is it that thou wast made to constitute the riches of the freeholder? What should we American farmers be without the possession of the soil? . . . This formerly rude soil has been converted by my father into a pleasant farm, and in return it has established all our rights; on it is founded our rank, our freedom, our power as citizens, our importance as inhabitants of such a district."

Thus secure in the possession of abundant agricultural land, Crèvecoeur is free to indulge in amateur naturalizing à la Thoreau, amateur philosophizing à la Rousseau, to sing in his raptures of wife and child, farm and freedom, the lyric apotheosis of the normal biological career.

But we must not close our examination of *The Letters of an American Farmer* without some consideration of the last letter which, on first reading, may seem to refute all that he has exultantly alleged in the opening chapters. This letter is devoted to "The Distresses of a Frontier Man." The outbreak of the Revolutionary War has placed Crèvecoeur in a painful dilemma. "If I attach myself to the Mother Country which is three thousand miles from me, I become what is called an enemy to my own region; if I follow the rest of my countrymen, I become opposed to our ancient masters." The frontiers are in constant terror of incursions by the enemy. Crèvecoeur who had "wanted nothing more than to live at home independent and tranquil" is forced to abandon the accumulated industry of nineteen years, leave the three hundred and seventy acres he has cleared, and plunge farther into the wilderness to begin again under the hospitality of an Indian tribe.

This closing episode, as Crèvecoeur tells it, is obviously vitiated by an admixture of romantic pose. But even after making allowance for the eighteenth century fashion of idealizing life among the noble red men, even after discounting Crèvecoeur's evident delight in dwelling on his troubles, and the grandiloquence of his "Farewell, proud world" gesture, we realize that his pose was struck upon a substantial platform of historical fact. The settler who through any vicissitudes lost his laboriously accumulated property and was forced to begin again, *could* begin again. A little farther on still lay untouched natural resources and the chance of a fresh start. So it had always been; so it seemed to Crèvecoeur it always would be. "There is room for everybody in America." If in his wildest speculations he looks forward to a time when America will have attained "a degree of population and power which Europe little thinks of," he refuses to worry about any possible diminution of its opportunities. "Long before this happen we shall rest beneath the soil." *"Après moi, le déluge!"*

IV. HAMLIN GARLAND

When we turn from the American Farmer of 1770 to the American Farmer of 1870, from Hector St. John Crèvecoeur to Hamlin Garland, we find a significant contrast. Instead of a record of success explicitly attributed to the presence of free land, we have a record of failure, expressly attributed to the disappearance of free land. The end of the trail has been reached in disillusion and bitterness of spirit. "The Song of Emigration has become the hymn of fugitives."

In *A Son of the Middle Border* Garland relates a frontier boyhood of driving toil, of constant moves, of squalid dinginess, of futile endeavor. He tells us of his break with the chronic pioneer his father, and of his striking out for himself, not like the earlier pioneers to go farther west, but to take the "back trail" to the east, to make a place for himself, not on some frontier homestead, but in the world of letters. Filled with the enthusiasm of his new environment, he goes on a visit west. As he rides across the plains of his country and looks out upon the ugly cabin homes of his people, he finds his theme:

> All that day I had studied the land, musing upon its distinctive qualities, and while I acknowledged the natural beauty of it, I revolted from the gracelessness of its human habitations. The lonely box-like farmhouses on the ridges suddenly appeared to me like the dens of wild animals. The lack of color, of charm in the lives of the people anguished me. I wondered why I had never perceived before the futility of woman's life on the farm.
>
> I asked myself, 'Why have these stern facts never been put into our literature as they have been used in Russia and in England? Why has this land no storytellers like those who have made Massachusetts and New Hampshire illustrious?'[1]

"The first actual farmer in American fiction," Garland undertook to tell the truth about Western farm life as he had known it. His representation of this life was so marked a departure from the conventional rustic idyl as to call forth a storm of protest at his indictment of farm conditions. This indictment may be considered as falling under two classes: first, those criticisms of farm life which arise from Garland's own distaste for farming; second, those criticisms of farm life which arise from his sense of the social injustice under which the farmer labors.

For our purposes the criticisms of the first class may be dismissed with casual comment. It is improbable that even in the days of the unexhausted frontier when the best of agricultural land was to be had for the asking, Hamlin Garland would have enjoyed the life of the

[1] The quotations in this book from "A Son of the Middle Border" by Hamlin Garland are used by permission of the Macmillan Company, New York, publishers.

farmer with the wholehearted zest of a Crèvecoeur. Farming was not his natural medium of creative expression; his share of the farm tasks was mere drudgery, work in which he felt humiliation rather than pride, work done with repugnance and thought of with resentment. This repugnance and resentment color the "realism" with which he puts into his fiction those aspects of farm life which had been most disagreeably real to him. "For me the grime and the mud and the sweat and the dust exist. They still form a large part of life on the farm, and I intend that they shall go into my stories in their proper proportions." Let Whittier sing of the cheery content of the snowbound family telling stories before the blazing hearth, making a jolly adventure of the daily excursion through the drifts to care for the cattle—

> Boys, a path!
> Well pleased, (for when did farmer boy
> Count such a summons less than joy)——

Whittier asks. Garland can tell him when. Here is the Garland version of *Snowbound:*

> One such storm which leaped upon us at the close of a warm and beautiful day in February lasted for two days and three nights, making life on the open prairie impossible even to the strongest man. The thermometer fell to thirty degrees below zero and the snow-laden air moving at the rate of eighty miles an hour pressed upon the walls of our house with giant power. The sky of noon was darkened, so that we moved in a pallid half-light, and the windows thick with frost, shut us in as if with gray shrouds.
>
> Hour after hour those winds and snows in furious battle, howled and roared and whistled around our frail shelter, slashing at the windows and piping on the chimney till it seemed as if the Lord Sun had been wholly blotted out and that the world would never again be warm. Twice each day my father made a desperate sally toward the stable to feed the imprisoned cows and horses or to replenish our fuel—for the remainder of the long pallid day he sat beside the fire with gloomy face. Even his indomitable spirit was awed by the fury of the storm.

Mr. Garland's distaste for farm life is personal. The more significant aspect of his frontier narratives is that in which he deals with men who, like his pioneer father, do want and seek a creative outlet on the farm, men, who, for all their indefatigable energy seek it in vain because of conditions over which they have no control. He sees in the defeat of his pioneer father the collapse of traditional American idealisms. Richard Garland, an experienced, energetic farmer, farming nearly a thousand acres, tells his son, "I can't get money enough to pay my taxes. Look at my clothes! I haven't had a new suit in three years." And Garland comments: "This statement of the Border's poverty and drought was the more moving to me for the reason that the old pioneer had always been so patriotic, so confident, so sanguine of his country's future. He had come a long way from the buoyant faith of '66, and the change in him was typical of the change in the West—in America."

In *A Son of the Middle Border* Garland tells how as a young man staking his claim in "The Land of the Straddle Bugs" he discovered *Progress and Poverty* and linking its doctrines with his own experience and observation, became an eager convert to the teachings of Henry George, joined the "Anti-Poverty Brigade" and by his writing and lecturing "entered the arena where problems of social justice were being sternly fought out." He analyzes the tragic significance of the march of the American pioneer to the sunset regions. "These plowmen, these wives and daughters had been pushed out into these lonely, ugly shacks by the force of landlordism behind. The speculative demand for land had hindered them from acquiring even a leasing right to the surface of the earth. . . . The free lands were gone, and so at last the price demanded by these speculators must be paid."

From Garland's new convictions and his old resentments sprang the grim group of stories collected under the title *Main Travelled Roads* and dedicated: "To my father and mother whose half century of pilgrimage on the main travelled road of life has brought them only pain and weariness." The stories in *Main Travelled Roads* are all variations of the same theme: the ugliness, the monotony, the bestiality, the hopelessness of life on the farm. An analysis of one will give the spirit of all.

In *Under the Lion's Paw* we find an apparent parallel to Crèvecoeur's story of Andrew the honest Hebridean. Like Andrew, Tim Haskins leaves his old home in the hope of bettering his condition. Like him he is assisted by kindly neighbors, who take him and his family into their own home until he can get a start, who lend him implements, cows, and seed corn, who introduce him to the leading magnate of the neighborhood with whom he makes an arrangement for leasing a farm. But here the resemblance ends. In the gratitude and hopefulness of the moment, Tim Haskins is unfortunately not as cautious as the canny Scotchman. He inquires the price of the farm from Butler. It is twenty-five hundred dollars. He is, of course, not in a position to buy, but makes arrangements for a three years' lease with the privilege of renewal or purchase at the end of the period. During those three years "they rose early and toiled without intermission till the darkness fell on the plain, then tumbled into bed, every bone and muscle aching with fatigue, to rise with the sun next morning to the same round of the same ferocity of labor." They repaired the house and planted a garden. They added fences and outbuildings. They transformed the neglected, run-down farm into a pleasant and profitable homestead. And so at the end of the three years with joy and pride and relief that his terrible ordeal is over, he offers to buy the farm from his landlord—who calmly informs him that the land is now worth five thousand five hundred, and he can buy at that price or get out.

The tragedy in this story is, of course, accentuated by Haskins' almost incredible blindness to the probability of Butler's making such a demand; this blindness makes possible the sudden reversal from high expectations to desperate rage and sullen despair as he realizes that he is caught "under the lion's paw." But Haskins' lack of foresight is not the cause of his misfortune. He would have been powerless to help himself in any event; without capital, he had to take land at Butler's terms or go without. It is not Haskins' simplicity but the disappearance of the frontier that makes possible Butler's demand for the unearned increment.

An even more bitter picture of a frontierless America is given in Garland's play *Under the Wheel* (written during the financial depression of 1889-90 when the Dakota drouth was at its worst). The opening scene is laid in a tenement. The city workers, hard pressed by constantly soaring prices and rents, voice their nostalgia for the soil:

> 'Phwat is the world comin' to whin the half av us nivir see the blissid sun rise 'r set; an' nivir a blade of grass n'r a shavin' o' mud f'r the childer t'roll on, savin' the gutter, an' a cop on the corner waitin t' braak y'r head 'r a placard sayin' kaape off the grass. Faith an' if this is free Amuriky what'll be the Amuriky that'l be comin' wid the fall o' wages and the rise o' rint?'

Goaded by notice of another increase in rent, lured by the gaudy "literature" of real estate promoters, the Edwards family decide to go west:

> 'Where there ain't no landlords and no rents, where there ain't no rich n'r no poor. Where people don't live in holes like this. Where they raise such ears of corn as that and have farms like that (displaying poster) with cows and pigs and clover and brooks near by full of trout.'

Later in the play, Reeves, Alice Edwards' Boston suitor, unsatisfied with the vague accounts given in her letters, follows them west to see for himself the conditions under which they are living. He finds them packed in a miserable shanty on a burning prairie; driven to long hours of backbreaking toil to wring from the land a bare living plus the interest due the speculators from whom they have bought. To Alice's appeal that the Judge either take back the land or remit the interest due on the mortgage, the Judge replies, "We don't want the land. We've got more land now than we know what to do with. All we want is the interest on the mortgages." To which Alice replies bitterly: "I see! It pays better to let us think we own the land than it would to pay us wages. We work cheaper."

Reeves visits the land sharks' office and sees their devices for cheating their victims. He visits the Edwards' shanty where old Edwards tells him: "We've tried our last chance and we've failed. This is the upshot of our dream. The great free West! Free t' starve in. Just as a desert is free. I've strained every muscle all my life and this is the result of it. If the blight 'r the frost 'r the drouth didn't take the crop, taxes and the railroads and the landlords did. Every year puts us deeper in a hole." Stirred by the tragic irony of their hopeful westering, Reeves cries: "If this is free land what in the devil would you call highpriced land! The settler pays for his 'free land' all that makes life worth living; these families have purchased their bare and miserable acres with blood and sweat and tears. Free land! Bah! For a century there has been no free land in America."

V. FRANK NORRIS

The class war between the farmers and the financiers opened with the skirmish recorded by Bellamy in *The*

Duke of Stockbridge, continued as a losing fight through the farm stories of Hamlin Garland, and found its swan-song in Frank Norris' *Octopus.* In *The Duke of Stockbridge* we have the uprising of the debtor farmers against the bankers, the demand for relief by "cheap money" which has always been a slogan of the farming west, which at this time culminated in Shays' rebellion. Garland's farmers face a more complicated situation; theirs is not only the loss entailed by fluctuations in the money market, changes in the value of the dollar which may make it better worth the farmer's while to burn corn than to market it; theirs is the problem of how to secure and keep up payments on desirable agricultural land. Norris' ranchers enact the last scene of the drama, make the last stand of the agrarian interests against the ubiquitous villain of the piece, the "Octopus."

These farmers of the last frontier, the wheat ranchers of the San Joaquin Valley, although well-to-do, are unable to buy the lands on which they have built their homes, the lands on which they have put thousands of dollars' worth of improvements. At the invitation of the railroad they have taken up and improved the "alternate sections" of the railroad lands, trusting to the deliberately vague assurances of the P & S W that they have an option on the land, and when the company is ready to sell, can buy at a price "based upon the value of the land without improvements." It is the old story of Tim Haskins and Butler over again on a larger scale. Fatuously confident in the belief that they can eventually purchase the land at $2.50 an acre, the ranchers are amazed and indignant when the company, at last ready to sell, offers them the land at $27.00 an acre. In a burst of fury the League is born; it struggles valiantly but in vain against the clutches of the railroad octopus. The deputies of the railroad "jump" the ranches and the resisting Leaguers are shot down. "The drama was over. The fight of Ranch and Railroad had been wrought out to its dreadful close." The scene of the epic of the wheat shifts from the land to the Pit. . . , Very appropriately does Paxson close his recent history of the American frontier by pointing out that the agricultural period dictated by the frontier has come to an end; that the new era opening before the American people is an era of industrial conflict.

VI. WILLA CATHER

With this disappearance of frontier lands, with the transformation of the United States from an agricultural to an industrial people, one outlet of creative expression is closed. After determined search, Jack London's Billy and Saxon find their "Valley of the Moon"; but the Billies and Saxons to come will search in vain. The homesteaders of whom Anne Martin writes find Nevada "a beautiful desert of buried hopes." Ruth Suckow's Country People are drudging automatons, devoid alike of the deep rooted satisfactions of old world farmer stock, and of the abounding enthusiasms of Crèvecoeur's emigrants. The generation of Selina De Jong may put heroisms into their truck farms, may find beauty in cabbages; the generation of Dirk de Jong fritter away their time in unproductive occupations and vapid amusements. "So Big" proves himself of smaller stature than his mother. If we look in American literature for a reflection of this transition, for a realization both of the creative energy of the peasant pioneer and of the vacuum left by his disappearance, we find its supreme expression in the novels of Willa Cather. No American writer since Crèvecoeur has made so vivid the love of land as a ruling passion. Her Antonia and Alexandra are strong peasant types; large, slow, enduring, intense, apparently unimaginative; dull and coarse if transplanted to another environment; rich passionate sources of life in their domination of the land.

Alexandra falls heir to her father's unsolved problem of taming the land that "was like a wild thing that had its ugly moods." By indomitable force of will she holds her ineffectual mother and her commonplace brothers to the executing of her purposes. When times are hard and neighbors are selling out at sacrifice prices, she horrifies her brothers by insisting on taking out another mortgage to buy more land. Her brother asks: "How do you know that land is going to go up enough to pay the mortgages and ——"

"And make us rich besides?" Alexandra put in firmly. "I can't explain that, Lou. You'll have to take my word for it. I *know,* that's all. When you drive about over the country you can feel it coming."

A pioneer, Miss Cather tells us, should have this mystic intuition, this creative premonition that "feels the future stirring," where others see only the bleak exterior. This faith, this love, bind Alexandra to her land: "For the first time perhaps since that land emerged from the waters of geologic ages, a human face was set toward it with love and yearning. It seemed beautiful to her, rich and strong and glorious. Her eyes drank in the breadth of it until her tears blinded her. Then the Genius of the Divide, the great free spirit which breathes across it must have bent lower than it ever bent to a human will before. The history of every country begins in the heart of a man or a woman."

It is this peculiarly intimate dedication and communion that makes the significance of Alexandra's life. She is an artist who has found her appropriate medium of creative expression. When increased prosperity made it possible for her to have "improvements" in her house she turned its furnishing over to a furniture dealer in the neighboring town who conscientiously did his worst.

The house and its furnishings are a mere gesture of propriety. "When you go out of the house into the flower garden, there you feel again the order and fine arrangement manifest all over the great farm; in the fencing and hedging, in the windbreaks and sheds, in the symmetrical pasture ponds planted with scrub willows to give shade to the cattle in fly time. There is even a white row of beehives in the orchard under the walnut trees. You feel that properly Alexandra's house is the big out-of-doors and it is in the soil that she expresses herself best."

This artistic expression through the soil provides a passionate ecstasy of union which takes the place of emotional raptures in her personal life. Her one romance seems very unromantic to her relatives, and perhaps to the more youthful of her readers. Of her final union with Carl Linstrum she says simply, "When friends marry, they are safe." Her own life is merged with the larger passion, the more abundant fruitfulness of the earth:

> Her personal life, her own realization of herself, was almost a subconscious existence; like an underground river that came to the surface only here and there, at intervals months apart, and then sank again to flow on under her own fields.—There were certain days in her life, outwardly uneventful, which Alexandra remembered as peculiarly happy; days when she was close to the flat fallow earth about her, and felt as it were in her own body the joyous germination of the soil.[1]

Not even for her husband can she break this closer union; they both recognize that she belongs to the land.

> 'I've lived here a long time. There is great peace here, Carl, and freedom.'
>
> 'You belong to the land,' Carl murmured, 'as you have always said. Now more than ever.'

[1] The quotations in this book from the works of Willa Cather are used by permission of Houghton Mifflin Company, Boston, publishers of "My Antonia" and "O Pioneers!"

'The land belongs to the future. We come and go, but the land is always here. And the people who love it and understand it, are the people who own it—for a little while.'

Antonia, too, is a true child of the soil. Her transplanting to Black Hawk threatens to ruin her life; but she shakes off the smirch of her tawdry romance, and with her child returns to the plains and the cattle and the grainfields. After her marriage, she holds her pleasure-loving, unstable little city husband to long, lonely years of grinding farm labor. At the end of her story, we see her triumphant on the farm they have evoked from the stubborn soil, among the trees which she "loved as if they were people," among her brood of sturdy children. She is "a rich mine of life like the founders of early races." She is Demeter, the peasant goddess, the incarnation of glorified labor on a rewarding earth. "She lent herself to immemorial human attitudes which we recognize by instinct as universal and true. She had only to stand in the orchard, to put her hand on a little crab tree and look up at the apples, to make you feel the goodness of planting and tending and harvesting at last."

Garland and Norris in telling of the defeat of the farmers on the last frontier, have viewed the defeat as an economic tragedy. Miss Cather sees the defeat of the peasant pioneer as an emotional desolation. "One of Ours" now finds no creative outlet on the farm, but has to seek on the battlefields of France the spiritual exaltation once realized on the prairies of Nebraska. "The Lost Lady" loses touch with the heroic traditions of her pioneer husband and becomes a mere dainty piece of flotsam tossed up in the wreckage of the frontier. Antonia's passionate genius for motherhood is a conserving force. The same potential energy is frittered away and debased in Marian Forrester; not because of innate weakness or depravity, but for lack of an adequate object. In Enid it is corseted and sterilized into a devotion to prayer meetings, prohibition, and foreign missions. It may seem a far cry from Antonia's farm to The Professor's House but here among a group of city sophisticates, Miss Cather has worked out in larger terms the tragic contrast between the heroic days of America's early history and the disillusions of the present. The passions which have given meaning to the Professor's life have been outreachings to a far-frontier: his engrossing research has been concerned with the Spanish adventurers and their part in the development of the continent; his one enduring love is for Tom Outland, the son of the West who comes like a burst of sunlight and fresh air into his stuffy academic routine. What is the whole book but a reënactment of the tiny tragedy buried in its heart, the story within a story? The priceless treasures of Outland's buried city, a legacy from the earliest American culture, had been neglected and finally bartered to aliens. The profits of Tom Outland's invention are similarly misused, until the one friend who had understood grew sick at heart watching the vulgarization of all concerned with the fatal legacy. Miss Cather began her work by writing of the open plains and the waving wheat, of the indefatigable effort and triumphant reward of the heroic age of pioneering. Now she is writing of the stagnating stupidities of small towns, of their vicious gossip and timid pieties, their futile aspirations and fermenting repressions, the aftermath of the vanished frontier.

We saw that at the end of the Leatherstocking Tales Cooper symbolized the passing of the trapper from the drama of the frontier by magnifying his solitary figure against the sunset sky. Miss Cather chooses the same symbol as she writes of the passing of the pioneer homesteader:

Presently we saw a curious thing: there were no clouds,

the sun was going down in a limpid, gold-washed sky. Just as the lower edge of the red disc rested on the high fields against the horizon, a great black figure suddenly appeared on the face of the sun. We sprang to our feet, straining our eyes toward it. In a moment we realized what it was. On some upland farm, a plough had been left standing in the field. The sun was just sinking behind it. Magnified across the distance by the horizontal light, it stood out against the sun, was exactly contained within the circle of the disc; the handles, the tongue, the share, black against the molten red. There it was, heroic in size, a picture-writing on the sun.

Even while we whispered about it, our vision disappeared; the ball dropped and dropped until the red top went beneath the earth. The fields below us were dark, the sun was growing pale, and the forgotten plough had sunk back to its own littleness somewhere on the prairie.

The free lands have gone, the frontier has vanished. The "nester" must seek in other occupations means of livelihood, in other mediums, an outlet for "the creative intention." Across the cold statistics of the Bureau of Agriculture echoes like a warning refrain the epigrammatical comment made to Chesterton by a New York waiter: "From the earth we come and to the earth we go; when we get away from that, we are lost."

BIBLIOGRAPHY

I. On Land Problems.

Adams, Romanzo
"Public Range Lands: A New Policy Needed" in *American Journal of Sociology,* vol. 22, Nov. 1916

Bentley, Arthur F.
The Condition of the Western Farmer
Baltimore; Johns Hopkins Press, 1893

Buck, Solon J.
The Agrarian Crusade
New Haven; Yale Univ. Press, 1921
The Granger Movement
Cambridge; Harvard Univ. Press, 1913

Cartwright, Otto
The Middle West Side
New York; Russell Sage Foundation, 1912

DONALDSON, THOMAS
The Public Domain
Washington; Govt. Printing Office, 1881
GEORGE, HENRY
Progress and Poverty
Garden City; Doubleday, Page & Co., 1906. Originally published in 1876)
HART, A. B.
"Disposition of our Public Lands"
in *Quarterly Journal of Economics,* vol. I, pp. 169–183
HILL, ROBERT T.
The Public Domain and Democracy
New York; Columbia Univ. Press, 1910
HUMPHREY, S. K.
"What is the Matter with Our Land Laws?"
in *The Atlantic Monthly,* vol. 102, pp. 1–9, July, 1908
MCCABE, JAMES D.
History of the Grange Movement
Philadelphia; National Publishing Co., 1873
QUICK, HERBERT
The Real Trouble with the Farmers
Indianapolis; Bobbs-Merrill Co., 1924
SANBORN, JOHN B.
Congressional Grants of Land in Aid of Railways
Madison; Univ. of Wisconsin Press, 1899
SATO, SHOSUKE
History of the Land Question in the United States
Baltimore: Johns Hopkins Press, 1886
TALBOTT, E. H.
Railway Land Grants in the United States
The National Land System, 1785–1820
TREAT, PAYSON
The National Land System, 1785–1820
New York; E. B. Treat & Co., 1910

II. On the Farm in American Literature.

CRÈVECOEUR, HECTOR ST. JOHN
Letters from an American Farmer
New York; Fox, Duffield & Co., 1904. (Original edition) London, 1782

Sketches of Eighteenth Century America; More Letters from an American Farmer
(edited by Henri Bourdin, Ralph Gabriel, and Stanley Williams)
New Haven; Yale University Press, 1925

GARLAND, HAMLIN
Main Travelled Roads
New York; Harper & Bros., 1891
Other Main Travelled Roads
New York; Harper & Bros., 1892
A Son of the Middle Border
New York; Macmillan Co., 1920
Under the Wheel
Boston; Barta Press, 1890

NORRIS, FRANK
The Octopus
New York; Doubleday, Page & Co., 1901

CATHER, WILLA
My Antonia
Boston; Houghton Mifflin Co., 1918
O Pioneers!
Boston; Houghton Mifflin Co., 1913

CHAPTER VIII

THE COMING AGE OF SPIRITUAL PIONEERING

THE landing of the Pilgrims marked the beginning of regional and spiritual pioneering in America. On the Puritan frontier these two trends of pioneering fused in a concentration of power, a simplification of purpose such as is possible only for brief periods and under exceptional circumstances. As the pioneer urge swept out of New England and across the continent, as new characters with new motives came in to play their part in the making of the frontier, the spirit of the first frontier underwent modifications. The religious element persisted, though sometimes attaching itself to grotesque objects. The deification of SUCCESS, the moral obligation of "making good," that is of making money, was an inevitable development of the frontier morale. The elements of sordidness, of greed, of chicanery increased, until the frontier spirit had apparently become identified with the acquisitive instincts, until apparently the glory of the creative intention had departed. It is this aspect of pioneering that modern critics have in mind when they deplore the American inheritance from the pioneer.

But if the pioneer was a bargain hunter, he was also a mystic. Never in the most crudely materialistic maneuvers of the pioneer was there completely lacking the redeeming motivation of the frontier spirit: the sense of something beyond, of the open road, of the best that was yet to be; the resolution to carry on a little longer; the passion to create values where none existed before —even if they were the fictitious values of speculation.

The lust for gain, the relentless drive to labor, were real enough; yet, though they for a time threatened to obscure the spiritual motives of pioneering, they were after all merely incidental, not fundamental.

And now statisticians and historians tell us that the drama of the frontier is played out—and so it is, from the standpoint of material resources. The geographical frontier, finite, is already exhausted. But not so readily does the pioneer spirit which it produced pass from American life. The urge that brought the Puritans to America may very probably have been as recent historians tell us, partly commercial. But it was also partly spiritual—the desire to make a Beloved Community after a pattern which seemed to them more true and beautiful than any they had found in the Old World; to build Jerusalem in New England's green and pleasant land.

Paradoxically enough, those moderns who are most vigorous in their onslaught upon the Puritans, who proclaim doctrines which would have brought them to banishment or death in the stern community of John Winthrop and Thomas Dudley—these iconoclastic moderns are the ones who are feeding the sacred fire, who are keeping alive the tradition of pioneering in America. In their zeal and in their humorlessness, in their raptures and in their intolerance, they are the spiritual descendants of the Puritan Fathers whom they disown.

It may be unkind to suggest that there is a tang of the fabled sour grapes in the unanimity with which, within a decade of the disappearance of the frontier, a group of young intellectuals discovered the undesirable characteristics of the frontier character and the industrial America which he created from frontier resources. Certainly what one of their own writers has called "America's Coming of Age" was marked, not by the receiving but by the dissipating of America's material inheritance. This coming of age was no matter of idle jubilation but of tremendous intellectual seriousness. It gives rise to a new school in American criticism—a revolt against the classic cultural traditions of Paul Elmer More, George Edward Woodberry, Bliss Perry, *et al.* This revolt was inaugurated by John Macy who in 1912 analyzed *The Spirit of American Literature* and found it tepid and meager. Van Wyck Brooks, Randolph Bourne, and Waldo Frank have carried on the tradition begun by Macy; they find the only hope for "Our America" in a break with Puritan inhibitions and pioneer incentives.

This new school has not confined itself to the criticism of literature with which its activities ostensibly began; it has dedicated itself to a criticism of life. It has sat as a coroner's inquest upon *These United States* and has found the trail of the pioneer over them still from Vermont to California. Thirty of its specialists have conducted an autopsy on *Civilization in the United States* and agreed in their report that the patient had no chance of survival after inoculation with the Puritan virus.

It is easy to poke fun at the solemnity with which these younger intellectuals take their self-constituted responsibilities. It is easy, on the other hand, to make the mistake of taking them as seriously as they take themselves, and becoming unduly excited about the importance of their findings. But quite aside from the validity of their findings is the value of their investigation. We have overthrown at least one tyranny of the frontier morale; Americans have attained the stage where honest self analysis is possible. Frontier conditions demanded solidarity. "Don't be a knocker, be a booster" was the first commandment of the frontier community. More polished societies refine that into the more urbane injunction: "Let your criticism be constructive rather than destructive." The spirit is the same, the tyranny the same, the resulting paralysis of free thought the same. If we owe nothing more to the younger critics of American literature and American life, we owe to them the emancipation from the demands of 100% Americanism.

The unfavorably analytical tendencies which spoke out in *Civilization in the United States* and in *These United States* have been thinly camouflaged in poetry and fiction. Masters' dissection of Spoon River, Sinclair Lewis' dissection of Zenith and Gopher Prairie, probe unflinchingly into the fatty degenerations that have grown from the poison of the Great American Myth. But these daring feats of surgery are already an old story. Satire implies a popular belief in that which is satirized. The old sacrosanct beliefs in the sweet neighborliness of the village, the democratic equality of rural America, the sturdy integrity of the American business man, the priceless value of the smokestained cities consecrated to his factories—these beliefs are dead, and the muckraker only wastes his efforts in disturbing their ashes. The belated and brief reign of naturalism in American literature is drawing to its close. The vogue of the naturalistic novel in America, like other manifestations in American literature, owes something to foreign sources. Other writers of other lands had anticipated Mark Twain and Herrick and Dreiser and Frank and Charles Norris in their theory that man is a pathetically or comically impotent creature of his environment, the butt of undignified jokes played upon him by tricks of his own chemistry. But writers need to be explained not merely in terms of other writers, but in terms of their readers. To the reading public must be allowed at least a rejective power. The public which welcomed *Main Street* and *The Domesday Book, Miss Lulu Bett,* and *One of Ours,* was a public already half disillusioned, a public already eager to have the writer tell them with polished irony or broad burlesque what they had secretly suspected. Many of these readers may have known little of Zola or Balzac or George

Moore; they may have known equally little of the westward retreat of the frontier from King George's royal proclamation of 1763 to Professor Turner's obituary monograph in 1893. But they felt obscurely that the daily grind was a little harder, the returns less rewarding, the impulses less heroic, than they had been told they were in the good old days. With the passing of the geographical frontier passed the inflated optimism which it engendered. The succeeding period of bitter naturalism has had its vogue and is already passing.

The progress of Sinclair Lewis might aptly be entitled Up from Naturalism. His three important novels have so much in common as to make their points of difference strikingly suggestive. In each case, the old struggle of an individual against his world is staged in the standardized world of our industrial America with an individual just a little less crude, just a little more skeptical than the yokels and Rotarians, the Baptists and Realtors who surround him. In each case the struggle ends in defeat.

It is the difference in tone which prevents *Main Street, Babbitt* and *Arrowsmith* from being a mere set of variations on the same theme. In *Main Street* Lewis sneers unsparingly not only at Gopher Prairie but at Carol Kennicott. Her half baked aspirations, her vulgar snobbishness, her tactless attempts at "uplift," her meaningless dabbles in philandering, in feminism, in culture, brand her as essentially a part of Main Street, rather more unprofitable and unpleasant than the more genuinely earthy of her neighbors. The satire in Babbitt has already become more kindly. In Babbitt's dreams of the fairy girl, in his strangled but only half dead ambitions as a lawyer, in his uncalculating friendship for Paul Riesling, we have hints of the Babbitt that might have been if Zenith had not trimmed him into a dutiful husband and enterprising realtor. If his bungled attempts at self-assertion and independence are grotesque, it is with a sort of wistful grotesqueness. The blame is laid with the environment rather than with Babbitt. Carol Kennicott we feel would have been flighty and ineffectual wherever it had pleased Providence to place her. Babbitt removed from the pressure of the Good Citizens' League might have put some meaning into his life. But as it is, both Carol and Babbitt feel that they have not gotten much worth having out of life, and with the eternal cowardice of the older generation, we find their books closing with their "passing the buck" to their children. Carol standing over the cradle of her daughter dreams that Vassar—or perhaps Bryn Mawr—may do for her all that Blodgett College should have done for her mother. Babbitt, who has gladly slunk back to respectability himself, greets with approval the runaway marriage of his son. "Practically I've never done a single thing I wanted to in my whole life! . . . I get a kind of sneaking pleasure out of the fact that you knew what you wanted to do and did it. . . . Don't be scared of the family. No, nor all of Zenith. Nor of yourself the way I've been. Go ahead, old man. The world is yours!"

This consummately ironic conclusion of *Babbitt* sounds a return to the old motif of triumph over environment. *Arrowsmith* sounds a return to the older idealism. Where *Main Street* and *Babbitt* are the records of failure, *Arrowsmith* is the record of many failures—and of an unquenchable idealism that frustrated all attempts of environment, all resolves of Arrowsmith himself to stifle it and play the game the easy popular way that leads to the approbation of his fellows, to immediate results and publicity and profits. Sinclair Lewis shows an increasing respect for his characters. He still falls into his old trick of caricature; but in *Arrowsmith* the caricature is done in such a forced, halfhearted way that Almus

Pickerbaugh and his ilk are utterly unconvincing men of straw. The hatred for sham, the contempt for the jocular hail-fellow show of solidarity, for the trumped up hurrah stuff, for the speeded up manufacture of shoddy results, still animates Mr. Lewis' picture of commercialized America. But in *Arrowsmith* he for the first time ascribes to his protagonist a rejective power over his environment.

In *Arrowsmith* we find a progression through the three phases of American pioneering. The book opens with an apparently irrelevant account—after the much ridiculed manner of old-fashioned novelists—of Arrowsmith's forbears:[1]

> The driver of the wagon swaying through forest and swamp of the Ohio wilderness was a ragged girl of fourteen. Her mother they had buried near the Monongehela—the girl herself had heaped with torn sods the grave beside the river of the beautiful name. Her father lay shrinking with fever on the floor of the wagon box, and about him played her brothers and sisters, dirty brats, tattered brats, hilarious brats.—She halted at the fork in the grassy road, and the sick man quavered, 'Emmy, ye better turn down towards Cincinnati. If we could find your Uncle Ed, I guess he'd take us in.'
>
> 'Nobody aint goin to take us in,' she said. 'We're goin' on jus' as long as we can. Going West! They's a whole lot of new things I aim to be seeing!'
>
> She cooked the supper, she put the children to bed, and sat by the fire alone.
>
> That was the great-grandmother of Martin Arrowsmith.

That impelling curiosity to see new things persisted in Martin Arrowsmith, brought him back to scientific research after each unsuccessful attempt to stultify his energies and prostitute his purposes, kept him from ever paying wholehearted allegiance to the demand of his superiors for immediate and practical results. In the

[1] The quotations in this book from "Arrowsmith" by Sinclair Lewis are used by permission of the publishers, Harcourt, Brace & Co., New York.

account of his dedication to abstract science we find a curious overtone of the religious fanaticism of the Puritan frontier. Arrowsmith says of his hero Gottlieb, "His just being in a lab is a prayer." Arrowsmith "exalts the search for fundamental laws above temporary healing as the religious exalts the nature and terrible glory of God above pleasant daily virtues." The fervor of his solitary experimentation finds a natural outpouring in an agnostic prayer:

> God give me unclouded eyes and freedom from haste. God give me a quiet and relentless anger against all pretense and all pretentious work and all work left slack and unfinished. God give me a restlessness whereby I may neither sleep nor accept praise till my observed results equal my calculated results or in pious glee I discover and assault my error.

Arrowsmith is like the Puritan pioneers in his contempt for the immediate and practical as compared with the abstract and eternal; in his suspicion that any form is tainted with insincerity; in his ruthlessness toward anything or anybody that gets in the way of his dedication. But while his resemblance to the Puritan is probably one of which he himself was unconscious, he is proudly conscious of his resemblance to the pioneer, so much so that he recurs to that figure to explain his purposes. When his wife seeks to hold him by the old plea of duty to herself and to their child, Martin replies impatiently: "I imagine it's just that argument that's kept almost everybody all these centuries from being anything but a machine for digestion and propagation. The answer is that very few ever do under any conditions willingly leave a soft bed for a shanty bunk in order to remain pure, and those of us that are pioneers——" And Arrowsmith whose ancestors were regional pioneers, whose contemporaries commercialize their science in deference to the competitive standards of industrial pioneering, joins his friend on one of "the new frontiers of unwon fields of science" which Professor Turner suggests may take the place of the old frontiers of wilderness. Like the transcendentalists, Arrowsmith must revert approximately to the conditions of regional pioneering in order to find opportunity for his adventure in spiritual pioneering. Martin Arrowsmith is the most recent incarnation of that familiar frontier character, the Refugee from Civilization. He and his partner Terry in their cabin laboratory in the woods joyously plan their work—not work for immediate results, for assured profits, for sensational publicity, but long, unrecognized, unremunerative work which may very probably in the end get them nowhere. A new note in American pioneering is struck in this exultant acceptance of failure:

> I feel as if I were really beginning to work now. This new quinine stuff may prove pretty good. We'll plug along on it for two or three years, and maybe we'll get something permanent—and probably we'll fail.

A new manifestation of the pioneer spirit, a call to a new frontier is already evident in American literature. The new frontier offers a new idealism—not, like the transcendental idealisms vehemently denying limitations, but serenely accepting them; it offers a new vocation—not the development of the continent but the development of the character; it substitutes for the assertive redblooded heroes of regional or industrial pioneering, a hero who has hitherto been merely a tolerated bystander—the artist. He may be an artist in the conventional sense that he "writes perfectly of beautiful happenings" or makes beautiful pictures, or builds beautiful houses. But whether or no he be an artist in this specifically limited sense, he must be an artist of life. He must care for experience, not as a means to an end, but as an end in itself; his standard of values must be qualitative not quantitative; he must reverence other human beings because in them he recognizes the potentialities which he prizes supremely in himself. He refuses to stultify his soul with the mendacious inducements of the Gospel of Wealth. In his hunger and thirst after perfection he "hurls himself into a battle in which is engaged against him all the accumulative genius of the world."

And curiously enough in this rejection of the code of industrialism, the American of the newest American literary coterie becomes European as Aldrich and Longfellow never were European. For they merely imitated externals—but the American artist of today has lived as a new genuine experience that old experience of the Old World that "with Renunciation life begins." Henry Adams feels in the Virgin of Chartres a power greater than that of the dynamo of Chicago. Sherwood Anderson voices a "Mid-American Prayer" for "what the Old World can bring to us—the true sense of real suffering out of which may come the sweeter brotherhood." The lesson of acceptance, of self-abnegation which Henry James' American had to learn in Europe, contemporary Americans are learning from the American scene.

Even in drama, that form of literature which traditionally extols the strong man of action, we find instances of this introverted emphasis in the new American literature. No advancement of industrial prosperity compensates man for being a mere adding-machine; no augmenting of national prestige is worth while if the price of glory is the debasement of men. The greatest of American dramatists pleads under varied symbols that human nature throw off the masks imposed by greedy commercialisms and timid conventionalities.

A disturbing sensitiveness to life, an insatiable desire to find reality and beauty in human relationships, haunt the tragedies of Eugene O'Neill. His sympathies are not with the crassly materialistic sons who ride away to the gold fields singing the old pioneer refrain,

O Susannah!
Don't you cry for me;
I'm off to California
With my washbowl on my knee,

any more than they with the Puritan patriarch who arrogates to himself the hurling of Biblical texts. The central figure of his pitiably twisted tragedy is the son whose longing for love, whose passionate devotion to the land that had been his mother's, involve him in incest and murder; who, even stained with these unnatural crimes, goes to his doom with some vestige of incorruptible purity, some flame of quenchless love still linking him to the faded wanton who had been his undoing. Even more suggestive than the objects of Eugene O'Neill's love are the objects of his hate. Someone has wittily said that Luther's hymn should be slightly paraphrased to serve as the American creed: "Ein feste bourgeois ist unser Gott." This God of American adoration is the Great God Brown whom O'Neill delights to dethrone, madden, and destroy.

Yet even this repudiation of the American philosophy of success betokens the spirit of the American frontier, the phoenix which rises always more beautiful from the ashes of its apparent death. So thoroughly has the frontier entered into the American consciousness that writers instinctively turn from the end of one of its manifestations in expectation of another. Harold Waldo in a recent *Bookman* voices the need of "New Wests for Old." Lloyd Morris writing in *The North American Review* on the work of Willa Cather points out that "the new frontier occurs within the imagination," that "the pioneers of yesterday become the artists of today turning from the conquest of the land to a fresh contest with an equally obdurate spiritual environment." After all, the conquest of the continent was valueless unless it resulted in the enriching of individual life. As the problems of material pioneering have been solved, the problems of spiritual pioneering become more insistent. The artist who dedicates his life to their solution is the hero of the new frontier.

A brief glimpse of two such artists will illustrate the type of pioneering that challenges the heroisms of the coming age. Vachel Lindsay prides himself on his descent from Kentucky pioneers. Among his favorite heroes are Johnny Appleseed, the American St. Francis who wandered on the farthest flung frontiers, planting his apple orchards among the forests for the pioneers to find long after, and Appleseed's comrade, Hunter Kelly. Lindsay himself is not merely figuratively but actually a pioneer, "making sundry explorations afoot and penniless in Florida, Georgia, North Carolina, Tennessee, Kentucky, New Jersey, and Pennsylvania," adventuring in the name of his Gospel of Beauty, trading his rhymes for bread.

The first article of his gospel of beauty denies the values of regional pioneering. "The things most worth while are one's own hearth and neighborhood," a proud provincialism, an ideal of the intensive rather than the expansive life which takes us back to the philosopher of Walden. Lindsay, too, finds voluntary poverty the only means of belonging to the truly leisure class. He longs for a return of St. Francis; he pictures himself as a sort of Franciscan troubadour. In revolt against the machine, he conducts a private agrarian crusade. He agrees with Carl Becker in finding Kansas the state which most completely realizes the frontier idealism, Kansas the heart of the west, Kansas the ideal American community. In the Proclamations with which he closes his letters from Kansas farms he calls the slaves of the empire of business back to the land, to the old-fashioned Americanism of our Puritan farmer fathers. "You to whom the universe has become a blast-furnace, a coke-oven, a cinder-strewn freight-yard . . . turn to the soil, turn to the earth, your mother, and she will comfort you."

This Gospel of Beauty with its idealization of agriculture, its glad acceptance of poverty, its prophecy of an American Renaissance, repudiates the values of industrial pioneering—the artist pioneer should expect "neither reward nor honors." Lindsay takes issue sharply with the assumption of the Gilded Age that "politics is business and business is politics and the only worth while citizens are those that get the money." But he wastes no time or temper in muckraking. Rather he lets the stupid regimentations of commerce dissolve before the compelling radiance of his vision of the City Splendid.

The Golden Book of Springfield might be read as an allegory of America. The seeds are planted by the heroic pioneer, Hunter Kelly, who received them from the saintly mystic, Johnny Appleseed. Kelly vowed to plant in his honor "a city like an apple tree with its highest boughs in Heaven." Entering into a Devil's bargain with the leader of the wolf pack, the pioneer, that he may facilitate the building of the city, submits to the torture of burial below his orchard. "In his living skull and heart were entangled the roots of the first Apple Amaranth trees." For centuries he endures his living death waiting for the birth of the City, for the promised hour when the children of men shall dare to eat of the Amaranth apples that they thought were poison. "For he who eats of the Amaranth apples is filled with a love of eternal beauty." And then the City stirs in glory in response to the surging call, "Springfield Awake! Springfield Aflame!"

All the assured faith, all the mystic ecstasy with which Edward Johnson lauded the *Wonderworking Providence* enters into Mr. Lindsay's vision of transfigured Springfield. But a new note is added, lacking in the pious rhapsodies of earlier patriotism—a note of humility and patience foreign to the spirit of an earlier frontier. The Springfield that is to be, the Beloved Community for which Vachel Lindsay prays, is one whose greatness cannot be measured by the speed of her growth or by the size and wealth of her population:

> Let not our town be large, remembering
> That little Athens was the Muses' home;
> That Oxford rules the heart of London still,
> That Florence gave the Renaissance to Rome.
>
> We must have many Lincoln-hearted men;
> A city is not builded in a day,
> And these must do their work and come and go,
> While countless generations pass away.

The second artist pioneer whom we shall consider, the figure who in his life and in his writings best illustrates the spirit of the new frontier, is Sherwood Anderson. His recent testament, *A Story Teller's Story* is unique in the annals of American autobiography, The most characteristically American autobiographies have been complacent records of material success. From the *Autobiography of Benjamin Franklin* to *The Americanization of Edward Bok,* American literature has been well furnished with these Horatio-Algeresque accounts of the type of "success" which Mencken scornfully says distinguishes the national letters—the ideally successful career being that of the poor boy who begins by sweeping out the office and ends by marrying the daughter of the owner of a hook and eye factory. More recent autobiographies have departed from this tradition, ending in a note of negation and despair like *The Education of Henry Adams* or in the supercilious scorn of Lewisohn's *Upstream.* Anderson writes of himself without the boastful egoism of a Franklin or a Bok or the intellectual arrogance of an Adams or a Lewisohn. Not only has he intentionally rejected the materialistic standard of success but so far from being sure that his superior intellectual caliber guarantees a finer success, he explicitly states his certainty that only at God given intervals can he achieve the goal of his own desire: "The kind of workman I had wanted to be I could not be, but I did not know it at the moment. I could only give myself with complete abandonment to the surfaces and materials before me at rare moments sandwiched in between long periods of failure" This realization of his own limitations gives an honest humility to his account of his life. A recognition of similar limitations in his fellowmen qualifies his judgment of them with deep tenderness. A recognition of similar limitations in his country prevents him from heaping upon it the fulsome panegyrics of a Carnegie, but a faith in its ultimate possibilities prevents him from flaying it with the philippics of a Lewisohn. With this humility, this tenderness, this faith, he tells in apparently disconnected notes "the tale of an American writer's journey through his own imaginative world and through the world of facts."

The early years of Sherwood Anderson's life recapitulate the familiar American story of the poor boy rising in the business world by energy and capability. His boyish ambitions were colored by the hero stories of regional pioneering. The earliest experience recorded in this fragmentary autobiography is playing *The Last of the Mohicans* with his brothers. He regrets that he was born too late to take an actual part in such exploits. "Deep within the breasts of my brother and myself there is a resentment that we were born out of our time. By what a narrow margin in the scroll of time have we missed the great adventure! Two or three or at the most a dozen generations earlier and we might as well have been born in the virgin forest itself." He consoles himself by believing that in his chosen craft he is a sort of successor to *La Longue Carabine* whom he admires and whom he represents in their boyish dramatizings: "I am the one destinied to follow the little crooked words of man's speech through the uncharted paths of the forests of fancy."

This childish admiration for the primitive heroisms of regional pioneering gives place to the gospel of size and hustle which intoxicated the young manhood of his day. "A new kind of hero—tarnished somewhat later—filled the popular eye. . . . Everyone was singing a new little song, 'Get on. Make money. Get to the top.' The factories were calling. . . . Oil and gas were spurting out of the ground in Ohio and the discovery of oil and gas meant the coming of factories, it meant the New Age, prosperity, growth going onward and upward." With the histrionic excitability which is evident throughout his narrative, Sherwood Anderson responds enthusiastically to the hero challenge of his own age, and decides to be "an empire builder." "There were the great cities of Chicago and New York which I had not seen although I had read much about them and about men who had grown from poverty to riches and power in them. Like all young Americans I had read innumerable tales of men who had begun with nothing and had become great leaders, owners of railroads, governors of states, foreign ambassadors, generals of armies, presidents of great modern republics. . . . Were these men any better than myself?"

Anderson's ardent response to the New Age is disturbed by the enigmatical Alonzo Berners. In this hopeless invalid he feels an inexplicable power quite at variance with the creed of the empire builder. What was the mysterious something that Alonzo Berners gave to those with whom he came in contact? Why had this painridden invalid "health and sanity within himself when almost without exception the others, including myself, had not?" Anderson begins to wonder if there is "a power greater than obvious power"; if the empire-builders of his hero-worship are not after all childish in their scramble for the spoils. "Did most men and women remain children and was Alonzo Berners grown up? Was it grown up to come to the realization that oneself did not matter, that nothing mattered but a kind of consciousness of the wonder of life outside oneself?" Baffled and disconcerted by the mystic force that he feels in this quiet invalid, he fights with irritation against his influence, only to find himself conquered by the "power of unasking love" only to emerge with a "new morality" . . . a morality so like an old one once proclaimed with angelic rejoicings that Anderson himself recognizes it smilingly as he tells of his kneeling in the dust in the moonlit road "having a ridiculous desire to abase myself before something not human. . . . A child cried in a nearby house . . . and I thought of the wise men of old times who were reputed to have come to worship at the feet of another crying babe in an obscure place."

Between his new morality and his business morale Sherwood Anderson leads for a while a dual life of the spirit, till the day of his great migration comes and he goes forth in search of himself, leaving his "poor little factory like an illegitimate child on another man's door-step." He tells with intimate detail of that crucial moment, one of the moments in which one really lives, the moments which shape lives. Like a true American he had been thinking in terms of size, had given himself with a sort of madness to his attempt to create a demand for the goods produced by his factory, to make it bigger and better; the Carnegie gospel of wealth still lends a touch of benign benevolence to his schemes. Suppose the day comes when he has a thousand workmen under him. He would build them model homes to live in "a town of model homes about my great factory. The workmen would be my children and I would look out for my children."

Some saving grace of humor and sincerity convicts him of the essential absurdity of this patronizing paternalism. How could he be a father to his workmen? What did he really know of them and their life purposes? What did he know of his own? Did he really want a large factory briskly turning out standardized goods in a model town? Did he really want to spend his life dictating letters to his stenographer, letters cunningly contrived to create a fictitious demand for those goods? He saw himself as a prostitute, selling his life to ends that were not his own. He wanted to leave the buying and selling, to take the six or seven steps that led to the door of his office, to pass through the door and never come back. And this secession, such a one as was futilely dreamed of by Babbitt in his rebellious hours of nonconformity, Anderson carried out. Thoreau's withdrawal from America took him two miles to the Walden woods; Sherwood Anderson's took him the seven steps to his office door. These two departures are the declarations of spiritual independence in the world of American letters.

Anderson's characters repeat his own experience. John Webster finds that there are more important things in life than being a manufacturer of washing-machines in a Wisconsin town. He arrives at the shockingly un-American heresy that "accomplishment is not the vital thing in a life" and determines to reconstruct his life so that it will have grace and meaning. The stalwart McGregor begins with a fierce contempt for the inefficient, stolid workmen, so obviously his inferiors. He determines not to be trapped and held down on their level, but to override them on his way to success. But he attains success only to perceive its emptiness; he sees the irony of "how men coming out of Europe and given millions of square miles of black fertile land, mines, and forests, have failed in the challenge given them by fate and have produced out of the stately order of nature only the sordid disorder of man." He cries, "There is a curse on my country. Everyone has come here for gain, to grow rich, to achieve. Suppose they should begin to want to live here." He resolves not to become part of the "great machine running crazily and without purpose," not to let his sluggish associates be mere cogs; yearning with a great tenderness for their inertia, inspired by the artist's passion to bring rhythm and order out of meaningless confusion, he organizes his marching men. Hugh McVey, imbibing from his conscientious foster mother the New England gospel of unflagging diligence, prods himself from being a poor white to becoming a brilliant and prosperous inventor. At the height of his success he is confronted by the revengeful bitterness of one of the little ordinary plodding men for whom his success had spelt failure. And Hugh recognizes that something is wrong with his laboriously acquired gospel of prosperity and sets to work to acquire another. He realizes that "the time of the comparatively simple struggle with definite things, with iron and steel, had passed. He fought to accept himself, to understand himself, to relate himself with the life about him. The poor white, son of the defeated dreamer by the river, who had forced himself in advance of his fellows along the road of mechanical development, was still in advance of his fellows of the growing Ohio towns. The struggle he was making was the struggle his fellows of another generation would one and all have to make." *Windy MacPherson's Son* begins like the conventional biography of an industrial pioneer, one of those successful supermen of the Gilded Age. But the moment of his attainment is the moment of his disillusion. "The great forward movement in modern industry of which he had dreamed of being a part, had for him turned out to be a huge meaningless gamble with loaded dice against a credulous public." Sam, the sturdy, independent, ambitious, resourceful pioneer type, had elbowed his way through life on a philosophy of self assertion. He had wanted "a work done by his own hand" and every form of self-expression to which he turned ended in mockery. He finds satisfaction at last in a creative intention devoid of any possible taint of egoism; assuming responsibility for the neglected children of a street woman, he returns with them to his estranged wife, and gives himself to the task of "understanding those other lives in love."

That phrase might serve as a summary of Sherwood Anderson's gospel. Grotesque it may often seem, as in the return of Sam with his ready-made family—but Sherwood Anderson has a great tenderness for grotesques. He sees in misshapen and broken lives the beauty of the intention, the pity of the frustration. He is the first of American writers to comprehend the full paradox of the failure of success and the success of failure. Is it merely fortuitious that the expansive days of the frontier saw a glorification of success, that with the passing of the frontier comes the sublimation of failure? Anderson himself suggests a connection between American philosophies and American pioneering:

> We Americans have believed that life must have point and purpose. We have called ourselves Christians, but the sweet Christian philosophy of failure has been unknown among us. To say of one of us that he has failed is to take life and courage away. For so long we have to push blindly forward. Roads had to be cut through our forests, great towns had to be built. What in Europe has been slowly building itself out of the fiber of the generations, we must build now in a lifetime. In our father's day at night in the forests of Michigan, Ohio, Kansas, and on the wide prairies, wolves howled. There was fear in our fathers and mothers pushing their way forward, making the new land. When the land was conquered,

fear remained, the fear of failure. Deep in our American souls, the wolves still howl.

Thus Anderson punctures the bravado of the frontiersman and substitutes for his blustering recklessness the cleareyed courage which accepts the certainty of failure. At the end of *Marching Men* David Ormsby, the "successful" man, comments on McGregor's failure: "Perhaps McGregor knew he would fail and yet had the courage of failure. I wonder if both Margaret and myself lack the greater courage, if that evening long ago when I walked under the trees I made a mistake? What if after all this McGregor and his woman knew both roads. What if they after looking deliberately along the road to success in life, went without regret along the road to failure? What if McGregor and not myself knew the road to beauty?"

The significant contribution of Sherwood Anderson is not his dissent from the accepted values of industrialism. Signs of restiveness under the Empire of Business were evident a far back as Mark Twain's earliest satires on the Gilded Age. Anderson is significant, not because he exposes the impotence of the old idol—scores of writers have anticipated him in that—but because he sounds the challenge of a new ideal. He is not interested in the specious brilliancy of the easy sneer. He gives himself to the infinitely harder task of patient understanding. He sees an America yet in the making, an America whose passion for size and speed is an unconscious confession of impotence, an America already half-sick of sterile standardization, almost ready "for the rediscovery of man by man." On the frontier of the spirit he discovers a wilderness to be reclaimed, power and beauty to be created out of barren wastes. Americans may have exploited a continent; they have not begun to utilize the potential riches of human relationships.

With these modern prophets of new gospels, the cycle of the frontier is complete. It began with a little group of obstinate zealots who in their obsession with spiritual pioneering almost forgot to mention the conditions of the actual frontier. As the frontier moved westward it offered freedom and elbow room to the lover of open spaces, release from social exactions to the incompetent, outlet for primitive instincts to the passionate; it promised adventure and wealth to the fur trapper; it guaranteed security and domestic satisfaction to the homestead farmer; it lent plausibility to the grandiose generalizations of the transcendentalists and their logical successors, the pragmatists. It scattered its largesse before the financier. And now when the frenzy of exploration and exploitation is over, out of the momentary reaction of depression, sounds again, sometimes fanatical, absurd and intolerant as on the Puritan frontier, but animated by the same ring of faith, the same conviction of boundless opportunity, the cry of spiritual pioneering.

BIBLIOGRAPHY

I. On the Modernist's Criticism of American Literature and Life.

BROOKS, VAN WYCK
America's Coming of Age
New York; B. W. Huebsch, 1915
Letters and Leadership
New York; B. W. Huebsch, 1918

FRANK, WALDO
Our America
New York; Boni & Liveright, 1912

GRUENING, ERNEST (editor)
These United States
New York; Boni & Liveright, 1923

MACY, JOHN
The Spirit of American Literature
New York; Boni & Liveright, 1912

MENCKEN, HENRY L.
A Book of Prefaces
New York; A. A. Knopf, 1917
Prejudices, 1st series
New York; A. A. Knopf, 1919
(Other series as indicated in general bibliography)
STEARNS, HAROLD E.
America and the Young Intellectual
New York; Geo. H. Doran Co., 1921
STEARNS, HAROLD E. (editor)
Civilization in the United States
New York; Harcourt, Brace & Co., 1922

II. On Sinclair Lewis.
LEWIS, SINCLAIR
Main Street
New York; Harcourt, Brace & Co., 1921
Babbitt
New York; Harcourt, Brace & Co., 1922
Arrowsmith
New York; Harcourt, Brace & Co., 1925
For critical comment:
SHERMAN, STUART
The Significance of Sinclair Lewis
VAN DOREN, CARL
in *Contemporary American Novelists*

III. On Vachel Lindsay.
LINDSAY, VACHEL
Adventures while preaching the Gospel of Beauty
New York; Mitchell Kennerley, 1914
The Golden Book of Springfield
New York; Harper & Bros., 1920
(Only the prose works are listed here, as they have the more direct bearing upon our investigation. The volumes of his poetry were published as follows:
General William Booth—1913
The Congo—1914
The Chinese Nightingale—1917
The Golden Whales of California—1922
Going to the Sun—1923
Going to the Stars—1926
For critical comment:

BOYNTON, PERCY
A History of American Literature
UNTERMEYER, LOUIS
The New Era in American Poetry

III. On Sherwood Anderson.
ANDERSON, SHERWOOD
Marching Men
New York; B. W. Huebsch, 1917
Windy McPherson's Son
New York; John Lane Co., 1917
Mid-American Chants
New York; John Lane Co., 1918
Winesburg, Ohio
New York; Boni & Liveright, 1919
Poor White
New York; B. W. Huebsch, 1920
The Triumph of the Egg
New York; B. W. Huebsch, 1921
Horses and Men
New York; B. W. Huebsch, 1923
Many Marriages
New York; B. W. Huebsch, 1923
A Story Teller's Story
New York; B. W. Huebsch, 1924
For critical comment:
FRANK, WALDO
in *Our America*
HANSEN, HARRY
in *Mid-West Portraits*
ROSENFELD, PAUL
in *The Port of New York*
VAN DOREN, CARL
in *Contemporary American Novelists*

GENERAL BIBLIOGRAPHY

On American Literature

Beers, Henry A.
An Outline Sketch of American Literature
New York; Chautauqua Press, 1887
Initial Studies in American Letters
New York; Chautauqua Press, 1895

Boynton, Percy
A History of American Literature
Boston; Ginn & Co., 1919
Some Contemporary Americans
Chicago; Univ. of Chicago Press, 1924

Brooks, Van Wyck
America's Coming of Age
New York; B. W. Huebsch, 1915
Letters and Leadership
New York; B. W. Huebsch, 1918

Brownell, W. C.
American Prose Masters
New York; Chas. Scribner's Sons, 1909

Cairns, William B.
A History of American Literature
New York; Oxford Univ. Press, 1912. (American Branch)

Erskine, John
Leading American Novelists
New York; Henry Holt & Co., 1910

Erskine, John and Trent, William
Great Writers of America
New York; Henry Holt & Co., 1912

Frank, Waldo
Our America
New York; Boni & Liveright, 1919

Kellner, Leon
American Literature (tr. Julia Franklin)
New York; Doubleday, Page & Co., 1915

MACY, JOHN
The Spirit of American Literature
New York; Boni & Liveright, 1912
MENCKEN, HENRY L.
A Book of Prefaces
New York; A. A. Knopf, 1917
Prejudices, 1st series
New York; A. A. Knopf, 1919
The second series was issued in 1920
The third series was issued in 1922
The fourth series was issued in 1924
PATTEE, FRED L.
A History of American Literature
New York; Silver, Burdett & Co., 1909
A History of American Literature since 1870
New York; The Century Co., 1915
Sidelights on American Literature
New York; The Century Co., 1922
The Development of the American Short Story
New York; Harper & Bros., 1923
PERRY, BLISS
The American Mind
Boston & New York; Houghton Mifflin Co., 1912
The American Spirit in Literature
New Haven; Yale Univ. Press, 1918
SHERMAN, STUART P.
Americans
New York; Chas. Scribner's Sons, 1923
On Contemporary Literature
New York; Henry Holt & Co., 1917
The Genius of America
New York; Chas. Scribner's Sons, 1923
TRENT, WILLIAM P.
A History of American Literature 1607–1865
New York; D. Appleton & Co., 1903
VAN DOREN, CARL
Contemporary American Novelists 1900–1920
New York; Macmillan Co., 1922
The American Novel
New York; Macmillan Co., 1921
WENDELL, BARRETT
A Literary History of America
New York; Chas. Scribner's Sons, 1907

WOODBERRY, GEORGE E.
America in Literature
New York; Harper & Bros., 1903

For extended bibliography as well as for critical articles: The Cambridge History of American Literature, 3 vol. edited by Erskine, Trent, Sherman, and Carl Van Doren.

On the Frontier

AIKMAN, DUNCAN (editor)
The Taming of the Frontier
New York; Minton, Balch & Co., 1925
COMAN, KATHERINE
Economic Beginnings of the Far West
New York; Macmillan Co., 1912
GARRISON, GEORGE P.
Westward Extension, 1841–1850
New York; Harper & Bros., 1906
GOODWIN, CARDINAL L.
The Trans-Mississippi West
New York; D. Appleton & Co., 1922
GREGG, JOSIAH L.
Commerce of the Prairies
New York; publisher not given, 1845, reprinted in Thwaites: *Early Western Travels*
HENDERSON, ARCHIBALD
The Conquest of the Old Southwest
New York; The Century Co., 1920
HINSDALE, BURKE A.
The Old Northwest
Boston and New York; Silver, Burdett & Co., 1899
HOUGH, EMERSON
The Passing of the Frontier
New Haven; Yale Univ. Press, 1918
The Story of the Cowboy
New York; D. Appleton & Co., 1898
The Story of the Outlaw
New York; The Outing Co., 1907
OGG, FREDERIC A.
The Old Northwest
New Haven; Yale Univ. Press, 1919

The Reign of Andrew Jackson: a chronicle of the Frontier in Politics
New Haven; Yale Univ. Press, 1919

PAXSON, FREDERIC L.
History of the American Frontier—1763–1893
Boston and New York; Houghton Mifflin Co., 1924
Recent History of the United States
Boston and New York; Houghton Mifflin Co., 1921
The Last American Frontier
New York; Macmillan Co., 1918
The New Nation
Boston and New York; Houghton Mifflin Co., 1915
"The Pacific Railroads and the disappearance of the frontier in America"
Amer. Hist. Assoc. Ann. Rept. for 1907, vol. I. pp. 105–122

ROOSEVELT, THEODORE
The Winning of the West
New York; G. P. Putnam's Sons, 1889–96, 4 vol.

RUSK, RALPH
The Literature of the Middle Western Frontier (2 vol.)
New York; Columbia University Press, 1924

SCHAFER, JOSEPH
A History of the Pacific Northwest
New York; Macmillan Co., 1905

SEMPLE, ELLEN C.
American History and its Geographical Conditions
Boston and New York; Houghton Mifflin Co., 1903

SKINNER, CONSTANCE L.
Adventurers of Oregon
New Haven; Yale Univ. Press, 1920
Pioneers of the Old Southwest
New Haven; Yale Univ. Prses, 1919

TURNER, FREDERIC J.
Rise of the New West, 1819–1829
New York; Harper & Bros., 1926
The Frontier in American History
New York; Henry Holt & Co., 1920

WINSOR, JUSTIN
The Westward Movement
Boston and New York; Houghton Mifflin Co., 1897

INDEX